ESSENTIALS
of Venture Capital

ESSENTIALS SERIES

The Essentials Series was created for busy business advisory and corporate professionals. The books in this series were designed so that these busy professionals can quickly acquire knowledge and skills in core business areas.

Each book provides need-to-have fundamentals for professionals who must:

- Get up to speed quickly, because they have been promoted to a new position or have broadened their responsibility scope
- Manage a new functional area
- Brush up on new developments in their area of responsibility
- Add more value to their company or clients

For more information on any of the above titles, please visit www.wiley.com.

ESSENTIALS
of Venture Capital

Alexander Haislip

WILEY

John Wiley & Sons, Inc.

Published by John Wiley & Sons, Inc., Hoboken, New Jersey.

Published simultaneously in Canada.

For general information on our other products and services or for technical support, please contact our Customer Care Department within the United States at (800) 762-2974, outside the United States at (317) 572-3993 or fax (317) 572-4002.

Wiley also publishes its books in a variety of electronic formats. Some content that appears in print may not be available in electronic books. For more information about Wiley products, visit our web site at www.wiley.com.

Library of Congress Cataloging-in-Publication Data:

Haislip, Alexander, 1982–
    Essentials of venture capital/Alexander Haislip.
        p. cm. – (Essentials series)
    Includes index.
    ISBN 978-0-470-61622-2 (pbk.); ISBN 978-0-470-91084-9 (ebk);
    ISBN 978-0-470-91085-6 (ebk); ISBN 978-0-470-91086-3 (ebk)
    1.   Venture capital. 2.   Business enterprises–Finance.   I. Title.
    HG4751.H343 2011
    332$'$.04154–dc22

                                                    2010018598

Printed in the United States of America
10 9 8 7 6 5 4 3 2 1

Contents

Contents

Contents

Contents

Preface

I left New Jersey in June of 2004 and drove my white Toyota across America on Interstate 80. After five days on the road, I pulled into the parking lot of a Residence Inn in Mountain View, California. It was the middle of the night.

Mountain View is in the heart of Silicon Valley, north of San Jose and south of San Francisco, and just a town over from Stanford University. It is a city of mixed residential buildings, low-slung apartment complexes, quarter-acre lots, and 1970s-style office parks. Tall redwood trees pop up between the buildings, punctuating an unremarkable skyline.

The city abuts Moffett Federal Airfield, which features the single most notable building in Mountain View, a 1930s dirigible hanger shaped like a gigantic caterpillar, three football fields long and 200 feet tall.

Giant gray C-130 Hercules turbo-prop planes buzz the town on Air National Guard training days, their massive bodies hanging fat and heavy against the blue sky.

Mountain View is a place practiced in the art of launching massive endeavors and has served as home to several large technology companies. Google was king while I was there and its employees seemed to have invaded the city. You couldn't walk down Castro Street, the city's main drag, without going past five or six people wearing T-shirts with the company's colorful logo.

They appeared so self-assured in the summer of 2004. Google was poised to go public and it was easy to imagine the employees smugly calculating the value of their stock options in their heads. The dot-com boom had come and gone, but the techies were going to cash in one more time. Google promised to be a phoenix flying out of the ashes of excess from four years before.

"Every few years, there must be that spectacular reminder that the merry-go-round still offers riders the brass ring," writes Silicon Valley Journalist Michael Malone.[1] After the dot-com bust, Google's initial public offering (IPO) was surely that: proof that entrepreneurs, engineers, and financiers could still launch lucrative new industries.

The process of going from idea to multibillion-dollar business fascinated me and I decided to learn as much about it as I possibly could. I spent my first year in Mountain View interviewing anybody who could teach me the business of technology.

One of the first lessons I learned was that there are two types of technology start-ups: those that *had* raised money from venture capitalists and those that were *trying* to raise money from venture capitalists.

Google raised over $25 million from Sequoia Capital and Kleiner Perkins Caufield & Byers, and was worth $27.2 billion the day it

---

[1] Michael S. Malone, *Going Public* (New York: Edward Burlingame/HarperCollins, 1991) p. 233.

went public. Kleiner Perkins's John Doerr and Sequoia's Michael Moritz had invested when Google was little more than two computer science dropouts in a garage. Five years later, it was an Internet juggernaut.

It snapped the Silicon Valley ecosystem into focus for me and helped me understand why venture capitalists were treated with such reverence. They were both technological clairvoyants and the gatekeepers to great wealth.

But the success of Google was a bright spot in an otherwise cloudy and confusing time for venture capital. The basics of the business were under constant question as investor performance waned.

What had once been a cottage industry of casual partnerships had been transformed by the dot-com boom but had yet to find a firm footing in its new role. Technology was no longer a part of the U.S. economy, it was *the* U.S. economy, and venture capital was one of its most important catalysts.

Venture capitalists raised over $100 billion in 2000, and the traditional models of investment were no more built for that kind of boom than a Volkswagen Beetle is built for the Indy 500. The industry was forced to evolve.

This book will help you understand how the venture capital industry is changing. It will show you the incentives that individual investors face and how those incentives dictate the evolution of the industry. If you're uncertain about how venture capital works, or want to understand recent developments in the business, this book is designed to quickly get you up to speed.

You can read the book straight through or pick out the chapters that interest you most.

Chapter 1 serves as an overview of both the basics of venture capital and the major changes and challenges the industry has faced during the past decade. This chapter will help you get up to speed on how venture investors operate and what makes them successful. You will learn how government regulation, industry consolidation, and new technologies have changed the finance of technology start-ups.

In Chapter 2, you will learn how to build a career as a venture capitalist. You'll see how different firms manage their staffing, growth, and succession, and understand how best to fit in.

Chapter 3 will show you several key fundraising strategies that work even in challenging macroeconomic environments. These will help you craft your pitch to potential investors. Understanding how firms market themselves will allow you to differentiate your approach and increase your chances of successfully connecting with cash.

Chapter 4 will introduce you to the basics of making investments. You will learn what venture capitalists look for in an investment and what factors affect their financing decisions. This chapter also describes how professional investors create special kinds of stock to protect their money.

Chapter 5 will show you how to find good investments. You will learn that venture capitalists have three major strategies for connecting with the best entrepreneurs and how to execute each strategy. Whether you are interested in how to make smart investments or in how to raise money for your own start-up from venture capitalists, this chapter will help you.

Chapter 6 is all about getting your investment dollars back. It compares taking a start-up public to selling it, which are the two major ways venture capitalists get their money back. It will help you evaluate the ongoing IPO crisis and introduce you to innovations designed to overcome it.

Chapter 7 is your guide through the ups and downs of the venture capital business. You will learn what drives the continual process of boom, bubble, and bust. You will be able to spot each part of the business cycle and execute strategies for investing effectively at any point in it.

Chapter 8 will walk you through the path to going global. You will see how successful firms have taken what works well in Silicon Valley and modified it to pursue opportunities abroad. This chapter will help you appreciate the difference between doing business in Israel, China, India, Russia, and other emerging markets.

Acknowledgments

Thanks to Larry Aragon, editor-in-chief of Thomson Reuters's *Venture Capital Journal,* for his mentorship and the opportunities he has afforded me while writing for VCJ. The magazine would not be the best in the business without his vision and tireless work.

Alastair Goldfisher, Joanna Glasner, Connie Loizos, and Dan Primack each provided me with invaluable research through their gold standard reporting and writing. I can always trust their stories to be well researched, thorough, and informative. They've helped me set high standards for what I do each day.

This book is informed by more than half a decade of research, and reporting on every aspect of venture capital and technology finance. I have spoken with well over a thousand investors, executives, entrepreneurs, and technologists, as well as a myriad of lawyers, accountants, and public relations executives too numerous to name. I am grateful to them all.

Still, there are those who have gone out of their way to help me. They invited me into their homes, took my calls at odd hours, read chapters, tipped me off to great stories, and selflessly offered me the benefit of their experience. A brief list of those I would like to specifically thank: Patrick Chung, Morten Lund, Alexandra Johnson, Mark Cecil, Venky Ganesan, Chris Douvos, Stewart Guenther, and two other high-ranking sources who wish to remain anonymous.

Knowing what to write is one thing. Putting words on paper is another. Thanks to Brian Caulfield, Joel Achenbach, Jim Willse, and Steve Isaacs for their mentorship and editorial encouragement throughout my reporting and writing career. Thanks to Ed Zschau for opening the world of Silicon Valley to me while I was an undergraduate at Princeton. Thanks to Sheck Cho, Helen Cho, and Laura Cherkas at John Wiley & Sons for their guidance and careful edits on this book.

Thanks to my parents for their constant encouragement, guidance, and support during this project.

Thanks to my lovely wife for sharpening the focus and logic of this book through her insightful edits. Her love fills my sails and carries me forward always.

CHAPTER 1

Industry Overview

After reading this chapter, you will be able to:

- Distinguish venture capital from other asset classes.
- Recognize the key functions and processes of venture capital investing.
- Differentiate between general partners and limited partners.
- Estimate typical investment returns for venture funds.
- Understand the seven reasons for the current performance crisis in venture investing.

What Is Venture Capital?

The best definition of venture capital comes from the man who created the industry. General Georges Doriot, a Harvard Business School professor and early venture capitalist, said that his firm would "invest in things nobody has dared try before."

Venture capitalists, sometimes called "VCs," look for new technology emerging from a government laboratory, a university research department, a corporate incubator, or an entrepreneur's garage that disrupts a big market. It may even create entirely new markets. Such disruption presents fertile ground for rapid growth and wealth creation, or wealth redistribution. Venture capitalists professionally invest money in businesses that are neither proven nor safe.

They advise and assist growing companies to achieve extraordinary investment returns. Venture capitalists often say they are "value-added investors" who offer important services to start-ups beyond just writing a check.

The three most common things they do to help start-ups are to give strategic advice, recruit executives, and make introductions to customers. Venture capitalists make their presence known in a company via the corporate board. A venture investor may sit on several boards of directors and can take an active role in company direction, finance, and staffing.

Venture capitalists professionally invest money raised from large institutional investors. They typically buy a minority share of any company they invest in, though a syndicate of venture capital investors might own the majority of a start-up's stock after several years. It is unusual for venture investors to push debt obligations onto their start-ups. Start-ups seldom have a predictable revenue stream to pay off the debt and few, if any, tangible assets that a lender could foreclose on.

Venture capitalists should be distinguished from "angel investors," who use their own money to invest in newly formed companies. Angels are typically retired executives who can give advice and between \$50,000 and \$500,000 of early investment capital. They do similar things as venture capitalists but are not professional investors.

Venture capital is a specific type of private equity investing. Private equity investors bankroll companies that do not have stock traded in public markets, such as the New York Stock Exchange or NASDAQ.

The distinction between venture capital firms and buyout shops, the other group of investors lumped into the private equity category, is the ownership level that they take in the companies they invest in. Buyout shops will buy up enough stock in a target company to be majority owners so that they can make serious changes to a company's operations. Exhibit 1.1 shows the differences between venture capital, buyouts, and private equity.

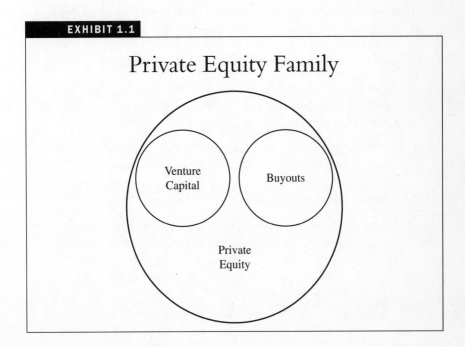

EXHIBIT 1.1

Private Equity Family

Venture Capital

Buyouts

Private Equity

I think of venture capital as investing money into small, private technology companies expecting rapid growth. But there is no formal definition of what kind of deal a venture investor can or can't do. They invest in corporate spinouts, leveraged buyouts, public stock, and just about anything else they think they can turn a buck on. A typical year may see anywhere from 2,500 to 3,500 venture capital deals, and no two are identical. Still, there are some norms that prevail and you can get a sense of what type of companies venture investors look for.

IN THE REAL WORLD

Done Deals

What types of investments do venture capitalists make? Here's a sample of representative deals from top-flight investors.

CANADIAN FUSION STARTUP POWERS UP WITH $22 MILLION[a]

A Canadian-based startup that is experimenting with fusion energy technology has quietly raised $22 million in early stage funding from venture capitalists.

Burnaby, British Columbia–based startup General Fusion plans to develop a prototype that will show its fusion technology can produce energy cheaper than coal-fire plants and safer than standard nuclear fission plants.

"What General Fusion is working on is game changing," says investor Rolf Dekleer, vice president of investments for Canadian venture capital firm GrowthWorks Capital. "If they were working on this 10 years ago, we wouldn't be talking about global warming today."

GrowthWorks Capital, Braemar Energy Ventures, Chrysalix Energy Ventures, and The Entrepreneurs Fund combined to provide $9 million for General Fusion. The Sustainable Development Canadian Technology Fund, a government entity charged with financing environmentally friendly technology projects, additionally kicked in more than $13 million, contingent on General Fusion's ability to meet key milestones.

MOTALLY RAISES $1 MILLION TO MONITOR MOBILE WEB TRAFFIC[b]

Metrics matter. That's especially true on the Web, where the number of "eyeballs" a site attracts helps to establish what a company charges advertisers.

But as people move from desktop browsing to accessing sites via mobile phones, tracking the exact number of visitors has become more difficult.

San Francisco–based Motally is working to help online publishers determine who is accessing their content and how visitors are interacting with their websites. The startup recently raised $1 million in early-stage venture funding from BlueRun Ventures and angel investor Ron Conway, according to regulatory filings and the company.

BIOTECH STARTUP RAISES $8 MILLION FOR ASTHMA TREATMENT[c]

Newton, Massachusetts–based NKT Therapeutics is looking for ways to subdue Natural Killers and now has $8 million in fresh funding to do that.

The company recently raised its first round of venture capital funding from SV Life Sciences and MedImmune Ventures to help it develop treatments for asthma and other diseases.

The company focuses on researching so-called Natural Killer T-Cells, which the company describes as a central component of the human immune system, playing a role in human health and disease. Natural Killers play a very different role in the 20 million asthmatics estimated to be living in the United States, waging war on otherwise normal lung tissue.

Companies that raised money from venture capitalists contributed 21 percent of the U.S. gross domestic product (GDP) and employed 11 percent of the workforce in 2008, according to a study financed by a venture capital lobbying group.[1] It cites several prominent examples of companies that relied on venture capitalists to get their start: Microsoft, Intel, Oracle, Google, Amazon, Staples, Netscape, AOL, FedEx, eBay, Apple, Cisco, YouTube, and others.

Venture capitalists have come to be associated with technology start-ups and California's Silicon Valley because the technology industry there has yielded some of the largest growth opportunities in the past three decades. Before that, the epicenter of technology innovation was the greater Boston area.

During the past 20 years, the majority of venture investors were white males in their late thirties to early fifties, educated at either Harvard or Stanford Business School with a background in either operations or entrepreneurship. They typically work in partnerships of 3 to 10 investors with offices within five miles of Sand Hill Road in Menlo Park, California, and make $774,000 a year, according to data from Thomson Reuters. These characterizations are changing as firms diversify and expand beyond their roots. The next 20 years of the venture capital business will see a new generation of investors that reflect the diversity of every other industry.

 TIPS AND TECHNIQUES

Venture Capital Spotting

If you spend enough time in Silicon Valley, you'll learn to spot the venture capitalists in any crowd. Here are a few tips on how to pick them out:

Clothes. Male venture capitalists wear blue button down shirts and khaki pants. Navy blazers are optional, though sometimes you'll see windowpane-style checkered jackets. I've never seen them with herringbone jackets or leather patches on their elbows. Most venture capitalists don't wear ties. Vinod Khosla has a closet full of mock turtlenecks. There are two notable exceptions: Kleiner Perkins's John Doerr and Draper Fisher Jurvetson's Tim Draper. Doerr has one tie he's worn for at least a decade that has broad black and silver stripes. Draper wears red ties from the Save the Children Foundation.

Early stage and seed investors dress more casually. Marc Andreessen wears flip-flops and shorts. European seed investor Morten Lund wears a blue Adidas hooded sweatshirt and Birkenstock sandals.

Female venture capitalists wear a range of styles. Blouse and slacks combos seem to be the norm, though one periodically sees variation ranging from pantsuits to a black Lacoste polo shirt with jeans.

TIPS AND TECHNIQUES (CONTINUED)

Communication. Investors love buzzwords and love to look intelligent. Here's a typical venture capital sentence that one might encounter in casual conversation: "His go-to-market strategy wasn't going to help him cross the chasm and deliver a scalable, robust solution in real time."

Eating. Favorite feeding spots tend to persist over time, and Buck's of Woodside is one which investors consistently favor. It's not unusual for the waitstaff at this rustic flapjack shop located in the suburbs around Stanford University to automatically bring whatever a venture capitalist typically orders. The place is full of real Silicon Valley history, from boxcar racers hanging from the ceiling to framed semiconductors and a California license plate that says GOOGLE.

Buck's has become well known to the point where it's unhip to be seen there. Other venture capitalist favorites in the Silicon Valley area include the laid back Palo Alto Creamery; Redwood City's upscale Chantilly (down the street from the Ferrari dealership); Menlo Park's Kaygetsu, a hot sushi spot right off Sand Hill Road; and Menlo Park's Dutch Goose, which makes killer deviled eggs.

Exercise. Venture capitalists could exercise like normal people, but don't. Consider Brad Feld, a managing director at The Foundry Group, who is shooting to run a marathon in every state before he turns 50. To balance his strenuous training regimen with work, Feld invented the *Treadputer*, a computer with three screens mounted to his treadmill. It's an IBM ThinkCenter with 19-inch flat screen monitors and voice recognition software.

How Venture Capital Works

A venture capitalist's job is generally broken down into three major functions:

1. Fundraising

2. Finding start-ups to invest in

3. Reaping the rewards

Fundraising

Venture firms are usually set up as investment partnerships rather than corporations or companies. Venture capitalists split the earnings from their work among themselves rather than giving it to shareholders. There are two components to a venture capital investing partnership, the *general partners* (GPs) and the *limited partners* (LPs).

The general partners are the venture capitalists. They are the active participants of a partnership agreement, investing in start-up companies. The money they invest comes from limited partners.

Limited partners are the passive participants in a venture capital partnership. They entrust their money to GPs and expect to get it back and more in several years. Limited partners are institutions, endowments, pension funds, or other large pools of money. They invest in a wide range of asset classes, such as stocks, bonds, real estate, and "alternatives," such as venture capital, private equity, and hedge funds. Examples of big limited partners include the Harvard University Endowment, the California Public Employees Retirement System (CalPERS), the J. Paul Getty Trust, and HarbourVest.[2]

Exhibit 1.2 shows the way in which limited partners invest in various asset classes and how the money eventually trickles down to start-ups.

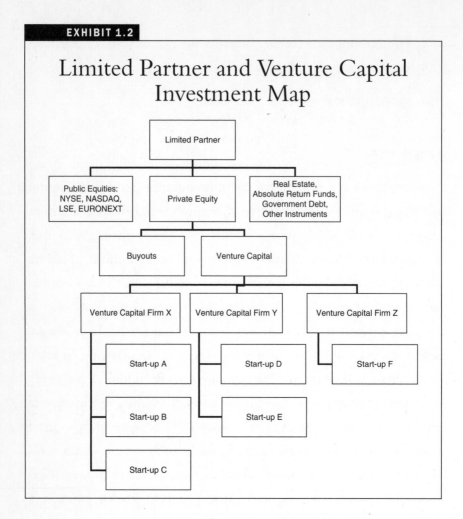

EXHIBIT 1.2

Limited Partner and Venture Capital Investment Map

These limited partners entrust the venture capitalists to invest money on their behalf for a period of time through a legal structure called a *fund*. The fund sets the parameters for the partnership, including what financial commitments the LPs will make, what compensation the GPs will get, and what types of investments GPs will make. A typical venture capital fund usually spends three to five years investing in companies and another five to seven years reaping the rewards and distributing the returns to its limited partners. The standard venture fund agreement is designed to terminate after ten to twelve years.

Many people have some small level of investment exposure to venture capital through pension funds, but most individuals cannot buy into a venture capital fund because they do not meet the requirements set by the Securities and Exchange Commission (SEC). The SEC requires individual investors to be accredited before they may invest in a venture capital fund. The rules for accreditation are complicated and subject to interpretation, but a good rule of thumb is that if you don't have a net worth of $1 million, you are unlikely to be able to invest in a venture capital fund.

From an individual investor's standpoint, venture funds are likely to be a poor choice. The main reason is that they are illiquid. Once you're in a fund, you should expect to hold that position for 10 years. There are a handful of firms that will buy positions in venture capital funds, but only at a steep discount. Even then, good venture capital firms may be able to choose the type of investors they allow into their funds and may prefer institutions that are stable instead of individuals whose commitment may fluctuate.

There's no formula for what percentage of an institution's money should be invested into venture capital, but it generally only accounts for a small portion of its overall portfolio. A big institution might invest as much as 15 percent of its capital in private equity funds.

IN THE REAL WORLD

Pension Fund Holdings

The California Public Employees' Retirement System (CalPERS) is the granddaddy of pension funds, managing around $175 billion on behalf of 1.6 million retired Californians. CalPERS is one of the more transparent retirement systems. Below is its portfolio allocation at the end of January 2009:[a]

- Domestic Fixed Income: 22.4 percent
- Domestic Equities: 21.3 percent
- Global Equities: 18.4 percent
- Alternative Investment Management (AIM): 13.8 percent
- Real Estate: 12.1 percent
- Cash Equivalents: 7.6 percent
- International Fixed Income: 2.3 percent
- Inflation Linked: 2 percent

The CalPERS Alternative Investment Management (AIM) program is the vehicle the pension fund uses to invest in venture capital and other private equity. The $23.9 billion CalPERS allocated to its AIM program only counts the money the pension fund has actually invested to date. It does not include commitments that CalPERS has made to general partnerships but has yet to actually write checks for. When you put the value of the investments CalPERS has already made together with the value of the commitments that it has made to write checks in the future, you arrive at the pension fund's "total exposure," to the AIM program: $47.9 billion.

[a] CalPERS web site, "Asset Allocation," June 2009, http://bit.ly/da0Utl. It's worth noting that after a terrible year on the stock market, the fund is likely overallocated to alternative investments at the point this data shows. Its target allocation for the AIM Program for 2009 was 10 percent.

Investing

Once a venture firm raises a fund, it invests in companies. Some venture firms have specific rules about what type of companies they can invest in, others are more flexible. Typically, venture firms invest in small, recently incorporated companies called start-ups.

When I think about start-ups, my first thought is two young guys in a garage. After all, it's Bill Hewlett and Dave Packard founding HP, Steve Jobs and Steve Wozniak founding Apple, and Sergey Brin and Larry Page founding Google. But the truth is that about twice as many U.S. tech entrepreneurs are in their fifties than in their twenties. And the average number of people employed in a start-up isn't 2—it's 42, according to a study by the Kauffman Foundation.[3]

Finding good start-ups to invest in isn't easy. Venture capitalists churn through thousands of business plans, hundreds of company presentations, and fund just a handful of start-ups. Picking the right handful relies on careful research and vetting called *due diligence*. The term comes from the standard of care a trustee must bring to the process of investing. In practice, it means interviewing the entrepreneur several times, testing the proposed technology, and speaking to potential customers or experts in the applicable technology field. Most venture capitalists feel more comfortable investing in companies that were introduced to them by someone they know or have worked with in the past.

Once a venture capitalist identifies a start-up to invest in, there are competitive issues and deal structuring concerns to be considered.

One of the biggest things to think about is whether to syndicate or share an investment with one or more other firms. Venture investors will choose to syndicate based on the macroeconomic environment and their beliefs about the risk of an investment.

A venture capitalist may write a small check to a start-up in the beginning, doing what is called an early stage or Series A investment round. The financing is intended to carry the company through a year or 18 months of operation and to a significant milestone. For example, an Internet start-up might use its Series A round to get its site up and running.

Once that major milestone has been achieved, some of the risk is removed. An Internet start-up with a working web site is a more stable investment than one without. The company may then decide to raise more money from venture capitalists in a Series B financing.

The first venture capitalist involved in the company's financing may want to participate again, though he or she is not obligated to. An entrepreneur typically looks to an outside firm to objectively determine the value of its stock before inking a new deal. The price of a company's Series B shares usually represents an increase in its value. Most start-ups don't go beyond raising a Series D or E.

Deal structures that worked well for semiconductor and software investments may not fit companies installing solar panels, hunting for cancer cures, or building hot new consumer applications. Venture capitalists tailor their deal structures to accommodate new technologies and evolving market opportunities.

Reaping the Rewards

Of course it doesn't matter where you find great deals or how you structure an investment if you can't get a healthy return. Venture capitalists typically plan to hold onto an investment for five to seven years. They used to rely on initial public offerings (IPOs) to value their companies and provide stock that they could distribute to their limited partners. That avenue has been all but inaccessible since the dot-com downturn, due in part to increased government regulation.

Start-ups increasingly sell to strategic acquirers, big corporations such as Cisco, Oracle, and Google. Those companies may pay cash or with their stock, which the venture capitalists are then able to pass out to their limited partners.

Venture capitalists get paid when one of two things happen. They collect money just for raising and managing an investment fund on behalf of large institutions. This payment is called a *management fee* and increases proportionately with the size of a firm's fund. A venture partnership that raises a $100 million fund might get a 2 percent fee of $2 million each year. Management fees generally decline as a firm moves from actively investing to passively managing the investments it has made.

Venture capitalists also get paid a portion of any profits they make from their investments. This compensation is called *carried interest* or just *carry,* and is a prearranged percentage of whatever the firm earns for its investors. Carried interest generally ranges between 20 percent and 30 percent of a fund's profits. A venture firm that raises a $100 million fund, makes $150 million for its investors, and has a 20 percent carried interest would get $10 million to split among the venture capitalists.

Performance Expectations

To determine how well any given venture capital firm is doing is tricky. You can't just look up its stock price or go to the SEC for its latest annual report. There are five major reasons why it is difficult to know how well a venture capital firm is doing.

1. Variability of the business cycle impacts industry-wide performance.
2. Different types of investors have different performance goals.
3. The investment time horizon is long.
4. A single excellent deal could drastically affect a fund's performance.
5. Little data is available.

The way to evaluate the performance of a firm is to look at each of its funds and compare its fund performance to other funds that operated at the same time and invested in the same stage of start-up development. Venture capital funds raised in 1997 typically did very well because they invested during a time of unprecedented economic expansion in the technology industry, and they harvested their returns at the peak of the dot-com boom. Funds raised in 2000 have not fared as well. Many invested in companies that seemed promising during the boom but proved to be duds during the bust.

Different types of venture firms have different performance expectations that make comparisons between funds difficult. An early stage venture capitalist will do extremely well if he or she can pick the next Google and buy its shares for pennies. The return expectation is high, but the variance in performance is also high, since there aren't many proto-Googles out there to find and because so much can go wrong going from a great idea in a garage to a public offering.

A late stage venture capital firm invests in companies that have fully developed products and at least some revenue. Since most of the risk has already been eliminated at this point, the late stage firm buys in at a higher price per share than an early stage venture firm. This leads to lower returns for the late stage–focused firm but also lower risk.

Each venture capital firm raises a fund that typically spans the course of 10 to 12 years, during the first half of which it makes investments and the second half of which it liquidates its holdings. A lot can happen during that time. Early stage investors often joke that the business of investing in a company that is little more than a team with a prototype is a lot like playing Russian roulette— only that you pull the trigger now and don't know if you're dead for another half a decade.

There's a lot of truth to that joke. The average time it takes a start-up to go from incorporation to being bought by a strategic acquirer was 6.5 years in 2008. It took the average company 7.9 years to go public in 2009, according to data from Dow Jones VentureSource.[4] Venture capitalists will own the company for most of that time.

It's easy to understand then why most funds are underwater, showing negative returns, for the majority of their decade-long life. Investors call this effect the *J-curve*. It comes from the fact that a firm spends at least the first three to five years of a fund's life just writing checks for start-ups, passing out money with the hope of collecting it in the second half of the fund's life, when its investments are mature and ready to be harvested.

The J-curve makes it hard to identify an underperforming fund, since negative returns are typical for the early years of any fund. There are two other major factors that also contribute to negative returns at the beginning of a fund's life: management fees collected each year that are used to pay the general partners and early failures that can be quickly identified and written down.

Success for a venture firm could always be just right around the corner. It may sound strange, but one major deal could take a fund from money loser to top performer. You can look at a venture firm's portfolio of companies and perhaps predict which will be successful, but nothing is certain until a start-up goes public or is acquired.

Averages are close to meaningless in venture capital. Looking at the distribution of returns on start-up investments is similar to looking at the average wealth of me, you, and Bill Gates: One data point skews the average so much that it jeopardizes logical conclusions.

Most statistics books would tell you to take the median of the set instead of the mean, but that's not particularly helpful in thinking about venture capital returns either.

Consider a top-performing venture fund of $100 million that invests its money evenly across 10 start-ups. Three of those start-ups will go out of business, and their value will be written down to zero. Four of those start-ups will be sold at cost, below cost, or just slightly above cost, but at least the venture capitalist will get his or her money back. Two will be sold for a profit. That, at least, salvages the portfolio and puts the investor on par with the

S&P 500. And then finally there's the one runaway success, the grand-slam home run, the Genentech, eBay, or Google. You can see these results tabulated in Exhibit 1.3.

The average return is $63 million on a $10 million investment, but most of the firm's companies will either break even or be money losers. The median return is $10 million on a $10 million investment, or 0 percent rate of return. But would you invest in that firm's portfolio? I sure would.

Venture investors are in the weird position of expecting most of their deals to fail and only one or two deals salvage their investment efforts. With so much variance in performance, how can a potential limited partner know what to expect from a venture fund?

EXHIBIT 1.3

Distribution of Returns from 10 Fictional Start-ups

	Amount Invested ($M)	Status	Return ($M)
Start-up A	$10	Bankruptcy	$ 0
Start-up B	$10	Bankruptcy	$ 0
Start-up C	$10	Bankruptcy	$ 0
Start-up D	$10	Sale at Cost	$ 9.5
Start-up E	$10	Sale at Cost	$ 10
Start-up F	$10	Sale at Cost	$ 10
Start-up G	$10	Sale at Cost	$ 10.5
Start-up H	$10	Success	$ 40
Start-up I	$10	Success	$ 50
Start-up J	$10	Home Run	$500
Total	**$100**		**$630**

The National Venture Capital Association (NVCA) and Thomson Reuters used to collect average returns data for venture investments over time—a job the NVCA has since offered to Cambridge Associates. You can see this data in Exhibit 1.4.

The data are broken down into time-horizons of investment. They will tell you the average return that firms expect in 1, 3, 5, 10, and 20 years. The data show that short-term returns are volatile, but venture capital, over the long run, outperforms other assets, such as the S&P 500 and the NASDAQ.

It's also worth noting that the 10-year data is artificially high. It includes the runaway success of the dot-com boom and will likely drop precipitously in 2010 when those peak returns fall out of the dataset.

Using an average of venture capital returns skews the data when there are a small number of big winners and a plethora

EXHIBIT 1.4

Investment Horizon Performance through September 30, 2008

Fund	1 Year	3 Years	5 Years	10 Years	20 Years
Early/Seed	0.2	3.8	5.1	37.2	21.6
Balanced	−6.4	7.4	11.5	14.9	14.7
Later Stage	8.6	12.0	10.5	8.9	14.7
All Venture	−1.6	6.6	8.6	17.3	17.1
NASDAQ	−21.4	−1.1	3.1	2.1	8.7
S&P 500	−22.0	−1.7	3.2	1.4	7.5

Source: Thomson Reuters/National Venture Capital Association, http://bit.ly/ahflF9.

of losers. Just as one or two start-ups can return big money for venture capitalists, only a handful of venture funds ever return money to their LPs. The top firms return 40 to 60 percent in a good year and return much, much more than that in a great year. Most firms lose money on their funds during a down market.

Getting a specific fund's returns isn't always easy. The best source for finding a single fund's returns is from a public entity that reports the performance of its individual investments. CalPERS makes its data on venture capital easy to find online.[5] But you won't find every venture fund on the CalPERS site. Some firms don't want to publicly report their returns and have opted to boot public-trust-style limited partners out of their funds so they won't be open to scrutiny.

But let's consider one firm that does take money from CalPERS and reports its returns to the giant pension fund.

Aberdare Ventures is a San Francisco–based early stage venture capital fund which invests in both biotechnology companies and medical device companies. Its returns, as of the end of 2008, are shown in Exhibit 1.5.

The CalPERS data in Exhibit 1.5 show several interesting things. The first thing to notice is the list of fund names. CalPERS has committed to three Aberdare funds so far. The fund "vintage" is the year that the fund was raised and began investing.

The "capital committed" is the amount of money CalPERS promised to put into each Aberdare fund. A firm such as Aberdare may go to many limited partners to raise a fund and CalPERS only has a small piece of each of the funds listed here. The firm's earliest

EXHIBIT 1.5

CalPERS Investment Returns for Aberdare Ventures as of December 31, 2008

Fund	Vintage	Capital Committed	Cash In	Cash Out	Cash Out and Remaining Value	IRR	Notes	Investment Multiple	Notes
Aberdare II Annex Fund, L.P.	2006	5,985,000	1,975,050	0	1,428,140	−19.2	N/M	0.70×	N/M
Aberdare Ventures II, L.P.	2002	20,000,000	18,999,996	5,538,889	19,707,777	1.3		1.00×	
Aberdare Ventures, L.P.	1999	2,500,000	2,218,900	1,361,751	2,046,379	−1.6		0.90×	

N/M = Not meaningful.

fund, called Aberdare Ventures, L.P., raised a total of $50 million, records show. Its next fund also raised $50 million, but later added a $15 million "annex fund," which extends its investment ability beyond the initial fund size.

Capital committed is a promise to invest a certain amount of money, but the "cash in" column shows how much CalPERS has actually given Aberdare. Venture firms never get all of the money they raise at once; they get it over time by making capital calls to their limited partners. A capital call is nothing more than the process of transferring money out of CalPERS's bank account and into Aberdare's.

As you can see from Exhibit 1.5, Aberdare has not yet called down all the capital from its first fund. It has only called $2.2 million of the $2.5 million CalPERS promised. Venture firms typically hold a small amount of capital back to support portfolio companies as they grow.

"Cash out" is where the rubber meets the road. It is the money that the venture firm has distributed back to its limited partner. When Aberdare's companies go public, it may pass out shares of stock. When its companies are acquired, it may pass out cash. However it comes, "cash out" is the ultimate measure of how much money a venture capital firm has returned to shareholders.

Of course each venture firm has at least some companies that haven't been bought or gone public. Those companies have value and the next column, "Cash out and remaining value," attempts to capture that fact. The remaining value of a portfolio is reported by the general partners.

Remaining value is difficult to judge, even for the general partners in charge of the investments. Shares in private companies are not liquid securities. You can't just look up the recent trading prices on the Internet. Is the right way to account for their value to use the price of the last sale of shares to a private investor? Those transactions can be years old. Benchmarking a company's value against similar companies is hard too. There just aren't that many public-market competitors to use.

It's important to remember that "remaining value" is a little bit squishy, especially when it comes to evaluating a fund's Internal Rate of Return (IRR). The IRR is a measure of annualized return on investment: the amount of interest you'd get each year you invested in the fund. The IRR includes "remaining value" as part of its calculation even though those returns have yet to be realized.

Few venture investors use the IRR metric when discussing fund returns. Instead, they talk about cash-on-cash return or *investment multiple*. This number measures the number of times a firm returns the size of its fund to investors. A $100 million fund with a cash-out and remaining value of $200 million would have "2X," or two times the return. You can see that CalPERS has yet to get more than a 1X return on an Aberdare fund. That means the firm has lost money for its investors.

The notes of the last column in Exhibit 1.5 offer some perspective on the returns information. You'll see that the Aberdare II Annex L.P. fund has the note "N/M" next to its investment multiple. That means the fund is still too young to expect returns. The returns data shown are "not meaningful" yet. It's important to remember that a venture fund is typically a 10-year investment vehicle and the Aberdare II Annex L.P. fund was, at the time the data were collected, less than three years old.

Not every firm has public data available as Aberdare does. For example, getting performance data for Kleiner Perkins Caufield & Byers usually involves having a close relationship with one of the firm's investors and seeing its private records.

IN THE REAL WORLD

Why We Don't Have Venture Capital Performance Data

Should the University of California be excluded from investments that returned more than half a billion dollars?

Sure. No problem.

That was the answer that Sequoia Capital gave when booting the school from its list of limited partners. The firm had counted the school system among its investors for 22 years (spanning from Sequoia III to Sequoia X), during which time it had taken $110 million of investment capital and turned it into $508 million.[a] But that relationship came to an end in 2004, when Sequoia unceremoniously blocked the school from putting money into its next fund.

The move came after the University regents lost a lawsuit to the Coalition of University Employees and the San Jose Mercury News in 2003. The plaintiffs demanded the school comply with the California Open Records Act and disclose the individual rates of return made by each of its private equity funds. The school had previously released only the aggregate returns for the entire private equity portfolio.

Disclosing individual fund returns could make it possible for a motivated data analyst to extrapolate the value of specific companies within a venture firm's portfolio. That information could then be used as the basis for a strategic acquirer's bid and would subsequently depress returns—or at least that's what venture capitalists feared would happen.

Even worse, start-ups might have to disclose their financials, revenue projections, valuation, or other proprietary information by virtue of having received some small sliver of public money. The fear was that disclosure requirements would prevent private companies from being private.

"Discretion and privacy are the handmaidens of successful venture capital firms," wrote Sequoia Investor Michael Moritz in a widely circulated letter to the University of California investment team at the time.[b] "Our portfolio companies are hurt when sensitive information about their activities becomes available to competitors."

The same day the California judge issued his ruling, Sequoia sent another letter to the University of Michigan, informing the public school it would not be invited to invest in Sequoia's next fund and asked its Chief Investment Officer to sell the University's positions in previous funds.[c] The school had earned $125 million on its $14 million investment in Sequoia VI, VII, and VIII, according to reports.

Sequoia wasn't the only firm to stop looking to public pension funds and university endowments. Benchmark Capital, Charles River Ventures, and the Woodside Fund are a few that turned exclusively to private sources of funding, according to reports.[d]

State legislators panicked over the disclosure issue and soon were proposing or passing laws to protect private equity data from public scrutiny. Michigan determined that IRR data was a "trade secret" and passed a law preventing the disclosure of top-line fund performance data or any data associated with underlying portfolio assets. Colorado determined it would permit top-line performance disclosure, but explicitly protected all information pertaining to portfolio companies.[e] Massachusetts and Virginia passed similar laws.[f]

Not all states reacted this way. Texas Attorney General Greg Abbott extended an interpretation of his state's Open Records laws to make information on the underlying assets of venture firms public. "There is no proof that secrecy will ensure good investments, but it is true that secrecy can conceal bad investments," he said in a speech to the Freedom of Information Foundation of Texas.

The University of Texas Investment Management Co., which manages money for state-run University of Texas, said that this expanded interpretation forced several firms to exclude it from investing. Those firms included American Securities, Barclays Private Equity, Foundation Capital, and Prospect Venture Partners. Perhaps most stunning was that the venture firm that took its name from the state's capital—Austin Ventures—said it would not raise any funds from Texas-based public funds in 2005, citing concerns it would be forced to disclose information about its specific portfolio companies.[g]

Disclosure requirements are one of the reasons we have little or no performance data from top performing funds. Good firms can call the shots on who gets a chance to invest and they'd rather not have their private performance data exposed to public scrutiny.

[a] "UC Files Appeal in Venture Capital Disclosure Case," *University of California Press Room*, September 5, 2003, http://bit.ly/cSJwJs.

[b] "Venture Capital Firm Severs UC Ties After Court Ruling" *The Berkeley Daily Planet*, September 2, 2003, http://bit.ly/beyC4V.

[c] "Sequoia Boots Wolverines," Thomson Reuters' *Buyouts*, August 25, 2003, http://bit.ly/a3uCOd.

[d] "VCJ Editor: Clip and Send," *Venture Capital Journal*, June 1, 2004, http://bit.ly/cdFt4l.

[e] "Battle Over Preventing Disclosure Data Shifts to the East Coast," *Venture Capital Journal*, July 1, 2004, http://bit.ly/d41wTj.

[f] "Disclosure and Exposure in the Private Equity and Venture Capital Industries: More to Come," Nixon Peabody Client Memo, March 30, 2005, http://bit.ly/cNoFvk.

[g] "Limited Partner News," *Venture Capital Journal*, May 1, 2005, http://bit.ly/9xVCTZ. Once the Texas disclosure laws were interpreted to protect underlying portfolio data, Austin Ventures relented and still counts the University of Texas Investment Management Co. as one of its major investors.

Venture Capital in Crisis

Looking at Aberdare's returns might surprise you. The firm has been invested for more than a decade and has yet to return the initial investment CalPERS made. The giant pension fund would have been better off hiding its money under a mattress.

But Aberdare is not unusual. Most venture capital funds lose money in anything but the most buoyant market.

The poor returns of the last decade have caused a massive crisis of confidence in the venture business and will force major changes on the industry.

"I don't know what kind of a career I'm going to have in venture capital," a managing director at a well-regarded Silicon Valley venture firm recently told me. His comment had little to do with his own interest or ability in the venture capital business. In fact, he's one of the more successful venture investors, with at least one major multi-hundred-million-dollar acquisition and a fistful of enviable portfolio companies. If anything, he should be one of the people who would keep his job in the coming venture shakeout.

His concern is that it would become increasingly difficult to sell start-ups or take them public and limited partner money would dry up.

He's not the only practicing venture capitalist to think that his or her career is in trouble—a recent survey found that nearly 53 percent of venture investors believe their business model is "broken"[6]—and that may be the biggest problem the venture industry faces. Would you bet on a baseball team where five of the nine players thought they were going to lose?

Finance is a confidence game, literally. One group entrusts its money to another with confidence it will produce returns. Venture firms overdrew their confidence account during the dot-com boom and bounced bad companies on the public market.

So where did the confidence go?

The past decade has seen seven major reasons for poor performance by venture capitalists:

1. The venture overhang

2. Investment banking changes

3. Sarbanes-Oxley regulation

4. Consolidation of customers and strategic acquirers

5. Institutional investor growth

6. Difficulty commercializing cleantech

7. The recession

The Venture Overhang

Venture firms raised too much money during the dot-com era—over $100 billion in 2000 alone—and became desperate to put it to work as entrepreneurship seemed to evaporate after the bubble burst. The "overhang" is the amount of money raised, but not yet invested.

Too many dollars chasing too few attractive deals depressed returns. Venture capitalists either invested in companies doomed to be unsuccessful or were forced to bid too much for promising companies. Some firms gave money back to limited partners, saying there were few attractive opportunities, but many more kept the money, continued to collect management fees, and hoped against hope for a hit.

The venture overhang was estimated to be $68 billion in 2004.[7] The size of the overhang is, in part, a reflection of an information or demand asymmetry between venture capitalists and their limited partner investors. LPs still wanted to allocate money to the venture asset class, even after the GPs started to see opportunities go away.

Investment Banking Changes

There were two major changes to investment banking after the dot-com boom. The first was tightening the regulations that separated an investment bank's services department from its analyst department. The concept of this type of "Chinese Wall" is intended to keep analysts objective. Analysts, the professionals charged with rating stocks on their investment potential objective, are supposed to give unbiased advice to clients.

But allegations of conflicts of interest tainted many I-banks. Investors burned by dot-com companies blamed analysts for pumping the stocks of companies they had hoped their firms would collect fees from. The practice of keeping the deal-making and analysis groups separate has been regulated since the 1920s, but the government has since put additional measures in place to ensure investors don't get hurt again.

Although no venture capitalist would argue in favor of knocking down the Chinese Wall in banking, many will admit that it's difficult for a newly public company to attract the attention of institutional investors without coverage by analysts. In fact, many large money managers have provisions against investing in a company unless at least one investment banking analyst writes about it.

Investment banks have a limit to the number of analysts they can employ and tend to focus their resources on the biggest companies first, leaving a lot of small companies out to dry.

The other major change in the investment banking industry since the dot-com boom has been the consolidation of small banks focused specifically on technology companies. These boutique investment banks built good businesses consulting start-ups and taking tech companies public. Their success running up to the dot-com boom attracted attention and many small banks were acquired by bigger investment banks or rolled up into consumer banks following the repeal of the Glass-Steagall Act, a long-standing law preventing just such business combinations.

Former National Venture Capital Association chairman and venture capitalist Dixon Doll specifically pointed to the consolidation of Alex Brown, Hambrecht & Quist, Montgomery Securities, and Robertson Stephens—all key boutique banks of the 1990s—as a serious problem for venture capital liquidity.[8] To make matters worse, even the big banks have had trouble as of late, with Bear Stearns, Lehman Brothers, and Merrill Lynch folding during the financial crisis of 2008.

Sarbanes-Oxley Regulation

A combination of investor pain after the dot-com boom and shock over the massive fraud at Enron and WorldCom resulted in government regulation of corporate governance. The main piece of legislation was the Sarbanes-Oxley Act of 2002, which had many facets, but two major ones that made venture capital investing harder.

The first provision that impacted venture capitalists was Title III of the Act, which made corporate boards individually responsible for the accuracy of financial reports. This made sitting on the board of a public company a potential liability for venture investors. Many interpreted the law to mean that if a company ran into any accounting error they might be forced to pay a penalty or even go to jail. Lots of venture investors determined the small chance of a big cost outweighed the big chance of no cost at all.

Title III was important to venture capitalists, but might not have significantly hurt their business. After all, their time might be better spent working with small, high-growth companies than advising established public companies.

The real blow to the venture capital business came in the form of the additional costs of complying with all 11 titles of Sarbanes-Oxley. A small company might expect to pay anywhere from $250,000 to $2 million to ensure its records were secure, correct, and in compliance with government standards.

It may not sound like a lot of money, but it could be the kiss of death for a start-up struggling to break even. It increased the amount of money companies had to make before they could afford to go public.

Consolidation of Customers and Strategic Acquirers

Start-ups are often viewed as being at war with entrenched corporations. The innovators are perceived to be poised to pounce on the incumbents. But the reality is that start-ups often need medium and large public companies to buy their products and to potentially acquire their stock.

The best type of environment for a start-up to grow is one with a variety of potential customers. Big companies may be more willing to go with an unknown brand or buy from a start-up if they think it may give them an edge over competitors.

Silicon Valley start-ups often find their first and best customers are other start-ups or the smallest public companies that are still in growth mode. These customers often give good product feedback, don't take a long time to commit to buying, and don't require the most stringent specifications. That's very different from a huge global conglomerate that may take months before making a purchasing agreement or can have too many middle managers with anxiety about buying from a recently founded company.

A start-up that can sell to five companies is better off than one that just sells to one company. The ability to sell to a variety of customers indicates a true demand for a start-up's products and doesn't tie the company to a single powerful customer that could stop buying at any time.

Just as smaller-sized public companies competing with one another make good customers, they can also make good strategic acquirers. When two public companies compete with each other, each may think that a start-up has the key technology it needs to win market dominance. This is how bidding wars begin.

Bidding wars are good for entrepreneurs and their investors because it drives the acquisition price up. If there's only a single potential acquirer, it has the power to set the purchase price much lower. A company without clear competition may not feel pressure to get ahead by quickly buying a start-up, especially when it may be able to build the needed technology itself over a number of years.

Overall, industry consolidation makes both selling products and being acquired more difficult for start-ups. At one time, it was possible to sell routers, switches, and fiber-optic connections—the guts of telecommunications—to Sprint, Nextel, SBC, AT&T, Verizon, and MCI. Now only three of these telecom companies control the majority of the U.S. market, and competition for new technologies has decreased. This slows innovation and depresses returns for investors in telecom equipment start-ups.

Institutional Investor Growth

Starting in the 1980s and throughout the 1990s, Americans put ever-greater amounts of their savings into the stock market through direct investments and mutual funds. More capital under management at big funds such as Fidelity meant they had an even harder time investing in small companies.

Just as tigers don't hunt mice, most big investment funds have provisions that prevent them from buying into small companies.

Not every large firm has explicit restraints; it's often just the way the math works out. Consider two typical provisions: The institution may not hold more than 5 percent of a company's outstanding shares; and it will not make any investments smaller than $10 million. Put these two restrictions together and it limits the institutional investor's ability to invest in any company with a market capitalization under $200 million.

That math makes it tough for small companies to attract stable, long-term institutional investors. Venture capitalists are increasingly forced to hold on to small companies until they reach a size that is attractive to big public market stock institutional buyers.

Difficulty Commercializing Cleantech

The emerging industry that focuses on environmentally friendly technologies looked like it could be the next big thing for Silicon Valley. Entrepreneurs turned their focus to producing better solar panels, ethanol distilling, and even manufacturing electric cars. Investors thought they might ride a wave of public interest and enthusiasm for combating global warming, substituting away from $100 per barrel "peak oil," and embracing efficiency.

But unlike software start-ups, dot-com companies, and semiconductor design shops, cleantech companies called for buckets and buckets of cash to actually build physical things. Many needed several hundred million dollars of investment before they could even get to revenue—a problem for private investors with limited resources and a need to flip companies into either the arms of acquirers or up to the public market.

The Recession

A recession has five major impacts on venture capitalists:

1. Entrepreneurs that might normally leave a stable job to start a company stay entrenched in large corporations.

2. A start-up's customers delay purchasing products as budgets shrink.

3. Plunging public market stock prices make the climate for new issues unfavorable. IPOs just don't happen.

4. Potential acquirers lower their growth expectations and put off buying start-ups.

5. Limited partner investors reduce their allocations to venture capital funds. LPs balance their portfolios a little like a chef making a cake balances different ingredients. If a chef finds he only has three eggs instead of four, he'll have to use less flour and milk to keep the recipe balanced. When an LP's public market investments decrease in value, she will look to cut her allocation to venture capital in order to keep her portfolio balanced. It's called the *denominator problem* and may prevent some limited partners from investing in venture capital firms for several years.

Need for Innovation

The poor returns venture funds have delivered combined with a decreased supply of limited partner investment dollars is going to be hard on the industry of innovation financing. Researchers predict half of the operating venture capital firms of 2009 won't be in business within half a decade.[9]

It's more important now than ever that investors think hard about how to adapt and evolve to the new environment they'll be doing business in.

"What creates change is pressure," says John Balen, a general partner at Canaan Partners. The big pressure for venture capitalists, nearly a decade after the dot-com boom, is finding new ways of organizing, fundraising, generating deal flow, and achieving liquidity. We'll consider each in the coming chapters.

Summary

A venture capital firm professionally manages money on behalf of investors by directing it to high-growth opportunities involving new technologies, markets, or business processes. Venture capital investors generally do not seek total control of a company's board of directors or a controlling share of its stocks as buyout investors might.

Venture capitalists invest at early stages of a company's development or at inflection points that precipitate rapid growth. They hold their shares until they can either sell the company to a strategic acquirer or take the company public.

General partners run a venture firm's day-to-day investing process and raise funds from limited partners, which are typically large financial institutions such as pension funds and university endowments.

The performance of a venture capital fund is hard to determine, since the companies held in its investment portfolio take years to mature and one major hit could drastically improve a fund's returns overnight. Industry statistics may be skewed by a handful of super-performers that offset the majority of money losers.

Venture capital funds have not performed well since the dot-com boom due to the venture overhang, changes to the investment banking industry, Sarbanes-Oxley regulation, consolidation of customers and strategic acquirers, institutional investor growth, difficulty commercializing cleantech, and the recession.

Investors face an opportunity to innovate on existing venture capital business models.

Notes

1. "Venture Impact: The Economic Importance of Venture Capital-Backed Companies to the U.S. Economy (Fifth Edition)," Global Insight and the National Venture Capital Association, 2009, http://bit.ly/aFJCg4.
2. Thomson Reuters publishes a directory of limited partners each year that can be a useful resource for anyone looking to raise funds.
3. "Education and Tech Entrepreneurship," Ewing Marion Kauffman Foundation, May, 2008, http://bit.ly/aoOslo.
4. "VentureSource: 1Q 2010 U.S. Liquidity Report," Dow Jones press release, April 1, 2010, http://bit.ly/cwgSQ1.
5. "CalPERS Performance Data: California Emerging Ventures I, II, III & IV," December 2008, http://bit.ly/9G4vDa. The data are continuously updated and CalPERs does not keep separate web pages for previous quarters.
6. "Polachi VC Survey: Pulse on the Industry," July, 2009, http://bit.ly/9H8tn1.
7. "Overhang of Venture Capital Funds at $68 Billion; Fundraising Increases in 4Q03, According to Quarterly Report from VentureOne," *PRNewswire*, March 29, 2004, http://bit.ly/cGug2g.
8. "NVCA Releases Recommendations to Restore Liquidity in the U.S. Venture Capital Industry," NVCAToday.com, http://bit.ly/aX52k1.
9. "Right-sizing the U.S. Venture Capital Industry," Ewing Marion Kauffman Foundation, June, 2009, http://bit.ly/awldEN.

CHAPTER 2

Careers and Organization

After reading this chapter, you will be able to:

- Launch your career in venture capital.
- Map a career path from the most junior levels of a firm to the most senior.
- Manage your career growth.
- Quickly evaluate any investor you meet using five questions.
- Distinguish between horizontal and vertical venture capital firms.
- Plan for the future of your firm.

Launching a Career

The accepted wisdom is that there is no direct career path to become a venture capitalist. There are a handful of investors who have come from disparate backgrounds that seem to justify this position. You'll likely hear about Michael Moritz, a journalist for *Time* magazine and the author of a book about Apple Computer before he became a venture capitalist. But Moritz is an exception rather than the rule.

Venture capitalists typically come from three different walks of life:

1. Entrepreneurs who have made good and want to stay in the game as investors.

2. Executives who have spent a long time considering a certain type of industry and are technical or execution experts.

3. Those who are business school–trained and plucked out of consulting, banking, and other professional positions.

There are several ways to get hired into a venture capital firm. The first, and best, is to know someone already working for a firm. That person can be a friend, a family member, or someone you've worked with in the past. Industry insiders have the best viewpoint into who is hiring, what they're looking for, and what your chances of getting a position are. Your connection may even help you get a job at his or her firm.

Venture capitalists have a lot of casual acquaintances. A big part of their job is to collect such people; so shaking hands and swapping business cards isn't likely to score you a position. Venture investors are most comfortable working with people with whom they have worked with in the past. That's one of the reasons so many former entrepreneurs find their way into the business: They are well known to the people who do the hiring.

You can tell what some firms look for in a new hire by seeing what their partners have in common. For example, Accel Partners prefers graduates of Harvard Business School or Stanford's Graduate School of Business who distinguished themselves as being at the top of their class. New Enterprise Associates picks people who have passed through the Kauffman Fellowship Program, which provides supplementary education and career opportunities to aspiring business school students. Kleiner Perkins has followed a different strategy. It has shown a distinct preference for women and minorities and has actively pursued a pro-female hiring strategy. When hiring, it also skews toward people with PhDs.

There is one other way to become a venture capitalist: Start your own firm. New venture firms pop up like mushrooms around Silicon Valley, but few actually are able to raise money and successfully invest it. There's more on how new firms get started in Chapter 3.

IN THE REAL WORLD

Job Wanted: Venture Capitalist

Venture firms don't usually advertise for their positions. But they do work with headhunters and talent scouts to find people who might fit their criteria. Here's an example of a recent advertisement for a "Pre-MBA Associate" level position at a venture firm in the Boston area. The listing first appeared in July 2009 in a posting by The Pinnacle Group, a headhunting firm:

Qualifications: Our client is a prominent top-tier investment firm with a stellar track record in the Boston area. Their principal investment focus is in technology-based companies in sectors such as software, business services, consumer Internet, and wireless. They make investments in both VC [venture capital] and PE [private equity], and have a substantial amount of their fund to deploy.

Position Summary: They are seeking an associate who will be an integral member of the sourcing team and would work closely with senior members of the firm. The position is a pre-MBA opportunity for three years, though there is the potential for a career track position for an associate with outstanding performance. The primary focus of this role is sourcing opportunities, conducting technical and business due diligence, market and competitive analysis, and monitoring of portfolio companies. They need this associate to start in late summer of 2009 to work from their Boston office.

Responsibilities:

- Assisting in the sourcing of private equity opportunities.
- Conducting due diligence of potential investment opportunities.
- Reviewing market research and developing market intelligence.
- Preparing financial models in support of investment recommendations.
- Monitoring performance of portfolio companies.

Requirements:

- One to three years of relevant sourcing experience in investment banking, private equity, or consulting.
- Experience in technology is preferred.
- Bachelor's degree with a record of academic achievement required.
- Ability to form independent investment judgments and work well independently.

- Outstanding interpersonal skills, persistence, and strong initiative required.
- Ability to analyze a wide variety of business plans.
- Strong due diligence and financial modeling skills.
- Strong teamwork skills and excellent work ethic.

Career Ladder

During the past 20 years, the majority of venture capitalists were white males in their late thirties to early fifties, educated at either Harvard or Stanford Business School and with a background in either operations or entrepreneurship. Venture capitalists typically work in partnerships of 3 to 10 investors with offices within five miles of Sand Hill Road in Menlo Park, California, and make $774,000 a year, according to data from Thomson Reuters. These characterizations are changing as firms diversify and expand beyond their roots.

Not all firms have defined ranks, and each firm may define its titles differently, but there are some industry norms. The compensation data for each rank presented in Exhibit 2.1 come from Thomson Reuters' annual compensation survey.[1]

Nurturing Your Career as a Venture Capitalist

Once you've scored that job as a venture capitalist, your future success will depend on your ability to pick mentors, build connections, establish a reputation, cultivate skepticism, learn patience, and enjoy what you do.

EXHIBIT 2.1

The Venture Capital Career Ladder

Position	Pay	Experience	Explanation
Analyst	$76,000 base and $48,000 bonuses	Hired after completing an undergraduate education.	The lowest professional position at a venture firm. One seldom runs into analysts at early stage venture firms, as there is less opportunity to crunch numbers or compile industry research for the type of deals early stage investors make. The bigger the fund an analyst works at, the higher his or her compensation is likely to be.
Associate	$107,000 base and $59,000 bonuses	Less than 5 years of work experience and lacks an MBA.	More common than the analyst position. Associates generally work a 2-year term before going to business school. They used to be culled from the ranks of entrepreneurs and engineers, but as firms move toward larger, more complex deals, associates are increasingly coming from financial and legal backgrounds. Associates at large venture firms make a slightly higher base salary than associates at small venture firms, but their bonuses over the past several years have been as much as 100% higher.
Senior Associate	$131,000 base and $76,000 bonuses	MBA graduates with typically less than 3 years of experience.	Support portfolio companies, oversee some aspects of execution and sit in on deals. Some will have a small taste of the carry. Senior associates at the biggest funds typically make about $110,000 more per year than their compatriots at the smallest venture funds.
Vice President	$177,000 base and $117,000 bonuses	More than 3 years of post-MBA experience.	Provide substantial support to portfolio companies and sometimes sit on boards. This position may be the fastest growing in venture capital as firms realize they need more experienced support as they tackle increasingly complex deals. The position is also considered to be a feeder for

Title	Compensation	Experience	Description
			future principals and partners. Nearly all vice presidents get carry, as much as five times more than senior associates.
Principal	$191,000 base and $121,000 bonuses	More than 6 years of post-MBA experience.	On track to become a partner who may or may not lead his or her own deals. Principals almost always get carry and may sit on boards of directors that a firm's senior partners don't want to deal with anymore.
Venture Partner	Not tracked	More than 6 years of post-MBA experience and slightly more experience than principals.	Typically half a step up from principals, but below full partners.
Partner	$436,000 base, $338,000 bonuses, and the carried interest	Experience varies, but most partners have 15 to 20 years of post-MBA experience either investing or running organizations.	The bosses of a venture fund. Most firms have between three and seven partners who get the majority of the carried interest.
Managing General Partner	Not tracked	Experience varies, but most partners have 15 to 20 years of post-MBA experience either investing or running organizations.	A title generally reserved for a firm's founder or highest-ranking investor. Managing general partners get more money than their colleagues, either as salary or in the form of additional carried interest compensation. This title is sometimes called *managing director*.
Controller	Not tracked	Experience varies, but a legal or accounting background is a big plus.	Makes sure that all the details of deals are in order. This partner-level position usually goes to someone from a financial or legal background. The controller does not make investments and does not take board seats. They act as a resource for other partners.
Human Capital Officer	Not tracked	A background in headhunting or executive placement is a plus.	Helps recruit talent into a firm's portfolio companies. Not every firm has one, but some of the most successful firms have in-sourced headhunters to ensure that they get the best executives and engineers for their companies.

(continued)

EXHIBIT 2.1

(Continued)

Position	Pay	Experience	Explanation
Partner Emeritus	Not tracked	Must be a retired partner of the firm.	A retired general partner who works more on his golf game than on making investments. Firms sometimes offer this honorary title to project a sense of continuity and to remind both entrepreneurs and limited partners of past success and excellence.
Entrepreneur in Residence (EIR)	Depending on an EIR's experience level, they might expect to earn as much inside a venture firm as at a mid-sized private company	Someone who has made a lot of money in the past.	Each firm has its own policy for EIRs, but it is generally considered to be a temporary position lasting up to 18 months where an entrepreneur works on a new start-up. The EIR sits in on deal pitches and advises the general partners, when appropriate, on the technical barriers or execution challenges startups face. During this time, the EIR is also looking for a compelling new opportunity to apply his or her particular skill set. Some firms call EIRs by different names. For example, Sequoia Capital calls them "Entrepreneurs in Action."

Picking Mentors

The first step to learning a new skill is finding a teacher. A good mentor in the venture business is someone who has spent more time doing deals than you have. This person need not be successful. In fact, there's a lot to be learned from failure and a lot to be taught about how to deal with it. Learning from a successful person is like learning from a captain that has only sailed on sunny days. You're most likely to need a mentor when the clouds darken, the wind kicks up, and the waves start rolling ever higher. Pick somebody who has weathered the storm. Venture capitalists may build great returns by spending time with winners, but they make their reputations based on how they work with the companies that look like losers.

Most firms assign junior investors as a subordinate to one or two general partners and it's easy to look up to that person as a mentor. After all, the senior people in your firm know best how business is done in your office and may spend a fair amount of time explaining it to you.

It's important to learn what you're told, but there are two good reasons to look for outside help as well. The first is that your interests and the interests of the firm's senior partners may eventually diverge as you take on more power and threaten their fiefdom. They also have an incentive not to share the rewards of investing with you— even when you deserve them. Experienced outsiders may help you view what goes on at your firm with greater skepticism.

The second reason to look to outsiders for guidance is that they may help you approach problems differently. Firms can suffer from uniform thinking, or can fall into patterns of operation. Creativity is seldom promoted inside an organization, but an outsider may have unique insights that can help you.

You can have many mentors. You may go to one person for help doing deals, another for help running board meetings, and yet another may be a source of insight into firm politics. The more sources you can cultivate, the better informed you will be.

Some people are reticent to approach potential mentors, thinking that these people are too important, too busy, or too disinterested. These perceptions couldn't be further from the truth. Most people love giving advice because it makes them feel knowledgeable and useful. Asking someone for advice is a great compliment.

Mentors can play one more important role—they can help you get your next job. A good mentor may know just the right opportunity for you and can be in a position to recommend you for it. At some level, they may feel invested in you and take great pleasure in seeing you do well.

Building Connections

Your connection to a mentor may be your first and most important connection, but it's only one of many you'll need to be successful. Constructing a powerful Rolodex takes time and effort, but pays off handsomely in the venture business. The three most important connections to make are to experts, engineers, and entrepreneurs.

Experts can help you evaluate new technologies and understand emerging opportunities, and may even be a source of innovation themselves. Experts can include university professors, engineers, or industry analysts. Making friends with these people usually means paying great compliments to their hard-won knowledge. If you'd spent your life trying to understand the complexity of optical division multiplexing (an important part of the fiber-optic communications business), wouldn't you be happy to have someone treat your insights as important?

Engineers may be your future employees. It's good to ingratiate yourself with them as you may someday be wooing them to work at one of your portfolio companies. Engineers are also a good source of practical understanding. The expert may know that a new technology is possible, but an engineer can tell you if the technology can be translated into a product. Many start-ups go under because they lack the ability to turn a product into something they can sell a thousand units of.

Entrepreneurs will pitch you their ideas. There's a funny psychology of formal pitches that puts an investor into the mind-set of saying "no." Informal pitches, by the beach or over a glass of beer, turn the adversarial tone of a formal meeting on its head. You're more likely to entertain an idea put forth by somebody you know and like than somebody that you may be meeting for the first time. Building friendships with entrepreneurs can also expose you to their ideas of what would make a good business. Often they have insights that others lack. If engineers can tell you how to turn a concept into a product, entrepreneurs will know how to make that product into something customers will want.

Over time, you may also want to cultivate connections to investment bankers, big company business development executives, other venture capitalists, and even journalists.

Establishing a Reputation

Junior investors try to make a reputation as deal-sourcing go-getters. After two years or so, an associate might expect to be promoted to venture partner. Venture partners are typically stuck sitting on corporate boards that nobody else wants—the real dogs.

This can be a big problem for emerging venture investors. A young investor can find himself putting out fires he didn't start. Eventually those companies fall off of people's résumés and out of people's minds. But at the time, it can distract from the business of finding new, more promising companies.

Worse, perhaps, when it comes to trying to establish a career, is finding a great company and then not getting any credit for your role in spotting it. Consider the case of a junior associate whose job it is to vet early stage investment opportunities for consideration by the firm. He works hard, networking with industry experts, calling customers, reading professional journals, and sifting through piles of potential deals to find just the right one.

And finally he finds a company that might be just right for his firm's investment focus and is poised to rapidly grow. His bosses at the firm are beside themselves with happiness and decide they want to invest $10 million in the start-up. But the senior partners want to negotiate the deal themselves. Then one of the partners will take a board seat at the start-up and shepherd it through its rapid growth phase.

On the web site, and to the outside world, the partner is given credit for the deal—even though it was the junior associate who did the work of finding and selecting it.

It may not seem like a big deal, but what happens if the invest-ment is successful and the firm is able to take the start-up public or sell it for several hundred million dollars? The partner will get credit for supporting the start-up and that will attract the next round of entrepreneurs to seek him out as a potential funder. He'll be in the virtuous cycle where a perception of success creates more success. Few, if any, will remember the crucial role the junior associate played in finding and advocating the deal.

This type of credit claiming is not unusual in business. It is often the way things are supposed to work. Each firm keeps track of the junior executives it considers to be its hot prospects and always faces the choice of promoting them or losing them to another firm.

Not every firm gets it right. In fact, the problem of promoting promising young people to positions of power is one of the most pressing for venture firms. It's gotten so bad, in fact, that industry pundits have given the process a name: "succession planning."

Cultivating Skepticism

Silicon Valley suffers from a mass hysteria of optimism and it's easy to be infected whenever you hear about a new start-up's amazing tech-nology and huge addressable market.

The sad truth is that most products never get off the ground. Most markets are captured by incumbents. Most of the time, things just don't work out, and it can be very painful to invest your heart in every company that comes along.

There's no formula for balancing skepticism with optimism when it comes to venture investing, but it's a daily necessity.

Learning Patience

Investors don't get instant gratification for their efforts. It takes years for companies to mature, launch products, sign customers, and make serious money. This is especially true for early stage investors who can expect a decade to pass before their companies fully grow up.

Beyond patience for results, young investors must also learn to be patient with the people they work with. Company founders make mistakes; they hide things from the board and can be difficult to work with as the going gets tough. These tempests are typically confined to their teapots and can blow over quickly, if an investor just waits it out and lets things happen. This is especially true when working with first-time founders or other junior executives. Tempers can be short when millions of dollars are on the line, but investors must learn to take the long view.

Junior venture capitalists must also have patience with their co-workers and senior partners. Gray-haired investors have been around the block and know which businesses work and which don't. Having the patience to listen to their concerns about a deal can pay dividends down the road.

Careers are not built overnight; no matter how smart you are, where you earned your MBA, or what success you've had in the past. Nobody goes from associate to managing director immediately. Your responsibility and earnings will grow with time, if you're patient.

Enjoying What You Do

This is something I have heard over and over from venture capitalists: If you're not enjoying your business, it's going to be hard to keep doing it. That doesn't mean you have to enjoy every part of what you do, or enjoy every day on the job.

Different people enjoy different things. Some investors love meeting entrepreneurs, others like deal-making negotiations and yet others enjoy nothing better than spending an evening reading technical journals. Find what makes you happy during the day and try to focus on doing more of that.

TIPS AND TECHNIQUES

Venture Capitalist Classification

How do you distinguish an experienced venture capitalist sitting on a big pile of investment funds from a junior associate? Here are useful questions to classify investors you meet:

How big is your current fund? This can have a lot of different meanings. Big funds are typically more successful than small ones, all other things being equal. Bigger funds typically mean bigger management fees for the partnership.

Following up is important on this question. You might ask what stage of investment the firm focuses on, because a firm that focuses on late stage investing may have a much larger fund than one that focuses on early stage investing.

Firms that employ more general partners have bigger funds. How much bigger? Well, balanced stage investors typically set aside $30 million to $50 million per partner for investing over three to five years. The calculus of how much each partner may be expected to invest is particular to each firm, and there are seldom formal rules put in place.

What sectors and stages do you specialize in? Talking to a late stage information technology investor about early stage biotechnology is a little bit like talking to a Martian about the weather on Venus. The two investors focus on completely different things.

What is your position at the firm? Knowing what rank a person has at a firm can help you determine if they write checks to start-ups or support the people who do.

What companies are or were you directly involved with? Firms take generations to build up a track record. Once a strong investment history is in place, everyone at the firm memorizes the hits and will drop the names of success stories willy-nilly. A general partner will typically tell you which companies they are a director of. Expect an answer of "I sit on the boards of X, Y, and Z." Associate-level investors may reel off a list of companies they did the legwork for. It's a good idea to follow up with a question about whether or not the person sits on company boards.

When was your last fund raised? This question is designed to give you a sense of how successful the firm is. The typical fund-raising cycle for a firm is every three to five years. Any firm that has not raised a fund in more than five years may be winding down.

Firm Structure and Organization

Venture firms organize themselves into two dominant structural partnerships: horizontal and vertical. Each has advantages and disadvantages. The way a firm is set up dictates how it does deals, how its partners are compensated and treated, and how the firm evolves.

Horizontal Partnerships

A horizontal firm treats every investor as equal. Imagine tenured professors at a faculty meeting, each with his or her particular specialty. Each partner has certain responsibilities when it comes to finding and evaluating investments, and each partner shares the returns when those investments pay off.

The most famous example of a horizontal firm is Benchmark Capital, a firm with a string of Internet investment hits, including eBay. When Benchmark formed its fund, it pulled together two sets of experienced venture investors and threw in an investment banking analyst and an executive headhunter. Each partner shares the proceeds of investing, called the *carry*, equally.

Author Randall Stross describes exactly how the partners did business at the time of the dot-com boom in his book *eBoys*. One of the partners would find a start-up to invest in and do an initial background check on the entrepreneurs, the market potential, and the technology. If the company seemed like a reasonable investment, the partner would bring it to the rest of the Benchmark team for a decision.

The Benchmark team would ask questions, grilling both the start-up's entrepreneur and the partner who was sponsoring the potential investment. Eventually, the partners would put it to a vote. A simple majority would approve the deal and put the sponsoring partner in charge of managing the relationship with the start-up. The gains from the investment would be split among the partners, so each partner has an incentive to pick winners and help make them successful.

Benchmark was not the first firm to establish a horizontal partnership. Many firms set themselves up similarly—it's a model that law firms, banks, and other enterprises frequently use.

Horizontal firms are incentivized to share information and decision making across the partnership. Such firms are built on collaboration instead of competition and can work well with the right people. It's particularly well suited to working with early stage companies that require a lot of hand holding and can benefit from the collective advice and wisdom of an entire partnership.

But there's a lot that can go wrong. There are five basic scenarios that can shake a horizontal partnership:

1. Great success

2. Great failure

3. Quick-changing market

4. An urge to invest in ever-larger deals

5. The passage of time

Good venture capital teams work together to make their best investors even better. Maybe investor X at the firm has a great relationship with the business development executive at a large corporation that investor Y is trying to sell his start-up to. Structuring a venture firm horizontally encourages this kind of teamwork among partners.

A bad baseball team has trouble fielding all-stars. When a player does prove to be good, he usually leaves for a better team and a bigger salary. Horizontally structured venture firms can have trouble keeping an investor who proves to be better than the rest of the general partners. What's the incentive to stay at a firm that redistributes a large portion of your investment proceeds to general partners who are not equally good?

The same question might apply to a different scenario. What happens when an investor is clearly not successful—investing in one dog of a company after another—and the rest of the partnership ends up paying for his yacht? It breeds resentment.

A partnership of equals cannot long stand when the partners no longer perceive themselves to be equal.

A rapidly changing market requires fast decision-making—something a horizontal partnership is not set up to do well. A strong leader can set strategy and change direction rapidly, but committees of equals generally can't.

The technology business is constantly changing. Sectors fall into favor seemingly overnight and can be out of vogue equally fast. Networking equipment was super hot in 2000, with start-ups collecting over $2.5 billion from venture capitalists, according to data from Thomson Reuters. By 2003, investment slackened to $101 million. Demand had been filled.

Moving out of the networking equipment business and into clean technology investing would have been a smart move by 2004. Not every firm is able to make such a sharp turn in direction, but firms with a strong centralized line of management are better equipped to do so.

This problem is acutely felt by horizontal firms set up to have a specific partner focused on a particular technology. A partner who spent his or her entire career working in the semiconductor business and has only invested in semiconductor-related start-ups may have a tough time adjusting to a market that no longer demands semiconductor innovations. A horizontal firm may not have the ability to either retire or repurpose its outdated partner.

Trouble with star partners, underperforming investors, and adapting to a rapidly changing market can affect any horizontal partnership at any time. But there are two major forces driving the venture capital business away from horizontal partnerships and toward vertical organizations: the demand for bigger venture capital funds and the maturation of the business.

Vertical Partnerships

The demand for venture capital, as an asset class, fluctuates with time. But limited partner demand to participate in the top funds stays insatiable. A good firm, which consistently provides returns in excess of 20 percent per year, will find itself able to raise hundreds of millions of dollars. Sometimes this is more than it can reasonably take. These high-performance firms will also see thousands of pitches from entrepreneurs each year—more than any small group could evaluate by itself.

A venture firm might find its sole limitation to be the number of hours its general partners can spend each day. To some extent, venture firms have solved this problem by focusing the time of their most experienced and successful partners on only those activities that require difficult decisions or careful negotiation.

They then hire a series of underlings to perform duties such as reading business plans, finding investment opportunities, and doing background checks on entrepreneurs. The junior staffers look for good investment targets. Middle-ranking employees evaluate those opportunities and the senior staffers make critical decisions about the investments and sit on the boards of directors.

Adding layers of support to a venture firm allows the partners to raise a bigger fund and invest in a greater number of start-ups. Bigger funds mean bigger management fees and more investments mean more chances at bat to swing for the fences. Limited partners, who are all too anxious to get a chance to invest in a top-performing fund, write bigger checks.

Sequoia Capital went to a vertical structure faster than most. Between 2006 and 2009, it hired 10 new junior investors to supplement its staff of 15 experienced partners. That was just for its U.S. investing practice. Its China, India, and Israel operations picked up even more junior staff to lighten the load for senior partners.

The new, junior employees primarily focused on Sequoia's "growth" stage investment team and its public market investment group. Each operational group was founded to invest an ever-larger sum on behalf of the successful early stage firm. The firm raised an $861-million growth fund to do both public company investments and large, late stage private investments in 2006 to supplement its $445 million early stage fund. It increased its growth operations again in 2008, raising a $929.5 million fund. These bigger funds came with big fees for managing them.

This type of progression is natural in almost any industry as the people who start a business move into higher management roles. Still, venture capital firms have been reticent to move toward a vertical organization structure for a number of reasons.

The first is that those in control are unwilling or unable to cede power to the next generation. There are substantial incentives for a senior partner to continue reaping the rewards of successful brand building well beyond the age of retirement. Succession planning is one of the most difficult problems a firm can face.

The second is a vertical structure decreases transparency. Who is responsible for arranging a successful investment? Is it the analyst that finds the deal, the vice president who vets it, or the partner who approves it? Transparency is important to limited partner investors. They need assurance that whomever they're committing money to is the person that will be able to find and finance promising entrepreneurs in the future.

The third problem is logistical. It is difficult to establish a career path for next generation venture capitalists. Some firms never get it right, holding promising candidates down, keeping them out of profit sharing, and milking them for years. Eventually those junior investors pull the ripcord and escape to higher-paying positions.

Planning for the Future

Venture firms are a lot like small, family-owned businesses. In both there's a core group of founders with a significant interest in seeing the business thrive. These founders do well, get rich, and see their wealth multiplied. They build good reputations and good people want to work with them. But the founders get old, tired, and may even become complacent as their hunger to succeed is sated.

As a company or firm gets further away from its founders, its chances of failing increase. Only 30 percent of family-run businesses succeed into the second generation, according to government studies. That number falls to 15 percent by the third generation, according to data from the U.S. Small Business Administration.

The story in family-owned businesses is familiar: Senior works hard to build the brand and give his family a luxurious lifestyle. Work is anathema to Junior, who'd rather party on the yacht than roll up his sleeves and get to work. The business slows and eventually fails.

Phasing a successful executive out and a younger executive in can be difficult. It's like giving your teenager the keys to the Porsche and closing your eyes as he roars out of the driveway.

At least when there is a family member involved there is some incentive to shepherd this person into a position of power and prominence. But because venture capital firms are partnerships, rather than hierarchical corporations, an established investor cannot automatically pass his stake in the partnership to a son or daughter. Plenty of sons (and at least one daughter) have gone on to be venture capitalists like their fathers—but usually at different firms.

Without that incentive to pass on an inheritance of control to a direct, biological heir, senior partners have an incentive to stay in their lucrative positions as long as possible. In fact, many do.

In larger, non–family controlled corporations, a company's board of directors may step in to put a cap on excessive tenures by key executives. It's not unusual to see a mandated retirement age for CEOs at large public companies.

But venture firms don't have a board of directors that can intervene. Instead, senior partners stay involved, which may mean picking up the lion's share of any financial return from deals done by the junior investors.

That's the most common complaint among junior investors and one that typically leads to the greatest friction between generations.

The most famously flubbed succession planning happened in 1999 when six junior investors left storied venture firms Brentwood Venture Capital and Institutional Venture Partners (IVP) to found tech-focused Redpoint Ventures.

The move was something you might have only seen during the dot-com boom. When else would six headstrong investors issue a press release saying they'd quit their jobs to launch a fund with a code name? The investors—Jeff Brody, Tom Dyal, Tim Haley, Brad Jones, John Walecka, and Geoff Yang—quit their jobs in August and closed their first fund in November 1999 at $600 million.

The junior partners that founded Redpoint could quickly reap all the rewards of their investing efforts instead of waiting in line to pick up a smaller piece of the carried interest left over after the senior partners of Brentwood and IVP had taken their share.

Successful succession planning requires certain key factors not found at every firm.

The first requirement is a strong, centralized power structure capable of driving change without total consensus. Usually this takes the form of a single managing director or firm founder. Just as firms with a vertical structure are better suited to adapt to external change, they are also more capable of driving internal changes. The best example is perhaps Sequoia Capital's Don Valentine, who founded the firm in 1972 and gradually transferred control to Michael Moritz. Valentine stays on as an advisor, but Moritz leads the firm's meetings and accepts more of the firm's investing returns than any other partner, sources say.

The second requirement is a desire to build a lasting brand. Some investors want to create a firm that people will continue to talk about decades later. When it was popular for founders to lend their own names to their firms, Valentine picked Sequoia Capital specifically so the firm could survive beyond its founder.

Steve Woodsum followed suit in 1984, naming his private equity fund Summit Partners for the same reason.[2] Beyond the branding, Woodsum knew he needed opportunities for his junior investors to grow and eventually take control of the firm. In 2000, Woodsum and his other cofounders handed Summit's management over to the junior executives they'd been mentoring for several years. It was a complete handoff and both the old partners and the new management had to make that clear to their limited partners.

The third requirement is the most likely to be overlooked, but may be just as important as the first two. Junior partners should be able to see a path of progression and career advancement. This can take several forms. Draper Fisher Jurvetson, for example, promoted one of its junior investors exactly one year after hiring him. It sent a clear signal that the firm wanted him to advance and showed other new employees what to expect.

Every firm benefits from having several investors who have progressed through its ranks to act as a beacon to other, more junior investors. Most firms express an either tacit or explicit set of steps that must be completed before an analyst can become an associate or before an associate can become a venture partner.

One of the best ways to structurally ensure that succession happens in a regular and programmatic fashion is to put promotions and pay increases in step with fundraising. Investor compensation is typically determined by agreement between the general partners and limited partners at the outset of a fund. Some firms will wait to split up the fees and carried interest for the end of each year or at the end of a fund's life cycle.

Firms such as Advanced Technology Ventures have migrated to shorter, three-year fund cycles instead of five- or six-year fundraising cycles specifically to ensure that their younger investors will get a shot at the carry sooner. One venture capitalist at an "evergreen" fund that invests the family fortune of a particularly rich Canadian, lamented his firm's lack of fundraising cycle, saying that all his buddies at other firms got promotions each time they raised a new fund.

Summary

Although there is no certain path to a career in venture capital, there are several jobs that funnel professionals into venture capital positions. If you look at the background of successful venture investors, you'll see that they were previously entrepreneurs, technical experts, or banking and consulting executives. There are plenty of notable exceptions to this rule however.

Many venture capital firms have ranks that differentiate duties and compensation. The ranks from lowest to highest are:

- Analyst
- Associate
- Senior Associate

- Vice President
- Principal
- Venture Partner
- Partner
- Managing General Partner

Once you get a venture capital job, you should pick mentors, build connections, establish a reputation, cultivate skepticism, learn patience, and enjoy what you do.

Determining what responsibilities and power an investor has is a simple matter of asking questions about his or her fund size, specialization, position, involvement with key companies, and the freshness of his or her fund.

There are two major types of firm organizational structures: horizontal firms and vertical firms. Partners at horizontal firms share the rewards of investment and treat each other as equals but can be slow to react to market change. Partners at vertical firms recognize a hierarchy of prestige and compensation and may quickly adapt to a changing investment environment, but can be easily dominated by an overbearing manager. Firms that start off horizontal may migrate to vertical structures over time to better leverage the experience and time of senior partners.

Planning the future of a firm isn't easy. Many firms do not outlive their founders. Building a lasting brand means consolidating power into the hands of a competent decision maker, committing to permanence even if it takes money away from the firm's founders, and laying out a path for junior investors to take over.

Notes

1. The 2008 Private Equity Compensation Report by Thomson Financial and Glocap Search.
2. "The Next Generation," Thomson Reuters's *Venture Capital Journal*, June 1, 2002, http://bit.ly/c4lvNi.

CHAPTER 3

Fundraising

After reading this chapter, you will be able to:

- Appreciate the incentives of general partners and limited partners in the fundraising process.
- Understand the macroeconomic drivers behind fundraising.
- Anticipate the needs of limited partners.
- Strengthen your base of institutional limited partners and protect yourself against downturns.
- Understand why poor-performing venture firms are able to continue raising funds.
- Raise your first venture capital fund.
- Increase your compensation and fund size over time.
- Anticipate the future of fundraising.

Fundraising Is a Venture Capitalist's Number-One Priority

A lot of people think venture capitalists invest money as their primary job. Don't be fooled; venture capitalists get paid when they raise money, not when they invest it. The ability to raise money from large limited partners separates the professionals from the tourists. It's the single most important thing a venture capitalist can do. If you can't raise money, you can't invest money.

A venture capitalist that can raise a fund is guaranteed a paycheck. When a firm manages a fund, its general partners get a fee each year to cover expenses and pay their salaries. Each year, a typical general partnership might get between 2 and 2.5 percent of the fund they raise in consideration for their management efforts, although management fees as high as 3 percent are not unheard of. For example, a firm that raises $100 million will get $2 million each year it actively invests that fund to split among its partners and pay for office space, flight tickets, and business lunches. Such a firm might actively invest that fund for five years, after which the management fee might decrease substantially.

Raising a $100 million fund ensures that the general partners will earn $10 million over five years, regardless of any investment success. It's a good job if you can get it.

Venture capitalists raise money from large investors entrusted with hundreds of millions or even hundreds of billions of dollars. These big investors, such as university endowments and pension funds, enter into a special type of legal partnership with the venture capitalists that defines their roles. The endowments and pension funds have little active participation in the partnership. They write checks and later reap the rewards of the venture capital firm's investing activities. Because their role is limited, they are called *limited partners* or LPs for short.

Venture capitalists are the *general partners* or GPs of the special partnership agreement and are actively involved with making investments in start-up companies.

When a venture firm raises funds, it doesn't actually get any money—at least not immediately. What it has secured is a promise from its limited partners to wire money to its accounts in small increments over several years. The venture firm "calls down" or "makes capital calls" for several million dollars at a time from its limited partners to make a specific investment.

To raise funds, general partners can introduce themselves to potential limited partners, seek introductions from other professionals, or hire a placement agent. A placement agent helps dozens of firms raise funds, typically representing a portfolio of both venture capital firms and buyout shops.

A good placement agent is constantly in touch with the managers of large institutional funds and chief investment officers, assessing their needs, and looking for ways to match their money with firms the placement agent represents. It's not unusual for a placement agent to collect a fee near 2 percent of the total amount a fund expects to raise, or much higher.

When a limited partner gets interested in a fund, he or she may request the *private placement memorandum* (PPM). The PPM is a formalized, legal version of a PowerPoint pitch that outlines exactly who the partners are, what they will invest in, how much they expect to raise, and other details. The document contains about 5 pages of actual content and another 45 pages of boilerplate legalese.

At that point, there are essentially two types of fundraising: easy and hard. Fundraising is easy for firms that have good returns or have been through the process many times. Well-respected venture firm Kleiner Perkins Caufield & Byers, for example, is said to send out only the name of the fund it is raising and the money it expects to collect from a given investor and a deadline to fax back a signed commitment. Newer firms can take years to raise a fund, especially if they don't have a track record of success.

The goal is to sign a *limited partner agreement* (LPA), which defines a partnership between the venture firm and its sources of capital. The LPA will set out the fund's size and the terms and conditions of how the venture capitalists will be paid and will pay back the money limited partners invest. Once the ink is dry on the LPA, the fund is said to have *closed*.

A firm will set a target of how much it hopes to raise at the outset of its fundraising. It can have multiple "closes" as it corrals signatures from limited partners before reaching its target. For example, a firm with a $250 million target might have a first close on $125 million. It would be halfway through its fundraising process.

Targets are flexible. If a venture firm finds it can't raise as much money as it set out to, it can always take the money it has already closed on and begin investing it. Similarly, a firm may face more demand from limited partners than it initially expected and abandon its target to accommodate a larger fund size. Such a fund is said to be "oversubscribed" and probably has many characteristics of what limited partners want.

What Limited Partners Want

Large institutions employ investment officers to make decisions about how to grow their endowments or pension funds. The investment officers are professional finance experts who pick and choose venture capital firms based on a number of criteria.

First and foremost, investment officers want to see a track record of successful investing from the general partners. At one level, investing with a firm that has been successful in the past is a safe strategy. It's an argument similar to "I never got fired for buying IBM." At another level, a firm that has been successful in the past is actually increasingly likely to be successful in the future thanks primarily to enhanced brand recognition among entrepreneurs.

If no investing track record exists, LPs look for GPs to have experience working with each other. The thinking here is that people who have worked together in the past are less likely to come into conflict with each other. That's surprisingly important in small firms where the partners have to be able to rely on each other and function as a team.

LP investment officers also look for impressive people who have experience either as entrepreneurs or executives in the technology field. Investment officers feel that since many successful venture capitalists come from operational backgrounds, GPs with this experience on their résumés have a good chance at being successful investors. A bevy of references from prominent technologists or other executives may be a deciding point in a venture firm's favor.

LPs also look for a differentiated investing strategy. They want to see that GPs have some kind of specific competitive advantage and will work to exploit that to make smart investments. A team of GPs with experience working in the software industry should focus on investing in software start-ups instead of trying to put money into every sector in the technology industry.

Marketing plays an important role in a limited partner's decision to invest. Not every LP investment officer will admit it, but a little flash goes a long way, especially when a team of investors has yet to establish an investing record.

Historically, limited partners have demonstrated a strong preference for funds that the GPs have personally committed their own wealth to. The idea here is that GPs that have a significant portion of their personal assets tied up in the venture fund they manage will be aligned with the institutions whose money they invest. For example, an LP considering an investment in a venture fund looking to raise $100 million might expect the GPs to commit a bare minimum of $1 million from their own wealth to the fund. Recently, limited partners have begun calling for higher levels of up to 6 or 7 percent of the fund's commitments to come from the GPs.

 TIPS AND TECHNIQUES

Learn the Guidelines

Complexity is a problem when it comes to contracts. Venture capital firms and other private equity firms developed increasingly dense agreements with their limited partners, often exceeding 100 pages, during a recent boom in the leveraged buyout business. The contracts were designed to protect the general partners from any type of financial loss.

Limited partner investment officers agreed to these complex contracts either because they desperately wanted to invest in the funds or they did not fully understand the protections that had been written in. That may seem incredible, but it's important to remember that a venture firm needs to understand only one contract, but a limited partner might have to read over a hundred in a year, depending on how many commitments it plans to make.

The Institutional Limited Partners Association (ILPA) wants to see simpler contracts with fewer protections for venture firms and buyout shops. The ILPA represents over $1 trillion in investment assets and has released guidelines for writing contracts. It wants to see fewer clauses that give opportunities for GPs to enrich themselves at the expense of their LP investors.

The list of terms and conditions to avoid putting into a contract primarily apply to buyout funds, but are a good thing for venture capitalists to be aware of too, especially when the issues involve compensation and capital gains distributions.[a] An investment officer at the California Public Employee Retirement System (CalPERS) recently stated that compliance with the ILPA guidelines was driving much of the investment decision-making process at the pension fund.

[a] ILPA Private Equity Principles, http://bit.ly/doSQkl.

Working with Limited Partners

Not all limited partners are created equal. Although most venture firms aren't lucky enough to be able to pick and choose whose money they take, successful firms do have some flexibility.

Venture capital firms that can choose their LPs have a standard set of preferences:

- Avoid money that comes from sources subject to public disclosure laws.

- Diversify the base of investors so no single LP can dictate terms or jeopardize the future of the GP.

- Avoid capricious investors affected by market fluctuation, such as corporations.

- Take money from endowments and nonprofits whose causes you support.

- Seek LPs that will support other fund initiatives.

- Determine if "funds-of-funds" are friends or foes.

The Problem with Public Money

We discussed in Chapter 1 some of the reasons general partners choose not to raise money from public entities such as the endowments of large public universities or public pension funds. Venture capitalists are concerned that disclosing information about their operations may endanger their returns. They feel that the start-ups in their portfolio might get lower bids from potential strategic acquirers should too much information about their financials be made public. Venture capitalists are also concerned that if data about their start-ups' operations are readily available that competing start-ups will benefit from the intelligence.

These concerns have pushed many venture investors to seek private sources of capital, such as the endowments of large private universities, corporate pension funds, and charitable organizations, such as the Ford Foundation.

Diverse Limited Partners Provide Protection

Limited partners are usually extremely stable. There's little concern that Princeton University will shut down its multibillion-dollar endowment, or that CalPERS will abandon its $24 billion alternative asset investment program.

Still, venture capitalists are anxious to move away from relying on just one or two limited partners for their funds. A diverse base of investors protects a general partnership from investors that go out of business. It also helps them weather turnover in investment officers.

Limited partners do go out of business. The financial crisis of 2008 was a wake-up call to that reality. Big investment banks such as Bear Stearns and Lehman Brothers either helped firms raise funds by aggregating smaller investors or had had direct corporate investments in venture funds. Insurance giant AIG had interests in several firms as well.

Some LPs faced short-term liquidity problems during the downturn and specifically asked general partnerships not to call down capital. Others found they had to sell their stakes in venture funds to other LPs. Having a diversified base of investors can protect a venture firm from the ups and downs of any one specific LP.

Each commitment to provide investment capital to a venture fund is based on a personal relationship between a LP investment officer and the general partners of a firm. The venture capitalists have to persuade, convince, and cajole the investment officer to put in money. But what happens when a major investment officer gets a promotion, leaves for another pension fund, or retires?

Limited partners see a lot of turnover. One large university endowment has had four investment officers in the past decade. The level of continuity of the portfolio from one year to the next is surprising, and suggests that investment officers seldom second–guess their predecessors. But there is always a risk that they will.

Perhaps most important, a diverse base of investors prevents any one LP from dictating the terms of a venture fund's compensation.

IN THE REAL WORLD

The Right Mix of Limited Partners

Sequoia Capital has a long track record of successful investments and the power to pick which limited partners it prefers to raise money from. Over the years, the firm has developed a diverse network of investors. For the firm's $400 million eleventh fund, raised in 2003, it had more than 65 investors, each contributing 1 percent or more of its funds. But 45 percent of the fund was made up of institutions or individuals who owned less than 1 percent of the $400 million, according to documents filed with the Securities and Exchange Commission.[a] (See Exhibit 3.1.)

EXHIBIT 3.1

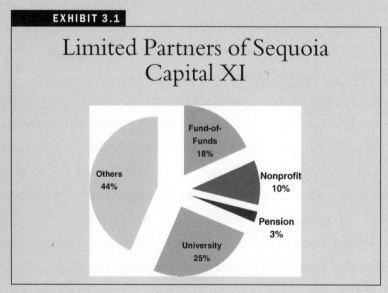

Limited Partners of Sequoia Capital XI

Fund-of-Funds 18%

Others 44%

Nonprofit 10%

Pension 3%

University 25%

Sequoia's biggest investors for its eleventh fund were the non-profit Ford Foundation, fund-of-funds HarbourVest Partners, the Trustees of Princeton University, the University of Notre Dame du Lac, fund-of-funds Commonfund Capital, Harvard Management Private Equity Corporation, the University of Southern California, Yale University, Vanderbilt University, and the nonprofit Barr Foundation. Each had less than a 3 percent stake in the fund, records show.

[a] Securities and Exchange Commission Files: An S-3 filed in conjunction with the sale of YouTube to Google, February 7, 2007, http://bit.ly/bOTAdi.

Capricious Investors

Venture capitalists are careful to avoid entwining themselves with LPs that have only a recent involvement in venture capital. During the dot-com boom, for example, many large corporations invested their excess cash into venture capital funds. When the bubble burst, CEOs typically terminated their venture capital commitments first, either by selling them to another limited partner or by refusing to finance further funds. This is one reason why venture firms generally do not market their funds to large corporations, hedge funds, or other investors likely to be affected by market cycles.

Venture Fund Allocations as Charity

One of the surprise beneficiaries of the sale of video-sharing company YouTube to Google in 2006 was the San Francisco Opera. The Opera earned shares of Google worth $800,000 through distributions made from Sequoia Capital.

The Opera's endowment weighs in at over $100 million but is not large in terms of LPs that typically invest in venture capital funds. The Sequoia Capital partners likely enjoy the Opera and felt that allowing the Opera's endowment to invest in their fund was a little like donating the investment returns to charity.

Having nonprofits as investors can make venture capitalists feel good about making money for them. More importantly, endowments and foundations have long investment time horizons that match those of venture capitalists. They have experience investing in alternative asset classes such as venture and seldom see spikes in their requirement for cash.

Leverage for Other Funds

A firm that earns great returns for its investors develops some power over its limited partners. For example, it can decide simply not to take money from an LP, or it can cut the *allocation* it gives to the LP. The allocation is the amount a venture firm allows the LP to invest in its fund.

Allocations can become a negotiating tool for successful firms. They almost always face a greater demand for investment allocations than they are able to supply. That allows them to dictate terms to limited partners.

One seldom hears about these negotiations unless they go wrong. This happened in 2007, when the Yale University endowment refused to invest in Sequoia Capital's China and Israel funds.

Sequoia had spent much of 2006 expanding its fund offerings into China, India, and growth stage investments. Some said the firm was leveraging the brand it built up investing in U.S. start-ups such as PayPal and Google to extract ever-greater fees from a wider array of funds.

Not every limited partner wanted to back these newer add-on funds. Sequoia had built its reputation on doing early stage U.S. deals and had no previous experience investing in India and China. There was no guarantee that it would be successful in these emerging markets.

The *Wall Street Journal* reported that Sequoia kicked Yale out of its Silicon Valley–focused fund in retaliation for not investing in its add-on funds.[1] Sequoia wanted a blank check from its investors, according to a 39-page memo from Yale's investment office leaked to the newspaper.

The venture firm denied the implication that it was holding its most successful, Silicon Valley–focused fund up as a reward to any limited partner that backed its other offerings.

Fund-of-Funds: Friend or Foe?

A *fund-of-funds,* as its name implies, is a fund that invests in venture capital and private equity funds. A fund-of-funds is a good way for small investors to gain exposure to the private equity asset class without having to spend the time to find the best general partnerships to invest in. A fund-of-funds can give LPs access to venture funds they might not otherwise be invited into. But the manager of a fund-of-funds charges a fee and a percentage of the profits from investing, which can make the service expensive.

Some top-tier venture funds don't look favorably on fund-of-funds investors. They feel that their brand equity is used to drive limited partner dollars to competing firms. The fund-of-funds managers tout their relationship with a single successful firm as a way of raising money for a handful of less successful competitors. Successful firms have been known to boot fund-of-funds investors from their limited partner roster for this reason.[2]

Why Invest in Funds That Lose Money?

One of the fundamental mysteries of venture capital is how firms that lose money are still able to raise new funds. In Chapter 1, you read about the investing results of Aberdare Ventures, a firm that had yet to return even the initial money CalPERS invested in it over the past decade at the time of this publication.

So how is the firm able to continue raising funds? I don't mean to pick on Aberdare, it was just at the top of the alphabetically organized list of CalPERS's holdings. And CalPERS has plenty of funds that do pay off.

Still, a large number of funds the pension invests in will lose money. The National Venture Capital Association's performance statistics presented in Chapter 1, which put the average return over 10 years at 17.3 percent, are misleading. The industry average may be that high, but that number includes a handful of super-performing funds that most limited partners don't have a chance to invest in. CalPERS, for example, probably never gets the chance to even look at private placement memorandums from firms such as Benchmark Capital, Kleiner Perkins Caufield & Byers, or Sequoia Capital simply because it is a public investor and subject to disclosure laws.

It's difficult to know how well CalPERS has done investing in venture capital firms. Since the inception of the CalPERS Alternative Investment Management (AIM) program in 1990, the pension fund calculates that AIM has had an annualized return of 5.5 percent. Venture capital makes up about 11 percent of the AIM portfolio, so it's not easy to figure out how the VC funds impact that overall number.

CalPERS has probably lost money investing in venture capital during recent years, or at least failed to make more than it would had it invested in the S&P 500. Since a handful of firms account for the lion's share of venture capital returns and CalPERS—or any other large public fund—is unlikely to be invited to invest in those top firms, it stands to reason that they're going to lose money investing in venture.

So why invest in venture capital at all then? CalPERS isn't alone in backing unsuccessful venture funds. There are plenty of other large limited partners that sustain an ecosystem of underperforming firms. To many, this may be one of the fundamental paradoxes of the venture capital industry. Why do LPs commit cash to firms that lose money?

Part of the problem lies with the people who make the decisions on what investments an institution makes, the limited partner investment officers. Investment officers are professional investors hired to invest money on behalf of the endowments, pension funds, and other large institutions they represent. They may be well intentioned, but the incentives they face often differ from those of the institution they represent.

There are five major reasons why limited partner investment officers put money behind losers:

1. They consider venture capital as an asset class and bet that an industry-wide boom will benefit every single fund.

2. They hope to get a hit with a first time fund and back a firm with little or no track record.

3. They are compensated based on hitting allocation targets instead of performance targets.

4. They act irrationally and invest in venture capital because they think it is fun or derive personal pleasure from it.

5. They get kickbacks or other sumptuous perks.

Betting on a Boom

Most firms will not make significant returns most of the time, but during a remarkable time, most of the same firms will manage to do remarkably well. For example, during the run up to the dot-com boom, venture capitalists almost had to go out of their way not to make money. As early venture capitalist Eugene Kleiner used to say, "Any turkey can fly in a high enough wind."

Venture capital, as an asset class, is pro-cyclical. That means that when times are flush and start-ups can easily go public or be acquired at attractive multiples, venture firms do very well. They do significantly better than the market as a whole. When times are tough, venture capitalists are hit harder than the rest of the market.

Investing in a portfolio of venture capital firms is like betting on the likelihood of a technology boom. Investment officers may choose to allocate dollars to venture in order to boost their overall returns during a bull market. As one limited partner investment officer once explained to me, "Buying a lottery ticket can cover up a lot of mistakes if you hit the jackpot."

Hoping for a Hit with First-Time Funds

A limited partner may end up with a bevy of money-losing funds because it is trying to score a big win on a handful of first-time funds.

Imagine investing in a completely unknown firm offering its first fund. The firm could be amazing, a come-out-of-nowhere runaway success as Benchmark Capital was when it debuted its first fund. And although a great first fund is not a promise of a spectacular second fund, it certainly increases the chances of having one.

Or the firm can be a dud.

In one scenario, you make an amazing investment that will boast great returns, make you look smart, and grant you access to a slice of the firm's subsequent funds. In the other scenario, it will be years before the firm ends up an obvious failure.

To make the incentives for investing in first-time funds even more compelling, research shows that it's actually just as likely that a first-time fund will be a top performer as a second, third, or seventeenth fund.

Investing in a first-time fund is a gamble. The only problem is that you don't know the outcome of your initial bet until after you're called on to make a second bet. The venture firm will likely invest the majority of its capital within three or four years and go out to raise a second fund. But it may have yet to prove it can make money, as some start-ups take as long as a decade to come to fruition.

A limited partner investment officer may feel compelled to invest in the second fund because of all the reasons it invested in the first fund. "It's always a two-fund bet," says one investment officer. A third fund may soon follow after that, even though the firm's first fund has yet to record returns.

Suppose then that the first fund reaches the end of its 10-year fund life and the venture firm liquidates its portfolio and returns money to its limited partners. Only then will investors know if the general partners are good at what they do.

It is even more disappointing to find at that point that you've invested in not just one sorry fund, but three.

Allocation Targets

Nearly every white-collar job today features some sort of incentive-based pay and the investment officers at pension funds and university endowments are no different. But what is the proper metric for compensation?

An easy answer would be performance. If an endowment or pension fund's investments do well in a given year, its investment officers should benefit. This isn't always easy to do though, in part because it is difficult to distinguish good investments because they usually perform in tandem with the overall market economy. Compensation based on performance alone may set up the wrong incentives for investment officers, encouraging them to take excessive risks for short-term gains.

But performance isn't the only measurement used in evaluating investment officers. Another common metric is the investment officer's ability to put money into certain types of assets in given ratios to each other. For example, the Pennsylvania State Employee Retirement System (PennSERS) had a mandate from its board of directors to put 47 percent of its assets into publicly traded stocks and 9.3 percent into private equity in 2009. Limited partner investment officers call these instructions on how to invest "allocation targets."

Each LP sets allocation targets differently, but at a large public pension plan the process can become political. Most pension funds are controlled by a board of directors, which includes elected officials. The board, advised by investment officers and outside analyst groups, comes up with a strategy for the fund to follow. The board then meets four or six times a year to approve potential investments and evaluate the fund's ability to pay out benefits.

Allocation targets may reflect political or popular beliefs instead of the best interests of the fund. Sometimes targets may just be slow to move, leaving an allocation set too high for investment officers to put the money efficiently to work.

That was the case immediately after the dot-com bubble, when pension fund boards looked at the positive performance of venture capital through the late 1990s and concluded that high levels of investment in venture funds should continue. But the limited partner investment officers actually charged with finding attractive funds to invest in would have been hard-pressed to find winning funds in the years after the boom—few, if any, firms were as successful after the dot-com boom as immediately before it.

An investment officer can, of course, hold back on making investments in venture funds when few funds appear to be capable of producing excellent returns. But many have a "use it or lose it" mentality and fear that if they don't find funds to invest in, their power will diminish.

Others may fear that investing less than a mandated allocation will be seen as a failure to meet the board's goals. Even if their variable compensation is not directly tied to how close they come to their targets, they perceive that they will be rewarded for following orders.

Irrational Reasons

Some limited partner investment officers enjoy investing in venture capital. Meeting with technology experts can feel more like science fiction than finance. Investment officers may find it just more interesting than real estate or oil refineries.

A venture fund may appeal to the personal interests of a limited partner investment officer. It is easy to imagine an investment officer with diabetes putting money into a health care–focused venture fund. The investment may never lead to a direct personal benefit, but there is an undeniable psychological gratification.

Venture capital is also more of a gamble than other asset classes. Holding a corporate bond may be a financially sound investment, but it will never give the wild upside that a venture capital fund will. Some investment officers may seek out this risk because it is a rush.

Others just like to rub elbows with world-changing innovators. "It's cool to go to the annual meeting and see the CTO [chief technology officer] of Facebook, or the CEO of Google," one former fund-of-funds manager told me.

Just for Fun

Some limited partner investment officers just enjoy being involved with venture capital. That's what Udayan Gupta found when he interviewed Sequoia Capital founder Don Valentine for his 2000 book *Done Deals.*[a] Below are Valentine's words, excerpted from the book:

> For approximately ten years I campaigned fairly aggressively with lots of our limited partners that they were putting out too much money. I did not make very much progress. Over the years, after getting to know several limited partners fairly well, I said, "We must talk about this, because I don't understand what you guys are doing. We have had limited partners with greater than $30 billion in assets. And, when they gave us $10 million and we compounded it at 100% a year, we had no impact on their fund. Why do this?" The answer was, "It was much more fun to do this than to invest in bonds. It's more fun than investing in real estate, where nothing happens for a long time." So, the reason why a significant portion of money is being deployed—for which I am eternally grateful—is that a whole bunch of people think it's fun.

[a] Udayan Gupta, *Done Deals* (Boston: HBS Press, 2000), p. 172.

Illegal Reasons

Not every investment officer is honest and the potential for personal gain when allocating state money is immense. Although no major cases of venture capital–related fraud have been exposed, the buyouts business is reeling from allegations that the New York State Pension Fund investment officers were accepting kickbacks in exchange for fund commitments.

The case is ongoing at the time of this writing, but the scheme was roughly this: The pension fund investment officers would ensure that a buyout firm got a multi-hundred million commitment if the buyout professionals agreed to pay a bribe.

The pension fund investment officers were unlikely to be held accountable if the buyout funds they invested in did not perform, therefore there was little incentive to pick winners. That makes fraud of this kind difficult to trace and hard to prove. The case in New York took two years of state and federal investigation to crack. It is very possible that a similar situation could be occurring inside the venture capital business but has yet to be detected.

IN THE REAL WORLD

Limited Partner Ethics

Increased scrutiny of the way public funds are allocated to private equity managers has caused some pension boards to beef up their ethics policies. For example, The Teachers' Retirement System of the State of Illinois (TRS) brought its Investment Management Agreement up to par with recent state laws regarding public funds.

It strengthened its ban on TRS representatives receiving finder's fees and rewrote its Code of Ethics and Conduct. Part of the changes require TRS trustees to take eight hours of ethics training each year, file annual statements of economic interest with the state and forbids them from receiving any gifts from those seeking state business. The updated Code of Ethics clarifies trustees' responsibility to avoid any personal benefit accruing to themselves or their relatives from TRS investment.

First-Time Funds

Raising a first-time fund isn't easy.[3] It's on par with a rookie base-ball player pitching a no-hitter. Limited partner investment officers want to see a track record, proof of previous investing success, or at least a clear indication that a new venture capital firm isn't going to burn through their money and come away with nothing to show for it. LPs also want to see some sort of proof that the team is robust—that its partners will stick together and not lunge for each other's throats when the going gets rough. How do you prove such things?

There are eight proven strategies for raising a first-time fund:

1. Demonstrate your skill by investing your own money or by making money for your close friends and associates.

2. Quit your job at an established venture firm and hang your own shingle. Be sure to bring your Rolodex.

3. Get a vote of confidence from some other venture firm by sign-ing on as an affiliated fund. But be ready to share your compensation.

4. Focus on a specific industry where you and your partners have the greatest strength and experience.

5. Get help from government programs designed to promote tech-nology and small business. This is especially useful in countries with a commitment to nurturing an emerging tech industry.

6. Prove you can pick good companies and help them grow even without money. Once you've established a track record, take it to limited partners.

7. Get a top-flight general partner at a marquee venture firm to vouch for you.

8. Attract a "bell cow" that every other limited partner will want to follow.

Use Your Money First

One of the best ways to prove you can successfully run a first-time fund is to establish a track record investing your own money. Calling on friends and family can also help get you started.

That's what the Founders Fund did. Started by successful executives from PayPal, the partners launched a $50 million fund in 2005 that came out of their own pockets and from their well-connected friends. Of course, they had some money to play with. PayPal was sold to eBay for $1.2 billion in 2002. The firm has had a number of successes and raised its $220 million second fund two years later.

Emergence Capital Partners followed a similar path. The firm focused on investing in the fast-moving business of "software-as-a-service," which is a way of delivering software to users via the Internet.

Emergence was the brainchild of Gordon Ritter, Brian Jacobs, and Jason Green. The three men put together a $1 million first fund by dipping into their own pockets and tapping their friends and family. The only problem in raising money from your friends and family comes if you fail and lose their cash. A big pension fund can write off a loss, but these people know where you live.

Fortunately for the founders of Emergence, the fund's only investment paid off handsomely. It invested in customer relations management company Salesforce before it went public. The investment netted a handy return and rocketed two of the Emergence investors to the Forbes Midas List for superior returns.

The investment proved the firm's ability to back a winner and supported their thesis that software-as-a-service was going to be a big business. Emergence put together its first institutional fund shortly after that, collecting $125 million in 2004 from large limited partners.

Spinout from Another Firm

Another good way to prove that you can find good deals and work well with your partners is to split off from some other venture capital firm. The history of Silicon Valley is replete with examples. Opus Capital jumps to mind. The firm spun off from Lightspeed Venture Partners in 2005.

Lightspeed, founded in 1971 as Weiss Peck & Greer Venture Partners, had a rich history, but poor recent performance. At the time of the split, data from CalPERS, a Lightspeed LP, showed that the firm's 2000 fund, LVP VI, had an IRR of −17.2 percent. In a time when most vintage 2000 funds were underwater, this one was particularly bad, lower than the average of −13.3 percent. So Gill Cogan and Carl Showalter jumped ship, brought on repeat entrepreneur Dan Avida, and set out to establish a new firm.

Less than a year later, Opus Capital had signed up $280 million. Much of the money came from limited partners that had backed Showalter and Cogan at Lightspeed. The firm was able to leverage those commitments to entice other limited partners to join.

Affiliate with an Established Brand

Limited partners are more likely to invest in a firm that they've worked with before, so it can make a lot of sense for a nascent firm to partner with an established venture capital brand.

That's something Draper Fisher Jurvetson (DFJ) has used to its advantage, setting up a syndicate of venture funds that share investment opportunities, industry connections, and back-office administrative functions. It can be an expensive option for first-time firms since DFJ doesn't lend its brand for free. Although the terms of its agreements with affiliate funds have never been disclosed, it is clear that the core DFJ partnership gets a taste of both its affiliates' management fee and its carry.

But the deal can work wonders for a new firm. Consider the path of DFJ ePlanet Ventures, a $650 million fund raised in 2000 under the Draper Fisher Jurvetson flag. ePlanet's plan was to invest in start-ups outside the United States.

ePlanet invested in amazing start-ups such as Chinese search engine Baidu, advertising company Focus Media, and European Internet telephone company Skype. Each benefited the investors immensely. The syndication experience allowed ePlanet Ventures to show a track record to investors when it went out without DFJ's backing for its second fund.

Focus, Focus, Focus

One of the biggest problems a new firm has is differentiating itself from others. A focused fund can be particularly attractive to limited partners looking to follow a specific investment thesis, insinuate themselves into an emerging industry, or diversify their holdings.

Focus can also be an indicator of future success. It's easier to do just one thing well than to do a handful of things well.

Glen Schwaber launched Israel Cleantech Ventures with these ideas in mind. The name of the firm says it all: The general partners are looking to invest in Israeli-based cleantech start-ups. It has both a geographic and sector focus.

Being exclusively focused on cleantech made Schwaber's firm attractive to limited partners anxious to appear environmentally concerned. Few firms were looking exclusively at these deals and there was a sense that anything short of a complete immersion in the new field would yield poor results. "The larger all-purpose funds are going to have trouble generating good returns," Schwaber said at the time. "There's an opportunity to be a first mover here."[4]

Get Government Help

Elected officials periodically think technology investment is important or that small businesses drive job creation and improve a country's standard of living. So they open the purse strings of public funds to help out companies and firms that can fit certain politically-set specifications.

Consider the case of New Orleans–based Advantage Capital Partners. The firm recently raised $55 million from investors for a venture capital fund focused on low-income communities in Illinois. The fund qualifies for tax credits under the state's New Markets Development Program, a $125 million stimulus plan passed in 2008.

"We take the tax credits, we sell them and then plow them into the program," says Advantage Capital Managing Director Louis

Dubuque. The firm knows how much it will earn from tax credits based on how much it plans to invest. It can guarantee a certain tax credit for its LP investors once the fund is invested. It's a form of guaranteed return that the firm can use to boost its fundraising efforts. "Instead of raising $1, we get, say, $1.30. That makes the fund larger and allows us to do things that not everybody else is doing," says Dubuque.

It's a nice benefit, but forces the firm to focus on investments in companies that have at least half of their assets and operations in impoverished neighborhoods. Fortunately for Advantage, it has a lot of experience working with this type of program. It has raised more than $318 million over from investors looking for tax credits under the federal New Markets Development Program.

Prove You Can Add Value

San Mateo, California–based Tandem Entrepreneurs launched a $15 million first fund based on the idea that venture capitalists should be similar to service providers—a sort of hybrid financier and head-hunter/consultant.

The firm makes an investment in a company and increases its equity stake based on how much help the start-up needs from the Tandem partners. For example, if the start-up calls on the firm to help it find a vice president of sales, the venture firm will get a swath of common stock for the service.

The cost of starting a software company decreased dramatically in the decade before Tandem Entrepreneurs launched its fund. Yet skilled executives and programmers became increasingly difficult to find. Tandem concluded that start-ups need skills, not fat checks.

The firm's web site summarizes its creed:

> We do not consider ourselves a VC [venture capital] firm. There are three primary types of capital that are required to make a start-up successful—Financial Capital (money), Human Capital (sweat), and Social Capital (friends). VCs bring mainly financial capital, some social capital and limited sweat. We bring value in the reverse order—sweat, friends, and money (much more like entrepreneurs).

The idea behind Tandem's unique plan is to align the incentives of the venture firm with the incentives of the entrepreneur. Company founders expect to get help with meeting customers, recruiting key talent, and managing growth-related issues. The benefit to entrepreneurs of Tandem's twist on the standard venture capital model is that they only pay for the services they actually get instead of blindly hoping their investors will help them grow.

Get Sponsored

Nothing quite wakes up a limited partner like a letter of recommendation for a new venture fund signed by a mega-successful venture capitalist. It's a guaranteed attention getter. A new venture firm looking for investors may turn first to well-established and respected venture capitalists with the hope they will open their Rolodexes and reach out to limited partners.

Venture capital firm Andreessen Horowitz used this technique to get its inaugural $300 million venture fund off the ground during 2009, one of the toughest years on record for fundraising. The firm's general partners, particularly Netscape cofounder Marc Andreessen, turned for help to the lead partners of three firms: John Doerr at Kleiner Perkins Caufield & Byers, Jim Breyer at Accel Partners, and Aneel Bhusri at Greylock, according to reports.[5] These investors made introductions to limited partners; and the new firm raised its first fund in record time.

Attract a "Bell Cow"

Entrepreneurs often complain that venture capitalists are lemmings that will follow one or two "thought leaders," even as they run off a cliff. No doubt venture capitalists feel the same about the people they get money from: limited partners.

The big limited partner investment officers are perhaps a little less lemming-like, thanks to the long-term nature of many of their investments. But they do watch for what the industry leaders are doing and try to emulate their success.

A successful institutional investor is like a "bell cow," or the one cow that knows enough to go home at night. She's just slightly smarter than all the other bovines, who only know to follow the sound of the bell that's attached to her neck.

Getting an investment from a limited partner that has successful experience backing venture capital firms can go a long way toward attracting other limited partners. Money from a major university endowment such as Princeton, Harvard, or Yale will suggest to other limited partners that a fund has been sufficiently well-researched and obtained a seal of approval.

Bigger Funds

For decades, venture has been one of the few businesses where it has paid to stay small. Venture capitalists have traditionally made their money in the earliest stages of company financing.

Having a big fund meant focusing on late stage companies well into their development. While early stage companies face problems like recruiting a CEO and getting their technology to work, late stage companies worry about securing international customers and going public. Venture firms have historically specialized in one type of investment or the other.

Yet at least half a dozen early stage venture capital firms have pitched what they call *growth funds* or supersized funds to their limited partners. A growth investment is different from a late stage deal and has characteristics similar to an early stage investment, but just requires more money.

The idea is that you can get the same risk-reward profile by investing in one $100 million deal as you would doing twenty $5 million deals. In fact, investing in early stage start-ups can yield invaluable insights into developing markets and technology trends, according to the firms pitching growth funds.

It's an attractive strategy for successful venture firms for several reasons. Bigger funds mean more management fees, for one. But more importantly, they allow general partners to put their skills to work with greater impact. A venture capitalist with one big investment can focus on making that company better, without worrying about doing anything else.

Limited partners have an appetite for venture investing and would prefer to invest with firms that have performed well in the past. Raising a growth fund can be a natural extension of a venture firm's regular operations, if managed well.

IN THE REAL WORLD

Putting Big Money to Work

New Enterprise Associates (NEA) was a traditional early stage venture capital investor, but has been actively looking for mega-sized deals since the dot-com downturn. NEA went very much against the grain when it decided to become involved in growth deals. Most industry experts thought that small deals yielded the best returns and that doing big deals meant sacrificing capital gains. "Common knowledge said you couldn't scale this business," cofounder C. Richard Kramlich said in 2007. "If so, it would be the only business in the world [that doesn't scale]. We pay attention to every dollar we invest."

The firm's criteria for making a growth investment are simple. It wants to see a company that needs its help for executive recruiting, strategic marketing, or technology improvements and can rapidly ramp up sales. "That's really no different from how we approach early and mid-stage deals," says General Partner Ravi Viswanathan.

NEA's investment in positioning company Tele Atlas showed that large, growth-style investments could pay off in a big way. The firm, along with another venture capital group, put $210 million into the company in July 2004. NEA helped the company think through its key hires, flesh out its board of directors, and develop a strategy for expanding into Asia.

The results of the effort were evident in December 2007, when navigation device maker TomTom agreed to buy Tele Atlas for $43.14 a share. NEA had bought into the company for less than $6 a share.[a]

[a] For more on growth strategies, see "Gaga for Growth," *Venture Capital Journal,* February 1, 2008, http://bit.ly/98wDfR.

The Future of Fundraising

Venture firms will likely raise funds in more or less the same way they always have, but there are a handful of emerging trends that may mold the way firms operate in the future.

Solo General Partners

One-man venture capital firms or "solo GPs" have had increasing success in attracting institutional investors. These firms may never manage massive amounts of money, but a handful of great investments have proven that this can work as a firm structure.

There are obstacles to this trend catching on. Limited partner investment officers traditionally prefer to have a smaller number of commitments. It is easier for them to research and approve investment in one $500 million fund than five $100 million funds or fifty $10 million funds. Solo GP funds may someday be encouraged to combine.

Longer Fund Horizons

Venture capitalists have always been associated with a buy and hold investment strategy—they often expect to invest in a company and wait five to seven years without seeing any return. It's like playing Russian roulette, only you pull the trigger now and don't know if you're dead or not for at least half a decade.

But the holding period of some investments is even longer. This is especially true in industries such as clean energy, where companies are working to not just develop technology, but build production facilities and begin massive installations. Venture firms are responding to this by increasing the time horizon of their investment and the lifespan of their funds to 15 or 20 years.

A longer fund life may help venture firms capture bigger returns. Some firms find themselves forced to liquidate their investment portfolios as their 10-year fund life draws to a close. That can mean selling start-ups before they meet critical milestones that would dramatically improve their valuation. A longer fund life would give venture firms more time to see these start-ups fully mature before selling.

Some limited partners already allow venture firms to extend the life of their funds in extenuating circumstances, such as a global macroeconomic crisis or major recession. Venture firms must annually justify extensions to limited partners, typically by promising that at least one of their start-ups will either go public or be acquired very soon.

Streamlined Limited Partner Agreements

Limited partner agreements, or LPAs, have taken on a mind-numbing complexity. These legal contracts establish the rights of investors and the requirements of the general partners and can run well over 100 pages.

There may be an opportunity to streamline the legal process and make these contracts simpler. Such collaboration between GPs and LPs would lessen the load for those engaged in the due diligence of investment opportunities and prevent hundreds of thousands of dollars going to lawyers.

Summary

Venture capitalists get paid once they've raised a fund, which makes fundraising of paramount importance.

Limited partner investment officers want to invest in firms that have a track record of success. Barring that, they prefer firms in which the general partners have worked together before or have been successful in other ventures. Many limited partners will require the venture capitalists to invest some portion of their personal wealth into the fund they raise, to ensure they are aligned with the interests of the fund.

Successful venture firms may try to pick and choose their limited partners to better protect themselves from public exposure, to diversify their base of investors, or to avoid limited partners who may disappear when times are tough. Some venture firms will save space for nonprofit endowments to invest in their funds, press their limited partners to invest in noncore funds, or may specifically exclude fund-of-fund investors.

Despite careful research and high standards, limited partner investment officers often invest in venture funds that don't make their money back. Making such a mistake once is understandable, but some investment officers consistently pick poor-performing firms. They do this because of the way they are compensated, because they hope for another industry-wide boom, because they are trying to get a hit with a first-time fund, or because of other irrational or illegal reasons.

Raising a first-time fund is very difficult, in part because LP investment officers evaluate a firm by its track record and first-time funds don't have any record. Venture capitalists looking to get a foothold may consider investing their own savings to prove they can make money or working with an established venture firm for a number of years before going out on their own. Other strategies include affiliating with well-known funds, focusing on an underserved technology sector, working within government programs, or proving they can help start-ups even without money.

Once a firm raises a fund, it may look to raise even larger sums from its limited partners. Bigger funds allow firms to make more investments and possibly get even bigger paychecks. These supersized funds have forced firms to seek new investment strategies.

Fundraising has changed little during the past several decades and seems unlikely to change much in the coming years. Still, a handful of interesting trends could catch on and add new wrinkles to the process. One-man firms are finding favor with investors, some firms are looking to invest for longer time periods, and there is a chance that streamlined limited partner agreements could make the process easier for both GPs and LPs.

Notes

1. "Venture Firms vs. Investors," *Wall Street Journal*, August 28, 2007, http://bit.ly/bbd4DP.
2. "Sequoia Tells Some of Its LPs to Forget about Fund XII: VC Firm Will Likely Not Accept Most Funds-of-Funds in the New Vehicle, LPs say," *PE Week*, May 29, 2006, http://bit.ly/csC2d8.
3. For more on first-time fundraising, consult an excellent article "A Fund Is Born," *Venture Capital Journal*, May 2004, http://bit.ly/99JEmZ.
4. "Israel Cleantech Holds First Close," *Venture Capital Journal*, April 1, 2007, http://bit.ly/cx84Qt.
5. "Made Men: Why Venture Capitalists Sponsor Other VCs," *BusinessWeek.com*, July 7, 2009, http://bit.ly/aOqRKY.

CHAPTER 4

Investing Basics

After reading this chapter, you will be able to:

- Evaluate potential investments as a venture capitalist does.
- Build a model of how venture capital investment into start-ups changes over time.
- Follow the process of how a start-up gets financing.
- Differentiate between classes of private company stock.
- Describe the process of deal syndication and start-up valuation.

What Makes a Good Deal?

Venture capitalists have remarkably uniform opinions on what makes a start-up suitable for investment. Ask venture capitalists what they look for and you'll get some combination of three major things:

1. Team
2. Technology and markets
3. Time horizon for success

The Team

Arthur Rock, one of the first venture capitalists to travel west in 1961 to what would later become Silicon Valley, said he didn't trust his ability to pick winning technologies. However, he did believe he could pick winning teams. And he picked quite a few, backing the founders of Intel and Apple, among others. Rock writes of his investment methodology:

> Good ideas and good products are a dime a dozen. Good execution and good management—in a word, good people—are rare. To put it another way, strategy is easy, but tactics—the day-to-day and month-to-month decisions required to manage a business—are hard. That's why I generally pay more attention to the people who prepare a business plan than to the proposal itself.[1]

Since then, venture investors often say they'd rather have an A+ team with a C+ idea than a C+ team with an A+ idea. It sounds a little convoluted, but the concept is that a great team should be able to overcome a mediocre idea, insufficient technology, a screwed up business strategy, or any other problem. If the team isn't good, even the best-sounding business will never make it to fruition.

A winning team can mean any number of things and each investor generally takes it to mean something different. At root, the team must have an entrepreneur who overcomes whatever obstacles come along and never gives up. Such people are often called "a force of nature," because they seem by sheer will to succeed. Spotting these people is an art.

Other key components to a top-notch team include the right technologists, salespeople, and product developers. Finding these people is one thing. Getting them to effectively work together is another. The right team is one that creates value that exceeds whatever the sum of their individual efforts would be.

Team matters to venture capitalists, and that's one of the reasons that successful entrepreneur presentations to investors will start by outlining the founding team's credentials. Teams that have had success working together in the past are more likely to connect with capital than those that haven't.

Technology and Markets

Not every venture capitalist is from the Arthur Rock school of investing. Although the value and importance of a strong team is indisputable, some investors are just more comfortable picking technologies instead of people. The most famous example of a technology-focused venture capitalist is Sequoia Capital founder Don Valentine:

> Arthur Rock and I have always had sort of a very friendly debate. Arthur disclaims any ability in technology, and any understanding of it. He makes his investments based on people—and he has proven to be a spectacular chooser. I was never very comfortable with that approach. I always felt that I could understand the market and the application. I would invest almost exclusively based on market size and momentum, and the nature of the problem being solved by the company. I always felt that trying to choose people was very difficult . . . .[2]

Valentine certainly proved this by investing in Cisco Systems, a start-up that he thought could capture a piece of the corporate data communications network. Valentine believed that corporations would increasingly swap information via data networks and would need devices such as routers and switches to help that data move around. He invested in Cisco when no one else would because he could see past the weak team and toward a time when customers would need the start-up's products. He later replaced Cisco's original founders with professional managers who could cope with the rapid growth that the start-up saw.

Start-ups need a competitive advantage to be successful. Often that means selling a product or service that has never been on the market before.

Venture capitalists feel the best path to developing these advantages is through new applications of cutting-edge technology. Of course there are many companies that create new markets and establish long-term competitive advantages by other means than through technology. For example, Federal Express started out with a more efficient delivery chain than its competitors.

Timing

Although investors may argue about which is most important—team or tech—everyone agrees that anything you invest in should have a reasonable time horizon for commercialization.

A start-up should have its product developed and selling within three years, profitability within five or six and be a size appropriate for an initial public offering within seven to nine years. Not every start-up adheres to this type of schedule, especially during tough economic times. But few venture capitalists will commit to a company unless they believe such a schedule is realistic.

Time to commercialization has been a big problem for industries that require a lot of primary research such as nanotechnology. Nanotech companies sprang up around Silicon Valley and many were funded with the hope that the technology would lead to specialized materials and microscopic machines capable of manipulating human biology, or fighting diseases.

Few of these companies survive today, despite raising tens of millions of dollars from venture capitalists. Many failed simply because it took too long to go from research to revenue.

Macroeconomics of Investing

Venture capitalists evaluate each potential investment on its own merits, but the sum of their individual actions is evident in the volume of investments made each quarter. Within the aggregate data presented in Exhibit 4.1, one can see that several key variables impact venture capitalist investment.[3]

Technology Trends

The first variable that appears to impact the number of deals done and the amount of venture capital dollars invested is the perception of new technology's potential to rapidly change big industries. When venture capitalists believed that the Internet and e-commerce companies were going to change every aspect of modern business, they invested.

The technology trend du jour is anything related to either alternative energy production or resource efficiency, two industries collectively called *cleantech*. Venture capitalists believe that solar panel

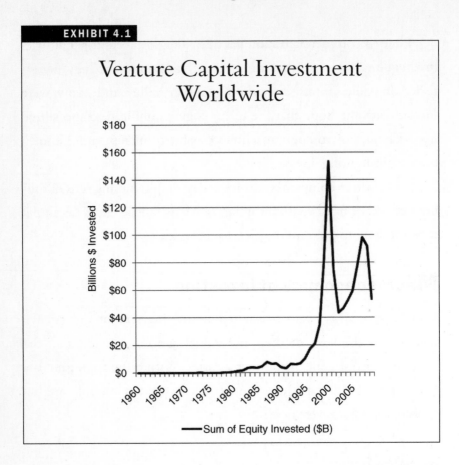

EXHIBIT 4.1

Venture Capital Investment Worldwide

Sum of Equity Invested ($B)

innovations, modern wind turbines, renewable fuels, and a host of similar technologies can rapidly revolutionize major industries.

Big new technologies emerge every six or seven years and venture capitalists invest based on their expectations for these innovations to impact big markets.

The Economy

Macroeconomic health matters to start-ups trying to sell new products or services. When times are good, people are more likely to part with their money and start-ups are more likely to see sales. When big corporations suffer losses, they are less likely to buy technology. The same thing applies to consumers watching their stock portfolios slide.

When sales slow, start-ups take longer to mature. If venture capitalists believe that it will take a start-up 10 years to reach $100 million in revenue instead of 5 years, they will be less likely to invest.

Still, fluctuations in the stock market and the overall economy have to be pretty serious to get a venture capitalist's attention. Most venture capitalists expect to hold a start-up's shares for five to seven years and anticipate some normal level of economic seesawing. It takes a serious crisis to put a dent in overall investment levels.

Fundraising

Investment slows when venture capitalists grow concerned about their own ability to raise funds. If a venture capitalist believes she will have a tough time raising a new fund from limited partners (LPs), she will conserve the cash sitting in her current fund. She will pick either low risk investments or start-ups that will make her look good when she goes before limited partners.

Profit Potential

The opportunity for a quick profit will boost venture investment. If investors believe that strategic acquirers are looking for start-ups to buy or that institutional investors are receptive to initial public offerings (IPOs), they will increase their investment to try to take advantage of the favorable timing. However, it is difficult to predict when the exit market will be good. This is especially true for start-up investors who expect to hold their investments for several years. It takes fundamental changes in the demand to acquire start-ups or buy shares in IPOs to radically impact investment levels.

Venture capitalists' beliefs about the potential of new technology, the overall economy, their own ability to raise funds, and the opportunities they will have to profit all impact the aggregate level of venture investment. Each of these variables is interrelated, and pointing to any one as the cause of a fluctuation in investment levels is difficult. Barring a major scientific breakthrough or a financial crisis, investment levels remain relatively stable over time.

IN THE REAL WORLD

The 2008 Financial Crisis

Venture capitalists maintained a relatively positive outlook as the credit crunch gave way to bank failures.[a] But they soon changed their tune when blue chip firm Sequoia Capital told the CEOs of its portfolio companies to assemble for a mandatory meeting toward the end of October and ordered them to get to cash flow positive as soon as possible. "Forget about getting ahead, we're talking survive," General Partner Michael Moritz advised the group.

Eric Upin, a public market investor for Sequoia, told the assembled CEOs that the credit crisis was going to be a long-term problem. "It's always darkest before it's pitch black," a source reported him as saying. "We are in the beginning of a long cycle. This could be a 15-year problem."

The CEOs took it seriously. In the 10 days following the meeting, three Sequoia-backed companies laid off employees and one shut down entirely.

Desperation radiated in waves from the meeting. One executive who attended took detailed notes and sent them to his team and other investors. The e-mail went viral and in no time half the venture capitalists in Silicon Valley had read it. Two days later, the PowerPoint Sequoia used at the meeting found its way onto the Internet. The opening slide—with the words "R.I.P. Good Times" written on a tombstone—was seared into the psyche of investors and entrepreneurs alike.

Things certainly seemed grim when the Dow Jones Industrial Average lost more than 20 percent during the week. "Maybe I should invest in canned foods and a gun," one venture capitalist said at the time, only half joking.

Other big name investors weighed in, begging their start-ups to conserve cash, get profitable, and take an acquisition offer if it came.

Angel investor Ron Conway repeated advice he'd given in the spring of 2000: "The message is simple: Raising capital will be much more difficult now."

Bill Gurley of Benchmark Capital echoed that sentiment in an e-mail he sent to portfolio company CEOs several days before the Sequoia meeting. It reads in part: "If we leave you with one message it would be this: Financings as we know it just got a whole lot tougher. Basically, the cost of capital is going way up."

But a week before Sequoia's meeting, the *Venture Capital Journal* conducted a survey of close to 50 venture capitalists and nearly 75 percent of them said they expected the stock market

Investment Process

Each venture capital investment comes together in its own way, so there's danger in generalizing—but most firms follow a fairly standard process for evaluating and making deals:

1. First contact
2. Initial pitch
3. Follow-up
4. Due diligence
5. Partner meeting pitch
6. Deal negotiation
7. Final close

First Contact

An investor will have some initial interaction with an entrepreneur—at a conference, in line at Starbucks, at a networking event, at a kid's baseball game, or by randomly reading business plans. Most investments are made on the basis of a referral from someone who has worked both with the entrepreneur and the venture capitalist in the past. This meeting, phone call, or e-mail exchange is a chance for the entrepreneur to give his elevator pitch: that concise explanation of what his start-up does and why it's going to make lots of money.

Initial Pitch

If the venture capitalist likes the elevator pitch, he or she will invite the entrepreneur for a formal, in-office pitch. The in-office meeting is designed to professionalize the relationship between investor and investee. It's a chance for both parties to smell each other and determine if collaboration is possible. This meeting will likely involve a formal PowerPoint-style presentation from the entrepreneur and an informal introduction to how the venture firm works.

It should be obvious at this point if the entrepreneur is pitching the wrong type of start-up to the firm—for example, a semiconductor start-up pitching to a health care–focused venture fund. Or a start-up with two employees in a garage may not be a good fit for a venture firm that only looks at companies with several million dollars of revenue. A venture capitalist might direct the entrepreneur to some other investment shop better suited to do the deal.

Follow-Up

If the start-up may be a fit for the venture firm's industry, investment stage, and general thesis, the investor will start asking follow-up questions. The post-pitch follow-up questions are designed to help the venture capitalist learn more. A venture capitalist considering an investment in a solar panel maker might want to know at what price the company will have to sell its panels to make a profit, or how exactly the company plans to integrate its new technology into existing manufacturing processes.

Due Diligence

Follow-up questions are just the beginning of a process called *due diligence*. The term comes from an old legal case that describes the standard of care a trustee must take when investing money on behalf of others. The trustee must do a reasonable amount of research on its potential investment to ensure it is viable. Venture capitalists have appropriated the term to mean any research one does in vetting a start-up for investment.

The due diligence process can involve any number of things. An investor might visit the company's offices, or drive around its parking lot on a Saturday morning to see how many employees are working hard on the weekend. He or she might call the entrepreneur's references, or anyone else that might have worked with the entrepreneur, to sniff out any scent of scandal. The venture capitalist might ask for the company's financials, or to see the schematics for its latest semiconductor. It's not unusual for an investor to hire a private detective to dig into the background of the start-up's founders or to tail them around Silicon Valley.[4]

Due diligence can be a difficult time for any start-up. Many entrepreneurs have concerns about releasing too much private information about their companies, or "opening the kimono."

Their fears may be well founded. Venture capitalists, as a whole, refuse to sign nondisclosure agreements, often called NDAs. The official reason any venture investor will give is that they are bombarded with start-up pitches and would be unable to effectively do their job if under the constant legal threat of violating an NDA. Entrepreneurs, however, feel that venture capitalists are not above passing their confidential information to a competitor, especially one that the venture firm may have an investment in.

Partner Meeting Pitch

Once the primary venture capitalist associated with the potential investment is satisfied that the start-up meets the venture firm's investment criteria, he or she will bring the opportunity to the rest of the firm for consideration. The partners' pitch meeting is more formal than the initial pitch and takes place at the venture firm's offices. General partners from the firm's other offices may join by teleconference. It will include a revised version of the PowerPoint slide, tailored to answer any questions that may have come up during the due diligence process. The entrepreneur will then field questions from any venture capitalist in the room.

Partner pitch meetings can seem intimidating and sometimes are. Each firm has its own process for deciding whether or not to make an investment. Some put the start-up to a vote and require a majority or supermajority to approve it. Others require two advocates beyond the vote of the venture capitalist who initially discovered the deal. Whatever the process, most firms take their time to decide. Waiting on an answer, which can take days, or even weeks, can be the most stressful part for the entrepreneur.

Deal Negotiation

If the partners decide they want to make an investment, they will then enter into negotiations with the start-up's founders. The negotiation will center around how much stock the firm will buy from the start-up and at what price. Other discussion points will center on the rights and provisions associated with the stock that the start-up sells. Both the venture firm and the start-up will likely bring in lawyers to help hammer out the details.

Final Close

Once the details are finalized, the deal is ready to close and both the entrepreneurs and the venture capitalists will put ink to paper. Depending on the terms of the stock sale, the start-up may expect to find a massive amount of new capital wired to its bank account within the week. The venture capitalist that made first contact with the start-up may or may not join its board of directors, depending on his or her experience level and the provisions of the financing.

Stock Classifications

There are two major forms of stock classification used in financing a private company's growth: common stock and preferred stock.

Common Stock

Common stock is the plainest-vanilla stock a company issues. It is the equity stake held by the people with the least power to negotiate specialized terms and conditions. Common shareholders may vote and collect dividends but have little power beyond that.

In practice, common stock goes to a start-up's founders and executives. It lacks many of the legal protections afforded to preferred stockholders.

Preferred Stock

Preferred stock is the type of stock venture capitalists buy when they invest in a company. Preferred stock can have any number of rights and provisions written in when it is created. If common stock is plain vanilla, then preferred stock is vanilla with sprinkles, chocolate chips, caramel sauce, and any other topping you can imagine. It's a more flexible security that lawyers can write almost any protections or rights into.

A company can, and usually does, have several different types of preferred stock, each with its own terms. Most preferred stock is *convertible*, meaning it can be turned in to common stock under certain conditions, such as a company sale or public stock offering. The conversion ratio may be 1-to-1 or it can be any other ratio specified in the terms of the preferred stock agreement.

Although preferred stock opens an infinite universe of features, venture capitalists usually are only interested in one major clause that comes with preferred stock: In the event of a company sale, the preferred shareholders are paid out first. Most of the provisions of preferred stock deal with exactly how the payments will be split up if the company is sold to a strategic acquirer or liquidated in some other way.

Typical Preferred Stock Clauses

Preferred stock is the ultimate custom-order. Venture capitalists can contract for any number of protections. Still, most firms ask for only a limited number of standard terms, each with its own minor variations.

There are plenty of other things to worry about when you work with a preferred stock agreement and it is sometimes useful to consult with a lawyer to help demystify things. Some law firms even offer easy explanations of these complicated stock clauses for free.[5] Fortunately, most preferred shareholder agreements are extremely similar.

The terms of preferred stock can be complex, but the reason for their terms can be extremely straightforward. Venture capitalists want to protect their investment. The terms of preferred stock are like a bundle of different insurance policies. They can give a venture capital firm choices on how to be paid when a start-up is sold and can be particularly useful when the acquisition price is disappointingly low and investors start arguing over the scraps of what's left. Liquidation preferences, participation and cumulative dividends, redemption rights, and antidilution clauses are all designed to ensure that when preferred shareholders sell their shares, they'll get a high price.

It's important to note that the investors may or may not decide to apply any or all of the rights conferred from their preferred shares. They will pick and choose which provisions give them the greatest gain when a start-up either goes public or is sold. A venture capitalist who goes down one path may not be able to later change his or her mind and go down some other.

Liquidation Preferences

If a company is sold, each stockholder will be treated differently. Preferred shareholders are first in line to be paid, but what will they get?

One of the most common clauses designed to answer this question is a liquidation preference. This clause guarantees that the preferred shareholder will get back the price he or she paid to buy the preferred shares. For example, a venture capitalist who invested $10 million to buy a swath of Series B preferred shares will get $10 million back if the start-up is sold. The payout takes place before anything is paid to the common shareholders, and unless there are additional provisions, the preferred shareholders will get back whatever they initially invested.

Liquidation preference is a pretty good thing for venture capitalists because it guarantees they will at least get their money back if the company is sold. The terms of these preferences have become an important negotiating point for venture investors, who expect many of their companies to be sold to strategic acquirers. Between 40 percent and 50 percent of the investments made each quarter involve some version of liquidation preference, according to the law firm Fenwick & West, which tracks deal terms and conditions. There are two major types of liquidation preferences:

1. *Senior liquidation preference.* This clause bumps a series of preferred stock to the front of the line for getting a payout. This is

particularly useful for venture capitalists who are investing late in a start-up's development. They may fear that the start-up will sell at a price that is so low as to not have enough money to pass out to all of the earlier investors, who may also hold liquidation preferences. If there are no senior liquidation preferences, each set of preferred shares is said to be *pari passu,* or on equal footing with each other.

2. *Multiple liquidation preference.* This makes a liquidation preference more potent by multiplying its payout. An investor may request that a series of preferred shares have a 2X liquidation preference, meaning that in the event of a company sale, the holders of these shares will get paid twice as much as they initially invested. An investor who pays $10 million to purchase a number of preferred shares with a 2X liquidity preference will be paid $20 million in the event of a company sale before anyone else gets paid. Some 50 percent to 60 percent of multiple liquidation preferences fall between 1X and 2X and another 40 percent are between 2X and 3X, according to data from Fenwick & West. One seldom sees multiples over 3X, but they are not unheard of.

To be clear, a liquidation preference only guarantees that the investor will get back what he or she paid for the preferred shares. Nothing more. That's fine if the start-up has a disappointing sale, then the investors are grateful for whatever return they can get. Liquidation preferences are less valuable if the start-up does well.

Consider what happens to an investor who pays $10 million to purchase 50 percent of a start-up's shares and has a 2X liquidity preference.

If the start-up sells for $30 million, the investor will be glad for his or her liquidity preference, getting $20 million back from the sale.

But if the start-up sells for $50 million, the investor would still only get $20 million from the liquidation preference. In this case, a venture capitalist would likely convert his or her preferred shares into common stock. Owning 50 percent of the common stock would yield a return of $25 million.

Not all venture capitalists will negotiate for liquidation preferences. Early stage investors, for example, may specifically avoid writing in these clauses for fear that they will set a precedent for all later investors. It's possible that if the later stage investors get too many liquidation preferences, there will be nothing to pass back to the early stage investors or the entrepreneurs.

Participation

An entrepreneur negotiating the terms of his or her financing agreement might be excited to hear that the venture capitalists were anxious to get *participation*. But the friendly sounding clause in preferred stock agreements is another way for venture capitalists to ensure they get paid.

When a company is sold, the proceeds first go to pay any outstanding liquidation preferences. Then, what's left is split among the preferred and common shareholders based on how much of the company each owns.

For a preferred class of stock to be paid from what's left, it must be participating. If the preferred shareholders own 50 percent of the company and are all participating, they'll get 50 percent of the returns from a sale after the liquidation preferences are met.

A participation clause can be included on top of a liquidity preference so that the venture capitalist gets the best of both worlds. More typically, however, the venture capitalist will only get one or the other. Participation may be particularly attractive to early investors, which will likely have paid a small amount of money to get a rather large ownership stake in the start-up. Although preferred shares can be customized to fit any need, it is hard to imagine a venture capitalist not taking either a liquidation preference or participation.

Let's look at what happens in the same scenario we considered in the previous section. A venture capitalist pays $10 million to purchase 50 percent of a start-up's equity, has a 2X liquidity preference and now has full participation on top of that.

If the start-up sells for $30 million, the venture capitalist gets $20 million by virtue of the liquidation preferences. That leaves $10 million to be split among the shareholders. The venture capitalist owns 50 percent of the shares outstanding and is fully participating. That means he or she will get half of what's left, in this case, $5 million. The total payout to the venture capitalist is then $20 million from the liquidation preference and $5 million from the participation rights, which sums to $25 million.

Had the venture capitalist owned just common shares, he or she would only have received 50 percent of the $30 million payout, or $15 million. The addition of liquidity preferences and full participation allowed a 50 percent shareholder to take 83 percent of the payout from the start-up's sale.

If the start-up sells for $50 million, the venture capitalist gets $20 million from the liquidation preferences and another $15 million from the full participation rights, summing to $35 million, or 70 percent of the total payout available.

A nonparticipating preferred shareholder is not nearly so well off if the start-up is sold. He or she is faced with a decision to either maintain the preferred shares or convert the shares to common stock. This comes down to which will yield a bigger payoff: any liquidity preference associated with the preferred shares, or the percentage of the payout that goes with owning a large swath of common stock.

The payout from a liquidity preference is based on the start-up's acquisition price. If the start-up sells for less money than the venture investors put in, the liquidity preferences may yield a bigger payout. If the start-up sells for much more than the venture investors put in, any nonparticipating preferred might be wise to convert to common stock.

The value of liquidation preferences and participation rights is inversely proportional to the acquisition value of the start-up. In our example, the preferred shareholders get 67 percent more than they would have if they were common shareholders if the start-up sells for $30 million. But as the payout increases, the difference between what the preferred and common shareholders are paid decreases. If the start-up sells for $50 million, the preferred get 40 percent more than they would have if they had been common shareholders.

Capped participation is a clause that sets an upper limit on what a preferred class of stock can be paid in the event of a company sale. Capping participation is an entrepreneur-friendly thing to do, and something that venture capitalists are likely to negotiate against.

Caps range from three to five times what an investor pays for the preferred stock and include whatever liquidation preference shareholders have already received. It's worth noting that if things go really well and a strategic buyer pays a bunch of money for a start-up, the venture capitalists may get a bigger upside by converting their preferred shares into common stock and thereby avoiding the participation cap.

Cumulative Dividends and Redemption Rights

The logic behind *cumulative dividends* is convoluted, but that doesn't keep lawyers from writing it into financing contracts. The idea is that a young company sells products, earns money, and becomes more valuable. Instead of paying out quarterly or annual dividends, as one might expect a mature corporation to do, the company holds onto the money. The presumption is that the company reinvests dividends it would have otherwise paid out.

Eventually the company is bought. Preferred shareholders with a cumulative dividend provision are then able to collect an additional payout based on how much they invested and how long they held the shares. Cumulative dividends are paid out after liquidation preferences and range from 5 to 8 percent annualized return based on a principal of whatever was paid for the shares of preferred stock.

Cumulative dividends work similarly to a certificate of deposit that you might get from a local bank. As long as the start-up is sold, the preferred shareholders that have this clause get an annualized rate of return. The dividends typically come on top of a liquidation preference.

Few financing agreements actually include cumulative dividend clauses. Fenwick & West puts the percentage of investments made with such clauses between 4 and 10 percent for each quarter over the past several years.[6]

Redemption rights are a part of a preferred stockholder agreement that looks a lot like a "gimme my money back" clause. It states that shareholders can, after some set time period, force the issuing company to buy back the shares. What's more, the company has to pay out at the price the shareholders initially bought in. One seldom sees redemption rights put into play since they require a majority shareholder approval and because most investors expect to get back more than they put in, thanks to all the other clauses written into preferred shares. Roughly 20 percent to 25 percent of the investments made each quarter include redemption rights, according to research by law firm Fenwick & West.

Antidilution

Writing in an antidilution clause allows a preferred shareholder to convert to common stock at a higher rate than initially established. The clause may be executed if the value of the company decreases.

Suppose each share of preferred stock could initially be converted for one share of common stock. The value of the company goes down and the antidilution provisions kick in, allowing preferred shareholders to trade in each of their shares for two shares of common stock.

Getting twice the number of common shares is like getting each share at half the initial price you paid and can ensure that the investor gets a healthy capital gain.

There are two major forms of antidilution provisions—weighted average and ratchet—which use different formulas for determining how the new conversion rate from preferred to common is set.

Seeking Simplicity

There is a movement to streamline the terms and conditions of early stage start-up financing, spearheaded by a handful of repeat entrepreneurs. They feel that some venture capitalists use the complexity of the contracting process to intimidate entrepreneurs into giving up rights and company ownership. They developed a "Plain Preferred" term sheet, which outlines typical clauses used in venture financing agreements. It may easily be found online,[7] and studying it may provide first-time company founders with a basis for discussing provisions in a financing contract.

Stock During Different Stages of Development

As a start-up goes from two founders in a garage with a business plan to an office full of people and real revenue, its financing needs change. So does its ability to negotiate with venture capitalists. Start-ups sell different "series" of stock as they grow. Each series of stock is sold for a different price to account for changes in the start-up's size, value, and risk profile. Each series is designated by a letter, with "Series A" being the first preferred shares sold, "Series B" being the second set of preferred shares sold, and so on.

Although any number of provisions can be included from one round to another, the biggest difference is typically the price paid for each share of preferred stock. Since shares of start-up stock are illiquid and cannot be traded in a market, their price does not freely move up and down like shares in a public company might.

A Series A investor may pay pennies for each stock, while a Series D investor may pay several dollars per preferred share. The Series A investor takes a great risk investing in a start-up that has not yet proven its technology or attracted the right management team.

A Series D investor may invest three or four years later in the start-up's development, after the technology has been shown to work and the company has recruited experienced executives. The Series D investors are likely to be concerned about the start-up's ability to respond to changing customer needs, access new markets, form strategic alliances, and eventually either go public or be sold to a strategic acquirer.

Series A investors who bought stock at a low price early in the company's development face all the same concerns as the Series D investors do. If the company can't access new markets, for example, both classes of stock suffer. For a summary of the different series of stock, see Exhibit 4.2.

An investor who purchases Series A shares may go on to purchase Series B, C, D, and all subsequent preferred shares sold by the company. Most start-ups sell a new Series of preferred shares every 12 to 18 months. There's no requirement that the early investors participate in subsequent financings, but many look at it as a sign of support that indicates that the Series A investor still has faith in the start-up.

EXHIBIT 4.2

A Summary of Series

Series	Cost of Shares	Stage	Risk	Typical Investment Amount
A & B	Low	Early	High: Functioning technology	$500,000 to $5M
C & D	Medium	Later	Medium: Getting customers	$5M to $20M

Some venture firms will only invest in early stage start-ups. They believe that they can pick founders who will navigate the problems of beginning a company, perfecting a technology and connecting with customers and feel that the risk they take will be compensated with great reward. They buy Series A and B preferred shares. Other firms will only invest in start-ups that have reached certain milestones, such as shipping a product or achieving $10 million in revenue. They buy Series C, D, and E preferred shares, take fewer risks, and generally experience lower returns than successful early stage investors.

A series of preferred shares are sold during a "round" of financing. During the round, venture capitalists negotiate a price for the shares with the start-up's management. Once the price for the shares is set, the investors and the start-up agree on a term sheet for the legal provisions of the stock class. Then there may be time allotted to bring in other investors who agree to the same price and terms. Completing a round can take anywhere from a week to more than a month. Once the round is closed, new investors must wait until the start-up is prepared to offer its next series of preferred shares for sale to negotiate a new price.

Syndication

There's safety in numbers. Venture capital firms often employ that thinking when they look at investing in a start-up. One venture capitalist may invite a friend at another firm to evaluate a promising start-up and, if both agree on its merits, they'll do the deal together.

There are several reasons for doing this beyond just having a second, or third set of eyes to evaluate an opportunity. The most obvious reason is that two firms may combine their resources to make an investment larger than either could have comfortably made on its own.

Venture capitalists often look to partner with each other when times are bad. It helps them spread their bets over a wider area. Having your eggs in a lot of different baskets is a good thing when all the baskets are getting knocked around by a bad economy.

Having many investors can help a start-up stay out of bankruptcy because it increases the chances that at least one of the investors will be willing or able to reinvest at any given point. "When you go through soft economy patches and you have to live through the cycle, having more muscle around the table can help," says Matthew Howard of Norwest Venture Partners.

But when investors expect times to be good, the tide turns and venture capitalists have an incentive to take as large an ownership stake in their start-ups as possible. "If you're going to have influence and impact in a company, you want to make it meaningful," says John Balen of Canaan Partners. "We'd rather have them rely on us instead of going outside and diluting us and taking away control."

Sharing

It's good to share. That's what an investor with Bay Partners discovered when his firm led a $3 million Series A investment round in a stealth hardware company.[a]

Bay Partners could have easily financed the entire round from its $300 million fund, but determined that the start-up needed more than money. It needed help working with Chinese manufacturers and customers. Executing in China would make or break the opportunity.

So Bay took the deal to three venture firms with a strong presence in China. The entrepreneur chose to work with Redpoint Ventures, which had experience investing in China. Bay Partners split the investment with Redpoint.

"Even early on in a company's history, we are comfortable trading off higher ownership to having the right DNA around the table to materially reduce the risk the company faces," the Bay investor says.

[a] This section is adapted from "Early Stage Syndication Drops," *PE Week*, March 31, 2008, http://bit.ly/bXJBx4.

For all the benefits of syndication, it is actually happening less at the early stages of company formation now than ever before, according to data from Thomson Financial. The average number of firms involved in a start-up or seed investment has fallen 32 percent over the past seven years. A typical early stage deal might now expect to garner investment from four venture capital firms, down from an average of nearly six in 2002, the data show.

There are several reasons for this. The first and most important is that many start-ups just don't need as much money as they used to. For example, information technology companies can use open-source software and commodity hardware to keep costs down. "We're seeing more deals that get off the ground with just a little money and reach critical mass without the traditional syndicate," says Tom Dyal of Redpoint Ventures.

Even if a start-up wanted to raise more money, cash is concentrated in a shrinking number of firms. Fundraising has gotten harder for firms without a strong track record. But the firms that can raise money are raising more than ever before. That puts pressure on venture firms to put more money to work in each of their deals.

"As funds get bigger, the need to write bigger checks has come with that," says Virginia Turezyn, the former managing director of American Capital Strategies's technology group. "I worked in the 1980s when your summary sheet was who wasn't in the deal instead of who was. That pendulum has swung the other way."

Valuation

One of the best reasons to bring other venture capitalists in to invest in a start-up is to help determine the price for a certain class of preferred shares.

Establishing a start-up's *valuation*, or the total worth of the business, is neither an art nor a science. It is a negotiation.[8] The start-up's management wants to have the highest valuation possible when it goes to sell a round of preferred shares. A high valuation allows management to either raise more money for expansion or retain a greater ownership stake in the start-up. The venture capitalists that are still prospective investors want the lowest possible valuation for the start-up. A low valuation makes the price of preferred shares cheap and allows the venture capitalists to either pay less money or get a bigger ownership stake for their firms.

A start-up's management and investors renegotiate valuation each time the start-up sells a new class of preferred stock. A start-up selling Series B stock will argue for a higher valuation than when it sold its Series A stock, pointing to the progress it has made since its first round of financing.

TIPS AND TECHNIQUES

Valuation Math

Imagine an entrepreneur who comes up with a great new idea. She maxes out her credit cards financing research and development of her breakthrough, incorporates, and starts to look for venture capital financing.

She meets with a well-known venture capitalist and after a while, they start talking about what her company might be worth. The venture capitalist thinks the work that the entrepreneur has put in and the idea's potential are worth $10 million. The entrepreneur argues that her innovation is really special and worth $30 million. They settle on a valuation of $20 million.

The venture capitalist offers to buy $5 million worth of Series A preferred shares at a $20 million valuation, or "five at 20." The first number is what is being invested and the second is the "pre-money" valuation, or what the company is worth before it takes on the investment. After the start-up has sold this swath of stock, it will have a "post-money" valuation of $25 million, which simply reflects the sum of the pre-money valuation and the new investment. The venture capitalist has paid $5 million for a 20 percent stake in the start-up, based on its post-money valuation.

After a year's worth of progress, the start-up is ready to raise capital again. The entrepreneur sets out looking for an outside investor to set the valuation for the sale of Series B preferred shares. A new venture firm offers "5 at 40," or a $5 million investment at a pre-money valuation of $40 million. The existing venture capitalist is also interested in investing and offers to buy $5 million worth of Series B preferred shares at the $40 million pre-money valuation set by the outside investor. Each firm is effectively paying $5 million for a 10 percent stake in the start-up.

Combined with the Series A financing, the entrepreneur will have sold 40 percent of her company after just two rounds of venture capital investment.

Setting the price for any series of preferred shares is not a simple matter. The venture capitalist that invested in the Series A finds him- or herself conflicted when it comes to negotiating the price for Series B shares. On one side, it is in the venture capital firm's interest to argue for a low start-up valuation, drive the price of Series B shares down, and subsequently pay less for its ownership stake. But the investor involved likely has taken a position on the start-up's board of directors, a position that has a fiduciary duty to maximize the value of the company for existing shareholders. As a board member, the venture capitalist's interests should be aligned with those of the start-up's management and he or she should be seeking the highest possible valuation for the start-up.

Rather than force this conflict on the Series A venture capitalist, the start-up typically goes hunting for a new investor to bring into the Series B round. The new investor will come to the valuation negotiation free of conflicted interests and will set the price of the Series B shares. The start-up's existing investors typically "re-up," or invest again at the price set by the start-up's negotiation with the outside investor. This frees the Series A investor from the conflicting requirements of being both an investor and a board member.

Not every start-up sees its valuation increase from one round of investment to another. If a start-up fails to deliver on a key technological development, experiences a drop in sales, loses key members of its team, or just faces a tougher macroeconomic environment, it may be forced to accept a "down round." A down round reflects a decrease in the start-up's negotiated valuation.

IN THE REAL WORLD

Changes in Value for Each Series

It is very difficult to find and track reliable data for how start-up valuations change over time. Still, there are a few sources that can be helpful in understanding how the process works.

One way to witness how valuation changes over time is to look at the value of the shares sold during each round of financing. A start-up that wants to go public often has to file this type of information with the Securities and Exchange Commission. To be sure, share price is not a perfect proxy for start-up valuation. Each series of shares may have a different set of liquidity preferences or other rights that can affect its value independently of the overall value of the start-up.

Consider the share prices paid by investors in lithium-ion battery maker A123 Systems,[a] shown in Exhibit 4.3. The start-up went public in September 2009, offering shares to the public for sale at $13.50.

EXHIBIT 4.3

Share Prices for A123 Systems

Series	Date	Share Price ($)	Valuation Change from Previous Round (%)
A	December 2001	1.00	
A-1	December 2002	1.50	+50
B	June 2004	2.08	+39
C	January 2006	3.37	+62
D	August 2007	6.56	+95
E	March 2008	16.59	+153
F	April 2009	9.20	−45

Notice the drop in share price from March of 2008 to April of 2009. It may be the product of the global financial crisis that began in June of 2008.

It's worth noting that the per-share price is less meaningful than the relative change in price from round to round. Consider two transactions: A start-up could sell 1 million shares at $1 per share and keep 9 million shares in reserve for future sales or it could sell 10 million shares for $0.10 each and keep 90 million shares in reserve for future sales. The only difference between the two is the number of shares issued and the price per share. The start-up valuation is the same as the amount of money it raises from the stock sale.

EXHIBIT 4.4

Share Prices for Tesla Motors

Series	Date	Share Price ($)	Valuation Change from Previous Round (%)
A	February 2005	0.493	
B	December 2005	0.740	+50
C	June 2006	1.081	+46
D	May 2007	2.440	+126
E	May 2009	2.512	+3
F	September 2009	2.969	+18

Consider the share prices paid by investors in electric carmaker Tesla Motors (shown in Exhibit 4.4), which has filed to go public but has yet to price its IPO as of this writing.

You can see the regular increase in share price corresponding to an improving company valuation. To be sure, some shares have special rights and their price likely reflects the value of those rights in addition to the underlying value of the company.

[a] Share prices from the company's S-1/A filing to the Securities and Exchange Commission made September 22, 2009, http://bit.ly/bPr7jy.
[b] Share prices from the company's S-1/A filing to the Securities and Exchange Commission made January 29, 2010, http://bit.ly/9HeatA.

There's no formula for how much a company's valuation should increase from one round to another. Each quarter, law firm Fenwick & West tracks the average valuation change that more than 100 start-ups see for their financing rounds.[9] You can see its results for a recent quarter in Exhibit 4.5.

EXHIBIT 4.5

Barometer Analysis—Fenwick & West VC Report

3Q 2009—*Price Change*	Series A	Series B	Series C	Series D	Series E+	Cumulative
Percent Change of All Rounds	n/a	23.12%	21.59%	−11.24%	−4.02%	10.69%
Percent Change of Up Rounds Only	n/a	65.70%	115.84%	49.93%	75.05%	76.70%
Percent Change of Down Rounds Only	n/a	−73.79%	−54.98%	−42.18%	−63.94%	−56.93%

The data require a little interpreting. Any one of the more than 100 financings the law firm tracks falls into one of the series and represents just one transaction, it's not as though a single company's progress is tracked over time, as some people mistakenly believe.

The top row, "percent change of all rounds" is an average of all the financings tracked for a given series. The row below that measures the average price increase for financings where the valuation improved and the bottom row measures the average price drops for financings where the valuation decreased.

The table shows that during the third quarter of 2009, start-ups raising a Series B financing round saw an average increase in valuation of 23 percent. Start-ups that saw an "up round" improved their valuation by more than 65 percent, and start-ups that saw a "down round" lost more than 73 percent of their value.

It's worth pointing out that the financial crisis of 2008 impacted late stage start-ups more than early stage start-ups, according to Fenwick & West's data. It's likely that the late stage companies were expecting to get a big boost in revenue that never materialized as would-be customers refrained from spending. The early stage companies, by comparison, may have only needed to prove that their technology worked to get an increased valuation.

Summary

Venture capitalists evaluate start-up investment opportunities by the quality of the team, the level of the technology, the size of the potential market, and the start-up's ability to be successful within a time horizon of five to seven years. Different investors feel differently about the relative importance of each of these measures of a start-up's potential. One major school of investing believes that people are a start-up's greatest asset. Another believes that technology is what matters most.

The aggregate level of venture capital investment into start-ups changes along with macroeconomic trends and the emergence of new technology sectors. Venture capitalists are more likely to invest in start-ups when they are optimistic about the ability of these small companies to make sales, attract strategic acquisition offers, or make an initial public offering.

A start-up looking to raise money from a venture capitalist can expect to go through six major steps before the deal is done. Venture capitalists make first contact with an entrepreneur, either via introduction or networking, and then may invite the entrepreneur into the office to make an initial pitch. The venture capitalist then follows up with questions for the entrepreneur and will begin the process of "due diligence," during which he or she researches the opportunity. If the venture capitalist still likes the start-up, he or she will invite the entrepreneur to pitch the rest of the venture firm's general partners. This may lead to a negotiation on the start-up's valuation and how much money the firm will invest. Once both sides agree to the deal's terms, it will undergo a final close and lawyers will draft an investment contract.

There are two major classes of private company stock: common shares and preferred shares. Venture capitalists buy preferred shares and leave the common shares to the company's founders and employees. Preferred shares have special legal rights that help investors protect their interest, but can be converted into common shares at any point. Protective clauses may include liquidation preferences, participation preferences, cumulative dividends, and antidilution provisions. There are free resources available to help entrepreneurs understand these terms and even a movement to simplify investment agreements.

Venture capitalists often share, or syndicate, investments with each other. Start-ups may seek multiple venture firms for investment to raise a lot of money or to tap different skill sets within different firms. Investors may look to syndicate deals in order to share risk and to set the terms for a new round of investment.

Start-ups sell shares of stock at different times in their development and for different prices. These stock sales are called "rounds" and require renegotiation with venture capitalists to determine the start-up's valuation. A start-up first raises a Series A round, by selling a swath of preferred shares to investors for a low price. Its Series B round preferred shares will usually sell for a higher price because some of the start-ups' risk as an investment will have diminished as the start-up progresses and grows.

Putting a value on a private company is not an easy thing. Venture capitalists and entrepreneurs negotiate the valuation of a start-up to determine how much shares of its preferred stock should cost.

Notes

1. Arthur Rock, "Strategy vs. Tactics from a Venture Capitalist," *The Entrepreneurial Venture*, 3rd ed., p. 351.
2. Udayan Gupta, *Done Deals*, (Boston: Harvard Business School Press, 2000) pp. 167–168.

3. Data from Thomson Reuters.

4. "Private Eye to the VCs Does 'Human Due Diligence,'" Dow Jones *VentureWire*, May 14, 2008, http://bit.ly/azMnBx.

5. See "Explanation of Certain Terms Used in Venture Financing Terms Survey," Fenwick & West, http://bit.ly/cbrEIM.

6. "Trends in Terms of Venture Financing in the San Francisco Bay Area," Fenwick & West (Fourth Quarter 2009), http://bit.ly/9Kdk2y.

7. "Plain Preferred" stock agreement from *The Funded: Founder's Institute*, August 24, 2009, http://bit.ly/dD90Nw.

8. Some believe that start-up valuation is a science and have devoted serious thought to what should be taken into account when determining what a start-up is worth. The best resource for those interested in the theoretical models of valuation finance is Andrew Metrick's *Venture Capital and the Finance of Innovation* (Hoboken, NJ: John Wiley & Sons, Inc., 2007).

9. "Trends in Terms of Venture Financing in the San Francisco Bay Area" (Third Quarter, 2009), http://bit.ly/d4p9ZK.

CHAPTER 5

Finding Investments

After reading this chapter, you will be able to:

- Understand the three ways venture capitalists find investments.
- Develop strategies for proactive outreach to entrepreneurs.
- Invest in and around major new technology platforms.
- Work with universities to commercialize innovation.
- Appreciate the emerging role of venture capital affiliated incubators.
- Create an Entrepreneur in Residence program.
- Understand how the needs of entrepreneurs and venture capitalists make opportunities for alternative strategies.

There are many resources for entrepreneurs looking for financing, but few for venture capitalists on where to find the best investments. This may be because if an entrepreneur doesn't connect with money to grow, he or she goes out of business. A venture capitalist, on the other hand, feels no similar sense of desperation. It's possible for an investor to go a year or more without writing a single check.

But eventually the investor must make investments. The question is where to look for the best opportunities.

It is useful to think of the venture capital industry as an early Neolithic society, dating back some 12,000 years ago, which relies on hunting and gathering for the majority of its subsistence and has only begun to experiment with agriculture.

Venture investors use those same three techniques for finding the majority of their investments. They gather business cards at conferences and business plans through online drop-boxes. They hunt for their own investments by making calls, connecting with their friends, or stalking down innovators working on new technology platforms inside universities. Venture capitalists can also grow their own investment opportunities by hiring Entrepreneurs in Residence or by working with start-up incubators.

We'll consider a handful of alternative strategies for getting in on good investments once we've covered how the majority of deals go down. Investors too new or too small to engage in the same practices as the established venture firms may find these alternative investment concepts particularly useful.

Gathering Opportunities

Entrepreneurs are always looking for investment capital. That can be a big help to venture capitalists. It's like a zebra inviting a lion to lunch.

One frequently sees entrepreneurs rushing up to investors who speak at technology conferences, thrusting business cards in front of them. It quite literally becomes a scrum tantamount to what you might see in a rugby game, full of pressed flesh and protruding elbows as one entrepreneur tries to edge out another for an investor's attention.

If an entrepreneur makes it through to the investor and successfully inserts his or her business card into the waiting hand, it's then time to fly into an "elevator pitch," where he or she tries to describe the opportunity in 15 seconds or less.

Venture capitalists will either be annoyed or thrilled by the attention, depending on their temperament. They tend to go to conferences early in their career as a form of self-marketing, specifically to collect a lot of business cards and see a large number of entrepreneurs. However, as an investor becomes successful, he or she is less likely to attend such events, since they typically yield a low number of really great investment opportunities.

In order to see an almost unlimited supply of start-ups looking for cash, a venture capital firm may invite entrepreneurs to submit business plans through its web site.

Pitches submitted through the web site are generally considered to be low-value opportunities. In fact, not every venture firm actually checks the submissions. The task of sifting through these pitches often falls to the most junior investor in the firm. About the best treatment such pitches can expect is to be printed out once a quarter to ensure that the venture firm has not overlooked some hidden gem.

John Doerr, a prominent investor from Kleiner Perkins Caufield & Byers who invested in Netscape, Amazon, and Google, said that his firm received 3,000 business plans from its web site each year. It financed zero of those plans, he told *The New Yorker* in 1997. "Most of these plans are crazy," he said. "People who want to put up a dome over Los Angeles to keep out the smog. Seriously."[1] Intel Capital, the successful venture investing arm of the semiconductor giant, sees a similar level of inbound submissions, says director of strategic investments Eghosa Omoigui. It has only ever invested in one such unsolicited business plan submission.

Venture capitalists can also take meetings with financing fixers, people who contract with start-ups to help them raise money in exchange for a fee. The fixers will meet with the venture capitalist and pitch half a dozen different start-ups at the same time.

Investors also attend special luncheons designed to showcase potential investments. They may pay a membership fee to participate in these pitch meetings. The luncheons typically feature mediocre food and an equivalent level of quality among start-ups.

Gathering investment opportunities in these fashions seldom gives serious venture capitalists enough high-quality deals to sustain themselves. It's like spending a day collecting nuts and berries instead of hunting for a substantial meal.

Hunting for Investments

Some firms don't wait for the best start-ups to come to them. Instead, they turn to proactive measures to find investments.

Few investors will talk explicitly about what they do. Each feels as though he or she has stumbled upon some secret of investing guaranteed to garner great returns. They're nervous that their competition would readily duplicate whatever trick they've developed for finding the best entrepreneurs or the hottest technologies.

Some venture investors, such as Vinod Khosla, obsessively read scientific and professional journals, looking for breakthroughs they might be able to commercialize. Others track government documents, such as new company registration filings, looking for start-ups that may have managed to slip under the radar. One well-known European investor says he calls a friend who works in the finance division of a large credit card company to find out what start-ups have managed to book big revenue recently.

Personal Connections

There's little secret to how most venture capitalists go hunting for deals though. They first look to the people they know.

More than anything else, this serves as a filter. It's easy for a venture capitalist to feel as though he or she is sitting on a duffle bag full of cash in the center of a gigantic sports arena, with everyone shouting their ideas and pressing forward with outstretched hands. Turning to friends, associates, and other connections first helps quiet the din. It makes the job of venture capitalist more like attending a noisy cocktail party.

The best connections are the people an investor has worked with in the past. It helps if those people have proven themselves to be successful already. These first-order connections can either be entrepreneurs themselves looking to finance a new start-up, or people who can point the investor to an entrepreneur that they know.

"Thou shalt come by way of introduction," says Intel Capital's Eghosa Omoigui to prospective entrepreneurs. And he's not joking. Venture capitalists like to rely on their acquaintances to vet potential investments for several reasons. Successful technology executives are likely to know entrepreneurs within their industry and may be able to offer some insight into what new venture has the potential to be successful. They may also be able to spot other people with the potential to be successful.

Other professionals, such as bankers, lawyers, or academics, may have a vague sense of what investors look for in a start-up and will steer promising investment opportunities to their friends.

Good investment opportunities are often referred by other venture capitalists. These investors may be looking to fill out an investment syndicate, or may be focused on bigger, smaller, or just different kinds of start-ups. Some referrals come from angel investors, or early stage venture capitalists looking to help their portfolio companies connect with a second round of financing.

A sly trick works well for some experienced entrepreneurs. They will approach a venture capitalist to whom they may have some tenuous connection and ask for advice. This can be someone that they swapped business cards with at a conference, someone that they went to business school with a decade or more ago, or even a friend of a friend of a friend.

They'll research what kind of investments the venture capitalist makes and start off a meeting by saying: "I know you don't invest in the kind of company that I'm working to build, but I thought you might be able to offer me some advice as to whether the business makes sense or who I might approach."

It's a great way to garner introductions. The venture capitalist will look seriously at the start-up, relieved of the burden of having to say "no" to its financing, and will likely offer solid suggestions of how to improve it. The venture capitalist is grateful for the opportunity to lecture. Once finished, he or she may be good for an e-mail introduction to another venture capitalist who actually does invest in whatever industry the entrepreneur is pitching.

Young venture capitalists may spend years attending networking events for entrepreneurs and going to technology conferences to build their network of connections. They pass out business cards and chat with people who may not be working on a start-up right now, but are similarly anxious to expand their own Rolodexes. Once he or she is successful, people will thrust business cards into his or her hands at conferences.

A venture capitalist may then turn to these people to either point them toward attractive investments or act as experts to vet other incoming opportunities. Venture capitalists are increasingly using social networking services, such as LinkedIn, to keep track of their growing number of connections.

The best investors know how to really work a room. Point in case: Ron Conway. The angel investor was one of the early backers of search engine Ask Jeeves, and later, of Google. He regularly invests several hundred thousand dollars at a time in 20 to 40 start-ups a year. Watching him network is like observing some kind of pendulous hummingbird, buzzing from one entrepreneur to another, whispering in ears, tugging on arms, and glad-handing other investors with aplomb. He seems to know everybody, no matter how big the gathering.

"Smile and Dial"

A common deal-hunting tactic employed at big venture firms with more than a billion dollars to invest is often disparagingly referred to as "smile and dial."

Under this process, the venture firm will set out a series of guidelines for what it is looking for and then employ a dozen junior associates to cull through long lists of company names and phone numbers. The associate will put on his or her best smile and then dial up each company's telephone number to learn if it is a fit for the firm's investment parameters. Senior partners then review any company that answers the phone and looks as though it might be a match.

The specific criteria junior associates look for varies from firm to firm. But the best-known implementations of such a strategy are at firms such as TA Associates and Summit Partners. These firms aim to be the first institutional investors in companies that are either historically family-owned or have successfully self-financed or "bootstrapped" to serious revenue of $50 million or more.

That net can dredge up any number of investment opportunities in diverse industries across the United States. Many will be unsuitable for a venture capital style investment because of the nature of whatever business they're in. Most companies will not be looking for venture capital investment and may need to be persuaded that they need money to grow faster or expand internationally.

The last mile of consulting, cajoling, and convincing a company that it needs investment capital is the role of the senior investors at the firm. They set the parameters of the junior investors' search, telling them where to fish. Once a junior investor has a company on the hook, the senior investors will reel it in. This dynamic makes "smile and dial" a strategy that works best in vertically structured firms.

Still, "smile and dial" has something of a negative connotation among venture investors, who would prefer to believe that their work is more art than simply the brute force of junior associates searching for prospects and banging the telephones.

Universities

Venture capitalists have always looked for innovation in and around university campuses.[2] Now, university research is becoming increasingly useful in venture capital-backed start-ups, especially as they look toward alternative energy and efficiency applications.

There's more innovation to take advantage of too. In fact, there's been a 45 percent increase in the number of patents granted to the top research universities over the last decade. And those patents are finding their way into start-ups, typically via licensing agreements. In fact, some 600 start-ups are formed based on university research each year, according to the Association of University Technology Managers.[3]

Still, many venture capitalists have a difficult time figuring out how best to approach schools. There are problems of licensing lab-created technology from the school and a generation gap between investors and undergraduate and graduate-level students. But there are a handful of strategies that do work when approaching universities; see *Tips and Techniques: Dealing with Universities.*

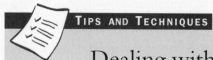

Dealing with Universities

University deals are difficult and time consuming. Even when you find the right technical founder, there's no assurance that the deal will work out. "Just because somebody's a great researcher doesn't mean that they've got the verve to start Amgen," says John Balen, a partner with Canaan Partners.

But if you absolutely must fight your way through the tangle of departmental politics or wrench intellectual property out of the grip of tech transfer officers, at least take some advice from the venture capitalists who have done it:

EDUCATE THE EDUCATORS

Dan Watkins, DFJ Mercury: "We like to get to know the university researcher and what they expect to get out of it. Some of them want just to further advance their research and this is just another source of money to them. They all typically have to learn what founders may expect to end up with if they acquire capital."

FIGURE OUT HOW TO PAY THE UNIVERSITY

Hanson Gifford, The Foundry: "Some of these things take easily over a year to conclude. There are a whole lot of compensation plans that can be created. Looking at different plans can help you find an arrangement that's mutually acceptable. Most universities have ended up focused primarily on royalties, and start-up companies are focused primarily on equity and are less sensitive to the impact of royalties, so everyone can come away feeling good about it."

WATCH OUT FOR CORPORATE SPONSORS

Todd Kimmel, Mayfield Fund: "Let's say I'm spinning something out of the chemistry department. Well, whoever is funding the chemistry department has to look at the IP [intellectual property] first to see if it's interesting. I don't have a problem with that, but I don't know why it has to take 60 to 90 days."

CONNECT WITH PEOPLE WHO CAN HELP

Carl Weissman, Accelerator: "It's just a relationship process. My prime relationship at Caltech was with Larry Gilbert [director of tech transfer] and at University of Washington it's Fiona Wills [director of invention licensing]. They get what it takes to move an early stage technology backed by venture capitalists to an exit. They've been extremely creative in coming up with deal structures that can work with our venture capital syndicate."

Platforms

When great white sharks swim through the ocean near the coast of California they're often accompanied by remora. The remora fish latches on to the stomach and sides of the great white and picks up the scraps that the enormous predator leaves behind. It's one of the classic examples of a symbiotic relationship.

Venture capitalists periodically want to invest in the remoras of the business world, start-ups that latch on to an enormous corporate technology platform and ride along with it.

Just as computers need software and the Internet needs web sites, large corporations sometimes need smaller companies to adopt their technology to make products people will find useful.

Investing in start-ups to populate an emerging technology ecosystem seems to be a popular thing for venture capitalists to do every half a decade or so. Sometimes the investors will launch a dedicated venture fund to target new tech platforms. It's a move that garners a lot of attention, especially from those entrepreneurs focused on developing applications using or targeting the new platform.

Few firms make this move with as much panache as Kleiner Perkins Caufield & Byers (KPCB). The firm opened a $100 million "Java Fund" to invest in start-ups using a powerful new programming language developed by Sun Microsystems in the mid-1990s. Sun, a large computer maker originally funded by KPCB and later acquired by database company Oracle, had developed the Java language to make Internet sites more interactive. The venture capital firm believed that more people using the Java language would make it more powerful as an alternative to other programming platforms.[4]

The fund had mixed results. It was a financial success, at least so says Ted Schlein, the KPCB partner who ran the fund.[5] But the start-ups it financed are largely unmemorable, and Sun was unable to take advantage of its burgeoning Java ecosystem in a meaningful way.

More than a decade later, KPCB launched another platform play, this one targeted at start-ups developing applications for Apple's iPhone. The firm's $100 million "iFund" brought many of the hottest iPhone application developers to KPCB's doors.[6]

Other firms have recently begun platform-play investment strategies targeted at different technology ecosystems. Accel Partners and the Founders Fund teamed up with social networking company Facebook to create a $10 million "fbFund," which invests in start-ups building games and tools to work inside Facebook's platform.[7] Bessemer Venture Partners and Bay Partners said they would work with customer-relations management company Salesforce.com to find and finance start-ups using the company's Internet-hosted software platform. The two firms committed a combined $25 million to the effort in 2007.[8] The technologies these platform funds are focused on come and go. Yet the underlying strategy of launching platform-focused funds to attract entrepreneurs periodically flares up as a popular thing to do.

A Fund for Friends

One of the most effective hunting strategies is to increase the size of your hunting party. The more people you take out into the woods, the more likely you are to spot big game and bring it down.

Venture capital firms have a neat trick for doing just this. They recruit lawyers, bankers, prominent executives, or other successful entrepreneurs to help find great start-ups.

Of course, these high-profile people don't work for free. So the venture firm creates a special fund and invites these people to invest in it. The special fund is called a *sidecar* because it invests beside the venture firm's main fund. Whenever the venture firm makes an investment, a small percentage of the money used will be pulled from the sidecar, and if the venture capital firm earns a return on its investment, some money will be distributed back to the investors in the sidecar. A typical sidecar fund is smaller than $10 million and may be collected from around 100 individuals.

This practice aligns the incentives of a variety of important players in the innovation ecosystem with the interests of the venture capital firm. It's a cheap way to recruit eyes and ears to the goal of finding investments.

IN THE REAL WORLD

Sequoia's Sidecar

The participants in most sidecar funds are a well-kept secret. But Sequoia Capital found itself forced to disclose who had invested in one of its sidecar funds when it sold Internet video company YouTube to Google in 2006.[a] The start-up had raised $11.5 million from investors before selling to Google for stock worth $1.6 billion.

The list of who received stock payouts reads like a Who's Who of Silicon Valley, with more than 70 names of high-profile entrepreneurs, executives, and even entertainers that had invested in Sequoia's sidecar. See Exhibit 5.1 for a sample of the winners from the fund and an approximation of what they made just from the YouTube sale.

EXHIBIT 5.1

Gains from Sequoia's Sidecar Fund

Person	Position	Payout
Carol Ann Bartz	Former CEO of Autodesk, now CEO of Yahoo	$160,000
Dan Warmenhoven	CEO of Network Appliance	$160,000
David Hitz	Founder of Network Appliance	$160,000
Jerry Yang	Cofounder of Yahoo	$160,000
T. J. Rodgers	Cypress Semiconductor Corp. founder and CEO	$160,000
Asheem Chandna	Venture capitalist with Greylock Partners	$120,000
Marc Andreessen	Cofounder of Netscape	$120,000
Michael Marks	Former partner at buyout firm Kohlberg Kravis Roberts & Co., now the founder and managing partner of Riverwood Capital	$120,000
Forrest Sawyer	NBC News anchor	$80,000
Maury Povich	Talk show host	$80,000
Ron Conway	Angel investor	$80,000

It's hard to say exactly what the big-shot insiders who participate in Sequoia's sidecar fund bring in when it comes to deal making—but if it didn't work, the firm probably wouldn't be doing it.

[a] "YouTube payoff benefits array of Sequoia investors," Thomson Reuters's *PE Week*, February 12, 2007, http://bit.ly/bic4oa.

Growing Your Own Investments

Gathering inbound investment opportunities from conferences and the Internet yields few substantive successes. Hunting through personal connections, smile and dial, and searching in universities can help venture capitalists connect with great companies, but it is always an uncertain process.

That's why some venture firms are increasingly growing their own investment opportunities. They're bringing entrepreneurs into their offices to germinate new start-ups and turning to incubators to nurture delicate companies through their most formative phases.

Both techniques give venture investors a high degree of control over the nascent start-ups.

Entrepreneurs in Residence

Why let innovation flourish in the wild when you can nurture it within the confines of your own office? That's the idea behind maintaining an Entrepreneur in Residence (EIR), an executive that may be found at any number of early stage venture capital firms.

The EIR is either a technologist or an experienced corporate manager who keeps an office inside a venture firm while working on a new start-up. EIR spots typically go to people who have proven their potential in some other role, such as successfully founding and running a start-up in the past.

Some people joke that EIR jobs are a form of venture capital welfare because they frequently go to out-of-work entrepreneurs or former founders who are just tired of hanging out at the golf course.

It's a good gig if you can get it. The venture firm pays the EIR a meaningful salary ($10,000 to $15,000 per month) for six months to a year.

During this time, the EIR typically offers part-time consulting to the venture capitalists, helping perform due diligence on potential investments or acting as a mentor to executives at other start-ups within the firm's portfolio. He or she also sits in on formal pitch meetings to hear what other entrepreneurs are working on. This can be a great way to brainstorm, learn about new markets, or take other people's ideas.

EIRs also spend this time working on their own start-ups—companies designed from the ground up to be attractive financing opportunities for the host venture capital firms.

The host venture capital firm may invest in the EIR's start-up once it reaches maturity. There is no obligation for the firm to invest in the resultant start-up. In fact, about half the time no start-up suitable for investment actually comes out of an EIR program. That doesn't seem to be a problem for the venture capitalists. It's cheaper for them to write off an EIR expense than to finance a start-up that's bound for failure. It's also cheaper than hiring someone to go out and look for investments.

There is seldom any contract in place that forces the EIR to pitch his or her start-up solely to the firm that has housed him and paid him for the past six months. However, it would be a major breach of decorum for an EIR to offer his or her start-up to a different venture capital firm first.

There are plenty of examples of successful start-ups born from EIRs. Consider the experience of Kai Li, a computer science professor on sabbatical. Li had been thinking about starting a company for some time, but had never fully committed to the idea. While on sabbatical, he ran into a friend from venture capital firm New Enterprise Associates and, a short while later, was installed as the firm's EIR. In 2001, Li founded Data Domain, a start-up that New Enterprise Associates invested in. Digital storage company EMC bought Data Domain for $2.3 billion during 2009.[9]

Beyond the salary and the exposure to great ideas, the EIR gets access to the firm's Rolodex of industry experts and executives. This can provide a big boost to an EIR hunting for help.

It can also be very useful to be associated with a marquee brand name, especially when an entrepreneur is working on the most formative stages of his or her start-up. A voicemail or e-mail from a random entrepreneur is easy to ignore, but no one in Silicon Valley would ignore the same message if it came from a representative of Accel Partners or Benchmark Capital.

Incubators

Incubator. Just the sound of the word may call to some minds raucous Internet entrepreneurs spinning around in Aeron chairs, burning through money.

Incubators are designed to give several start-up companies a place to work and some degree of back-office support while they are in their most formative stages. The idea is that half a dozen start-ups can occupy the same office space when each has only three or four employees and can move out into bigger offices when they raise venture capital dollars or develop a level of self-sustaining sales. It's a good way for small companies to pool their resources and save money.

The dot-com boom changed the way many people perceive incubators. Several real estate firms in San Francisco opened trendy office space in South Park and other areas in the South of Market area of the city to start-ups looking for a home. The real estate owners took stock options in lieu of rent, hoping their tenants would create billion-dollar Internet companies.

It was a scheme that worked for some, no doubt. But real estate owners are not especially well suited to evaluate early stage start-ups. So a decade after the boom, incubators are seen by many as a cesspool of amateur entrepreneurs and poorly executed start-ups.

Venture capitalists have since adopted the idea of incubators and made them a part of their operations to further vet interesting start-ups and keep costs low while companies develop their first products.

This is particularly useful in the health-care and life-sciences industries, where start-up costs are high due to the need for expensive prototyping equipment and laboratories. For this reason, several venture firms have banded together to provide space, tools, and management skills to the most promising medical innovations and researchers.

Two of the most prominent incubators are The Foundry, which focuses on medical device start-ups, and Accelerator, which works with health care–focused biotechnology start-ups. Each is designed to do a lot of the hand-holding that is necessary for an early stage technology venture without taking up lots of resources.

The Foundry is backed by Split Rock Ventures and Morganthaler Ventures, each a well-known venture firm with significant life sciences experience. It works with one or two start-ups at a time, helping them navigate intellectual property agreements with universities, giving them office space to work, loaning them tools to prototype their medical devices, and lending a hand with the management and administration of the start-up.

Accelerator is a management company created by a group of health care–focused venture firms, a real-estate firm and the Seattle-based Institute for Systems Biology. Its aim is to utilize the same management, office space, and resources to save on costs for the three to five start-ups looking to prove their worth. Accelerator's executives focus on getting start-ups to critical milestones as quickly as possible. That can help the start-ups raise less money when they go on to collect later rounds of venture capital investment.

Working with The Foundry or Accelerator doesn't oblige a start-up to raise venture capital dollars from the firms that support each incubator. But it does give the venture firms a close relationship with the start-up, making it likely that they will work together for a subsequent financing round.

Alternative Methods

Most venture capitalists are content to gather, hunt, and farm investments. Yet not all are able to. Some firms are too new, too small, or just too content doing what they do to engage in the same invest-ment strategies as the established venture firms. Instead, these inves-tors have developed their own ways for getting cut into good deals.

Some of these strategies are designed to lure entrepreneurs by solving the problems they face. A venture capital firm called the Founders Fund created a special class of stock to help entrepreneurs who face increasingly long holding periods for their shares. EB Exchange Funds invented a stock-swapping program that allows founders to diversify their holdings.

Another set of adaptive strategies is targeted at alleviating the problems venture capital firms have. Follow-the-leader firms set valuations for later round start-up financings, a service many early stage venture firms welcome. Venture debt and leasing firms give start-ups expansion capital without further diluting the existing venture capital shareholders.

One seldom sees these methods in practice. Today they are at the fringes of the venture capital industry. But they are innovations and have the potential to gain wider adoption if they prove to be successful.

Founders Fund Stock

The Founders Fund is a peculiar venture capital firm created by Peter Theil, a founder of PayPal, and several other former entrepre-neurs. The firm began as a formal version of the successful angel investing Theil and the others were doing.

The investors took a number of lessons from working closely with entrepreneurs in the earliest stages of start-up development. The most salient was the long time start-up founders had to have their personal wealth locked into the common stock of the start-up.

The entrepreneurs involved in a start-up typically leave well-paid jobs to begin their own companies and work for a salary substantially less than they might earn working elsewhere. They may even mortgage their house and max out their credit cards.

The Founders Fund wants to join the best investments and offers a deal to entrepreneurs who are looking at a decade or more wait before their start-ups go public or are acquired. If the start-up agrees to take an investment from the Founders Fund, the venture firm will help the entrepreneurs see cash payouts at regular intervals.

The setup is simple. The Founders Fund first makes a major, multimillion-dollar investment in the start-up, just like any other venture capital firm. Then it agrees to buy a certain number of additional shares at some point in the future. These shares come from the entrepreneur's holding of common stock and the entrepreneur can pick when he or she wants to sell them. The Founders Fund agrees to pay the entrepreneur the same price that the most recent round of preferred shares sold for.

This provision gives the entrepreneurs a guaranteed buyer for their shares and a way to sell their stock at higher prices as the start-up grows. It provides a convenient way for the start-up executives to experience some measure of payment before the start-up goes public or is bought. It's like offering a swig of water to someone crossing a desert.

That helps the Founders Fund find its way into investments it otherwise might not have had access to.[10] Other venture capital firms have attempted to create similar entrepreneur-friendly solutions, such as establishing credit lines secured by common stock for entrepreneurs who may need money.

Stock Swaps

A small San Francisco firm offers a creative solution to entrepreneurs looking to diversify their holdings while they wait for their start-up to mature to a point where its shares will be liquid.

The firm, EB Exchange Funds, lets entrepreneurs contribute 10 to 15 percent of their common stock to a pool, from which they each share distributions when any of the companies in the pool goes public or is sold.[11] Firm founder Larry Albukerk vets participants and manages the holdings on behalf of the pool, which may include shares from 20 to 30 start-ups.

Steve Larsen, former CEO of Krugle, a start-up search engine for computer code, contributed stock to participate in EB Exchange's third investment pool. He thinks it's a great idea. "Having been through situations where a lot of my family's wealth and savings were in a single stock, having the opportunity to diversify that with people who were in the same boat as me seemed like a great idea," says Larsen, who started four companies prior to Krugle.

The firm's first pool of start-ups had one big hit from the 11 companies that contributed stock. San Francisco–based OpenTable, an Internet-enabled restaurant reservation service that went public in 2009, distributing a fair swath of valuable shares to the other participants in the EB Exchange Funds stock swap.

Albukerk notes that even small returns can have a big impact for an entrepreneur. For example, if an entrepreneur's company fails, he or she would be thrilled to get just $500,000 from stock in an initial public offering (IPO) delivered to him through the fund, he says. "To the guys that have had an IPO, the difference between $65 million and $60 million doesn't mean much," he says, "but the difference between zero and half a million is big for everyone else."

Follow-the-Leader Investing

Some firms only invest behind well-respected early stage venture capitalists. These follow-the-leader firms will be invited into a Series B investment round by the existing investors to help ratify a start-up valuation and provide a measure of additional capital. They may or may not take seats on the board of directors.

Follow-the-leader firms are ultimately beholden to the leaders for access to good investments. That can mean several things. For example, it can encourage the following firm to arrive at a lower valuation for the start-up's round than a completely independent firm would. This would allow first round investor to continue buying shares in the start-up at a low price.

Although follow-the-leader firms have a fiduciary duty to any start-up on which they take a board seat, they have a strong, long-term financial interest in aligning themselves with whatever the leading venture firms want to do.

The most well-known venture firm to effectively employ a follow-the-leader strategy to gain access to promising investments is Duff Ackerman & Goodrich, which often just goes by DAG Ventures. The firm invests primarily in tandem with Accel Partners, Benchmark Capital, Sequoia Capital, or Kleiner Perkins Caufield & Byers. Each is a well-respected early stage firm. DAG has made 100 deals over the past decade, only 13 of which were not made alongside one of those four firms, according to data from Thomson Reuters.[12]

Venture Debt and Leasing

Start-ups usually finance their growth by selling equity—that's stock that represents an ownership stake in the company. But they can also borrow money and go into debt. Debt is a tricky proposition for many start-ups, which have no certain stream of revenue or even any major assets to use as collateral. Few banks will make loans to businesses that have yet to sell to customers or don't even own an office building that they can foreclose on.

Still, a handful of firms have sprung up to lend to start-ups. These firms expect both higher risk and higher return on their investment than a traditional bank would. Their role as a lender gets them involved in deals that can turn out to be very lucrative.

The lenders may, for example, write provisions into their contract that would convert the debt notes they hold into a certain number of shares of common stock in the start-up. If the start-up is bought, it could trigger this conversion and the lender's debt would become shares of common stock. That could significantly improve the return on their investment, but it is more generally used to ensure the lender gets paid if the start-up is subsumed into another company.

Entrepreneurs are more than happy to take on debt, when they can get it. Loans are *nondilutive*, meaning a founder doesn't have to trade shares for the cash that comes from a venture lender. That can be very attractive to a founder who has seen his or her slice of the equity pie dwindle through a series of financing rounds with venture capitalists.

The venture capitalists appreciate venture lenders for the same reason. Fewer claims on a start-up's stock mean fewer people to pay if the start-up becomes successful and makes it to a liquidity event. They're generally very welcoming of venture lenders for this reason, though they may attempt to cap a lender's conversion ratio.

This is why lenders typically enjoy only a limited upside to their investment. About the best they can hope for is to have their principal returned with double-digit interest. The equity holders, such as the founders and the venture capitalists, may enjoy an unlimited investment return. They own a percentage of the company and the company may skyrocket in value.

Missed Opportunities

Few firms will admit to missing out on the next big thing, but it happens all the time. A general partner will fail to spot an emerging industry, or won't be able to see past a brilliant start-up founder's long hair or lack of experience.

Bessemer Venture Partners maintains an "anti-portfolio" of start-ups it had the chance to invest in but, for whatever reason, passed on. The firm's successes are numerous, but its list of misses is impressive. Most notable was David Cowan's shot at Google:

Cowan's college friend rented her garage to Sergey and Larry for their first year. In 1999 and 2000, she tried to introduce Cowan to "these two really smart Stanford students writing a search engine." Students? A new search engine? In the most important moment ever for Bessemer's anti-portfolio, Cowan asked her, "How can I get out of this house without going anywhere near your garage?"[13]

Cowan's story goes to show that you can be in the right place at the right time and still miss out on the right investment.

Summary

Finding promising deals isn't always easy for venture capital investors. There are three major ways to get investment opportunities.

The first is to gather them from the environment. Entrepreneurs pitch venture capitalists on their ideas at any opportunity. An investor need only appear at an industry conference to go home with several dozen business cards and a fistful of business ideas. Unsolicited business pitches from unknown entrepreneurs are unlikely to get much attention from venture capitalists, but sometimes it works.

The second way to get investment opportunities is to hunt out the best entrepreneurs, innovations, and technologies. Most venture capitalists will only look seriously at investments that have been referred to them by a connection, either someone they know or have worked with in the past. Some firms engage in brute-force outreach programs that involve calling lots of companies and trying to convince a handful to accept growth financing.

Hunting for investment opportunities in universities can be difficult because the innovators there are not necessarily focused on commercializing their ideas. There are techniques that work for approaching researchers and their institutions to extract useful technology.

Investing in start-ups that develop modules for emerging technology platforms is a good way for venture capitalists to benefit from the success of corporate giants.

Successful venture capital firms enlist a community of mutual interest to help them find investments. Firms such as Sequoia Capital use a sidecar fund to invest a wider group of people in the success of the firm. The hope is that these executives, lawyers, bankers, and industry luminaries will refer exciting start-ups to the venture firm.

The third way venture capitalists cultivate investment opportunities is to grow them at home. Firms pay EIRs to work on new ideas inside their offices. This can be a low-cost way of connecting with a great start-up in its most formative stages.

Incubators can also help venture capitalists nurture start-ups to a point where they will be ready for serious investment. Sharing resources between early stage companies can help them achieve critical milestones inexpensively.

Beyond the three most basic ways of finding potential investments, firms on the fringe have developed a handful of alternative strategies for getting in on deals.

Some are tailored to fit the specific problems that start-ups and entrepreneurs face. For example, the Founders Fund developed a class of stock that allows entrepreneurs a measure of liquidity before they sell their company or take it public. Stock swapping consortiums, such as EB Exchange Funds, give entrepreneurs the opportunity to diversify their holdings by trading a small portion of their equity with other, similarly situated executives.

Other strategies give investors a way to play a role in promising start-ups by supporting the most successful venture capitalists. DAG Ventures, for example, is well known for cultivating relationships with top early stage firms to gain access into those firms' promising investments. Venture lending and leasing firms provide cash to start-ups without diluting shareholders. That's a big help to venture capitalists and ensures that the venture lenders can have a seat at the table when it's time for a start-up to raise cash.

Notes

1. "The Networker," *The New Yorker*, August 11, 1997.
2. Adapted from "Scaling the Ivory Tower," *Venture Capital Journal*, June 1, 2008, http://bit.ly/cbjjDA.
3. AUTM U.S. Licensing Activity Survey: FY2008, http://bit.ly/cQ2pqL.
4. Java was considered a potential competitor to Microsoft as a programming platform. CNet has a detailed story about the corporate investors who partnered to help the fund and information on the start-ups it backed. See "Java Fund Looks to Long Term," CNet, June 15, 1998, http://bit.ly/9RX5T0.
5. Ted Schlein told me the fund was a financial success. Others have reported the fund earned 50 percent IRR. See "Correcting the Record: Java Fund Not a Flop," *SiliconBeat*, July 20, 2005, http://bit.ly/9LfmRM.
6. The "iFund" is a bit of a misnomer as it is not actually a fund. Rather than establish a $100 million venture fund, the firm decided to pull the money from its existing funds. This affords

the firm greater flexibility, as it may choose to stop investing in Apple applications at any time without the legal restrictions imposed by having a dedicated fund which must invest a certain amount of money for a certain number of years. For a full profile of the fund, read "Kleiner Takes a Shine to Apple," *Venture Capital Journal*, April 2008, http://bit.ly/d82oTi.

7. The fund was initially conceived as a grant-giving program. See "Facebook, Accel and Founders Fund Launch fbFund; To Give Grants to Facebook App Startups," TechCrunch, September 17, 2007, http://tcrn.ch/b7vWi7.

8. Bay Partners had previously launched a program similar to the fbFund, targeted at financing start-ups developing for the Facebook platform called AppFactory. Salesforce.com approached Bay about starting a similar program for developers building apps around its Force.com platform. It turned out that the software-as-a-service (SaaS) giant maintains an internal list of the 50 or so strategic companies that are developing on its platform. "We came to know that six of them were our investments," says Bay Partners's Salil Deshpande. "They saw the success of our AppFactory announcement and saw some of the deals we were doing and it just made sense for both sides." For more on this, see "How to Reboot a Venture Firm," *Venture Capital Journal*, November 1, 2007, http://bit.ly/cQ8Qcf.

9. "6 Months, $90,000 and (Maybe) a Great Idea," *New York Times*, February 28, 2010, http://nyti.ms/a7lV4R.

10. "'Little Rewards' Keep Founders Happy, Motivated," *Venture Capital Journal*, May 1, 2007, http://bit.ly/c5PmrT.

11. For more on EB Exchange Fund, see "Creative Solution for Founder Liquidity Problem," *Venture Capital Journal*, May 1, 2008, http://bit.ly/9Usprz.

12. For more, see "Can DAG Nab It?" *Venture Capital Journal*, October 1, 2008, http://bit.ly/cn40la.

13. From Bessemer Venture Partners's web site, http://bit.ly/a7KuFa.

CHAPTER 6

Getting the Money Back

After reading this chapter, you will be able to:

- Distinguish the ways in which a venture capitalist secures gains from an investment.
- Differentiate between initial public offerings (IPOs) and acquisitions.
- Evaluate the pros and cons to either selling a start-up or taking it public.
- Assess the importance of the current IPO crisis.
- Evaluate proposals for structural changes designed to stem the crisis.
- Develop alternative strategies for getting liquid in a changing exit market.

Gains from Investment

The business of venture capital is a waiting game. Venture capitalists put their money into a start-up and may wait up to a decade to see any type of capital gain from it. It's understandable that getting their money back, along with a substantial payout, is an important milestone.

After holding on to highly illiquid private company shares for years, they're happy to get either cash or public company stock, which can be easily converted into cash. Venture capitalists call these transactions *liquidity events*. A liquidity event is also called an *exit,* because the venture capitalist uses it as a way out of a long-term investment.

There are two major types of exit. The first is an initial public offering (IPO), where a start-up sells stock to the general public and its shares are available for trading on an exchange such as the New York Stock Exchange (NYSE) or NASDAQ. In this scenario, venture capitalists convert their preferred shares into publicly traded common stock. Then they are able to distribute this stock to limited partners.

The second major exit path is an acquisition. A big corporation can pay cash for a start-up or use its own shares as a cash-equivalent to pay off the start-up's investors.

One of the most interesting aspects of any liquidity event is how much the venture capitalists take home from the deal. If a start-up goes public, it may disclose how many preferred shares its investors own via a filing to the Securities and Exchange Commission (SEC). There are regulations that require a company to list its major shareholders when it anticipates selling shares to the public. From these documents, and the trading value of the stock, you can determine how much the venture capitalists stand to gain.

Determining how much money investors make when one of their start-ups is acquired is harder. It isn't always something that the parties involved talk about. After all, these are private investors in a private company. Still, it is possible to get a rough idea of how well the investors did on the transaction by making a few assumptions and doing some simple arithmetic.

Imagine a situation where a start-up sells preferred shares to venture capitalists for $10 million in its Series A investment round. A year later, the start-up sells to a strategic acquirer for $100 million. How much the venture capitalists stand to make on the transaction depends on what percentage of the company they initially bought.

It's safe to assume that the investors got between 25 percent and 50 percent of the start-up's equity in the Series A. That would mean a payout, based purely on their equity stake, of between $25 million and $50 million. Not a bad day's work.

There's a lot more going on in such a transaction, but our simple example shows how lucrative an exit can be for the investors involved.

Measuring Success

There's a funny thing about how venture investors score their successes that can confuse people familiar with investing. They seldom, if ever, talk about *internal rate of return* (IRR). IRR is a common metric for evaluating the annualized performance of a portfolio of stocks. You might hear someone on Wall Street say that she earned a 20 percent IRR on her portfolio, and you'd know that she increased the value of her holdings last year by 20 percent.

Venture capitalists hardly ever use this metric for their investments. They prefer "cash-on-cash accounting," which measures the profit against the principal. A $100 million fund invested over several years that returns $200 million is said to return 2X, or two times the money invested.

The primary reason venture capitalists prefer this method is that it does not take into account the amount time it takes to get this return. A firm that invests for 10 years and delivers investors double their money at the end of that time has an IRR of only 6.5 percent, which is not as impressive sounding.

The measure of a great investment is one that returns 10X an investor's money over a normal five- to seven-year venture-investing time horizon. That means that a venture capitalist that puts $1 million into a start-up hopes to get back $10 million or more in a matter of years. It's a rare occurrence, but that's the goal.

Going Public

The best way to get to 10X returns and beyond is to take a start-up public. Going public means selling a start-up's common shares to institutional investors via a stock offering. Those large financial institutions can then sell the shares on a government-regulated exchange, such as the NYSE or the NASDAQ.

The businesses that run stock exchanges impose certain requirements on companies that wish to trade stock on their markets, and each exchange has slightly different rules. More important to a start-up looking to sell shares to the public are the rules and regulations imposed by the federal government, which mandates company financial disclosures and certain corporate governance practices. Federal regulation plays a big role in how start-ups think about going public, but we'll discuss more on that later.

Interestingly enough, there are no provisions from either the government or the exchanges themselves that require listing companies to be profitable, or even to have any revenue at all. So there are no lower bounds on company size, assets, or operations. In fact, there's a whole class of companies—special purpose acquisition corporations (SPACs)—that go public with no assets or operations at all!

Could two graduate students in a garage go public? Yes. The only real question to consider is whether people would buy the stock.

That's something that investment bankers spend a lot of time trying to determine. A company, or its venture capitalists, will hire bankers to consult on a start-up's chances of connecting with public market investors.

But going public is something of a misnomer, as companies don't actually sell their shares to the public in the process. Most of the time, they sell their shares to an investment bank that underwrites the IPO. The investment bank then sells those shares to its large institutional clients. The bank may promise to give a "best-efforts attempt" to sell the shares to its clients or may offer a "full commitment" to either sell the shares to its clients or buy them itself.

Either way, going public means selling shares to professional investors at big investment institutions that have several billion dollars at their fingers. If the bankers determine that a public offering may be viable and that its institutional clients will be interested in buying, they start running a book.

Book Building

Book building is the process of collecting commitments from large institutions to purchase stock in an initial public offering. The investment bank goes to each of its major institutional investing clients and asks a simple question: "If we offered you the chance to buy shares in this company, how many would you want to buy and at what price?"

The idea behind the process is to get shares into the hands of those institutions that will pay the highest price for them. If an institutional investor bids high, it will receive more shares than one that bids low. So the incentive is for those mutual funds, hedge funds, and other institutions to tell the truth about their valuation estimations for the start-up. It's a great way to get the pulse of potential stock buyers and assess the best value for a new company's shares.

Book building is a process of polling. But the results aren't always heeded, thanks to the sometimes conflicting incentives of the participants in the IPO process.

The start-up going public wants to ensure that it gets the highest price for its shares possible. That means more money in its coffers and a higher valuation for the shares owned by executives and employees.

What the bankers want is a little complicated. The start-up pays a fee to the bank that typically works out to 7 percent of whatever it is able to raise in its offering. If the start-up gets a high price for its shares, the bankers profit.

But the bank is also selling IPO shares to each of its large institutional clients, and they expect to get a good capital gain from buying the start-up's shares.

If the bank underprices the IPO shares, its clients will be able to buy them low and sell them high the next morning, when the company lists on a stock exchange. Banks sometimes slice as much as 15 percent off the price they believed the shares would sell for on the open market. The clients, happy from the windfall, are then more likely to engage the investment bank for other business. It is a complex form of bribery.

In some cases, the bank's incentive to underprice an IPO as a form of reward to its best customers can be stronger than its incentive to earn the highest possible fee from the start-up that hired it.

For a summary of the relationships at work here, see Exhibit 6.1.

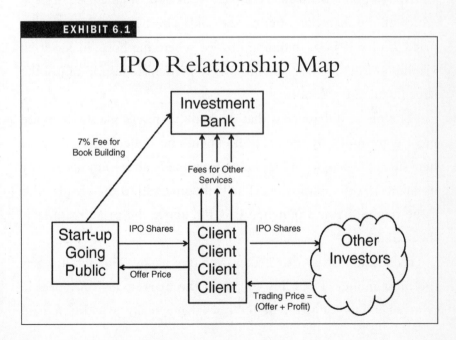

EXHIBIT 6.1

IPO Relationship Map

Dutch Auction IPOs

This conflict of interest has led some banks to pursue innovative new ways of helping start-ups go public. Perhaps the most well known of these is the "Dutch auction" that investment bank W.R. Hambrecht & Co. helped popularize. The firm's strategy for such an auction is to open a web site where anyone can visit and bid to pay a certain price for a certain number of IPO shares.

Similar to a traditional book building operation, the web site's software ranks the bids from highest to lowest. Then the bank goes from the top of the list and sums the number of shares that the would-be buyers bid on. As it goes down the list, eventually the number of shares being bid on will sum to the aggregate amount the start-up is looking to raise from its offering.

At that point, the bankers stop and look at the highest bid price at which all the shares on offer can be sold. This becomes the offering price. It's like a book-building process where the book makes itself via the Internet, but allows everyone to participate instead of just the large financial institutions.

The major difference is that the bank then sells the shares at the price determined by the auction. There's no underpricing at work here since the people buying shares from the bank are not necessarily its clients in other businesses. The bank only sells to the people who came to the site and punched in a bid above the price that clears the market.

It's a neat strategy that makes everyone happy. The start-up gets the most money it possibly can from the market; the only people who get to buy the stock are the ones that actually would have paid much more for it. The bank gets a nice fee, and because the Internet auction is so open, it doesn't have the option of underpricing the IPO as a payoff for its institutional clients.

It is a more democratic process. Instead of passing out shares just to a bank's large institutional clients, the Dutch auction is open to anyone with an Internet connection and money in their bank account.

The Dutch auction IPO is still relatively rare, but a handful of companies, including Google and Morningstar, have helped to popularize the idea.

IN THE REAL WORLD

Google's Modified Dutch Auction IPO

The highest-profile technology IPO since the dot-com bubble was also one of the strangest. The founders of Google wanted very much to appear different than the dot-com companies that had come before them. This urge compelled them to try something completely different when it came to the company's initial public offering.

They opted for a Dutch auction IPO that would minimize the first day "pop" that many tech stocks saw during the dot-com boom and would allow small investors to buy shares shoulder to shoulder with large institutions. The founders expressed this desire in the IPO prospectus, a document that explains the offering, the company's operations, and any risks shareholders should be aware of:

> It is important to us to have a fair process for our IPO that is inclusive of both small and large investors. It is also crucial

that we achieve a good outcome for Google and its current shareholders. This has led us to pursue an auction-based IPO for our entire offering. Our goal is to have a share price that reflects an efficient market valuation of Google that moves rationally based on changes in our business and the stock market.

Many companies going public have suffered from unreasonable speculation, small initial share float, and stock price volatility that hurt them and their investors in the long run. We believe that our auction-based IPO will minimize these problems, though there is no guarantee that it will.[a]

The odd thing was that the company executed its auction online and then ignored the results. Google determined it would sell 25.7 million shares and found that the online buyers interested in investing bid it up to $135 per share.

But something changed at the last minute. The company cut the number of shares it planned to sell down to 19.6 million and lowered its price to $85 per share. For whatever reason, it was essentially ignoring the results of the auction that it had set up and shaved a substantial slice from its would-be market capitalization.

As part of the price reduction, the venture capitalists opted not to sell their shares. Sequoia Capital and Kleiner Perkins Caufield & Byers had planned to sell a total of 4.5 million shares through the IPO but now would be forced to hold on to them beyond the company's 180-day lockup period. Google's founders and CEO also cut the number of shares they planned to sell through the IPO by half.

When the stock offered at $85 per share it experienced only a modest pop, rising to $100.34 by the end of the first trading day. By the end of 51 days it had hit its initial $135 target market. After a year, a share of Google stock was worth $280.

[a] Google S-1 SEC Filing, August 18, 2004, http://bit.ly/dzJzYa.

Pops and Lockups

One of the peculiarities of the IPO process is that a company actually goes public the day before its shares start trading on a major exchange. The investment bank sells the company's shares to its big clients after the stock market closes for the day. Their clients then begin selling the shares on the open market the next morning.

Once a company begins trading on a public exchange, it's typical for lots of regular investors to buy its shares and for the price to rise. The IPO process generates attention from journalists and hype among small investors. Even if the banks did their best to accurately gauge the market and establish an appropriate offer price, the belief that shares will rapidly rise can inflate a stock's price immediately after its IPO.

These factors make a newly public company's stock the target of speculators looking to cash in on a quick frenzy of buying during the stock's first day of trading. One often sees a stock get a nice first day pop in its price that can range from 20 percent to as much as 698 percent.[1]

A pop like that can be peculiarly frustrating for venture capitalists and their limited partners who hold on to the company's shares. Pops are likely to be followed by a drop in share price. Depending on the initial IPO agreement and government regulation, venture capitalists either sell their shares as part of the offering to institutional investors or are forced to hold onto their shares for a predetermined period.

The fear that birthed the restriction on private investors selling immediately after the IPO is that they might knowingly dump a bad company onto unwitting public investors and try to manipulate the market up in the first several days of trading. Venture capitalists and other "insiders" have to hold onto their shares for at least three months after the IPO to comply with federal securities laws.

But the investment banks may require the company insiders to hold onto their shares even longer. This gives their institutional clients a chance to liquidate their IPO holdings before the venture capitalists or executives can cash out. So venture capitalists have to hold onto their shares for a predetermined "lockup" period that typically lasts 180 days after the company goes public.

Some venture investors say that they're happy to hold onto a public company stock. They say that a newly public company usually increases in value faster than when it was a private company. They cite examples of companies that have seen their stock soar beyond the first day pop and for years after an IPO.

Sometimes it can be a very good idea to hold onto those shares. John Doerr, a venture capitalist with Kleiner Perkins Caufield & Byers, told audiences at an Internet conference in November 2007 that his firm still owned half the number of shares it had gotten through its early stage investment in Google, more than three years after the company went public.[2] At that point, Google shares were worth more than six times the price they had offered to the public in 2004.

Unfortunately, companies such as Google are the exception. Most start-ups that go public lose value after their initial pop. There is a wealth of academic research showing that you'd be better off investing in government bonds, or even keeping your money hidden under your mattress, than buying into an IPO the day it offers and holding the shares for three to five years.[3]

Distributions

Even if the share price of a public stock falls from its IPO, the venture capitalists are still going to make money. It's almost impossible to not get a gain when you buy shares for a dollar or two apiece during the start-up's most formative years.

Exactly how much gain the general partners get from their investment depends on exactly how and when they distribute stock to their limited partners. Just to be clear, the limited partners already own this stock, since it was their money that was used to buy it in the first place. The distribution isn't a sale. It's an endpoint to measure the capital gain the venture capitalists made on behalf of the limited partners.

It may seem like a minor technicality, but it is an important issue for one big reason. The value of the shares distributed will determine how much the venture capitalists are paid in carried interest—that 20 percent slice of the profits they get. Subsequently, limited partners are wary of exactly how such gains are accounted for.

Yet most partnership agreements offer the general partnership some flexibility as to when it must distribute shares to limited partners. In fact, they may not want the shares at all, preferring instead to let the venture firm sell the shares and pass cash back to them. This is usually something that the two groups work out in advance.

Still, things can get complicated if a start-up goes public and experiences intense volatility in its share price. The lockup period has expired and the venture capitalists are trying to determine how best to account for the value of the shares they will distribute to their limited partners. What's fair?

The partnership might just hold on to its shares until the stock volatility has settled down. It could try to time the market for a particularly good day and distribute shares then. Or it might give the shares to the limited partners at the end of the month and apply a 30-day average of the stock's closing price as a fair measure of its value.

Sound confusing? It is, which makes it a great opportunity for venture capitalists to pull a fast one on limited partners occupied with other things. There are even professional distribution consultants venture firms employ to help them maximize the value of their exit by timing the market.

Getting Acquired

An IPO is a very noisy thing, replete with public disclosures, media coverage, and discussions with any number of bankers and public investors. It is about as subtle as a ton of TNT explosives. An acquisition, by contrast, can be a very quiet business, like *le soupir amoureux*, the "loving whisper" of a champagne bottle opening.

There are only a few cases where any public disclosure is actually required in an acquisition. It usually happens when the buying company is public and the deal may affect its stock price. But most of the time there's little or no requirement for either side of the transaction to say anything about the terms of the deal.

Still, details sometimes slip out—offers, counteroffers, valuation determination, prices paid, and executive buyout bonuses—any deal that goes down has any number of backstories and plenty of behind-the-scenes intrigue.

One crucial difference between acquisitions and public offerings is the potential upside. When a start-up is bought, there's a sort of upper boundary on the gains the investors can hope for. You can only ever get what the acquirer pays. You don't have that kind of ceiling on returns in an IPO.

As much as a venture capitalist may prefer his or her portfolio companies to go public, strategic acquisitions have become an increasingly common and acceptable path for investor liquidity. You can see how this trend has evolved over the past two decades in Exhibit 6.2.

Why Corporations Buy Start-ups

Big corporations buy start-ups to enter new markets, to reduce their research and development expenses, or to fend off competition. They also make acquisitions for a bevy of irrational reasons that can lead to poor outcomes. Understanding these motivations can help both venture capitalists and entrepreneurs find the best buyers for their businesses.

The first concern any corporate CEO has about new technology is how it will affect his or her existing business. Is the technology a threat or an opportunity? Can it help the company to cut costs or expand into new businesses? What will the competition do?

If the CEO decides that the technology is likely to be a critical part of the corporation's strategy in the coming years, he or she will be faced with a choice: buy or build?

Building a new product inside a corporation is an expensive, time-consuming, and risky proposition. Hiring researchers means

EXHIBIT 6.2

The Shift to Acquisitions for Venture Liquidity

paying them, insuring them, and providing a raft of other benefits. Finding the right people to build a certain technology takes time, too.

Once you have the right people, it can take years for R&D to yield any real advancement. Even then, there's no guarantee that the lab will actually produce the desired innovation.

Buying a technology that has already been developed by a start-up may be much easier. It's like outsourcing your research and development. Acquiring a start-up allows the corporation to get the technology it wants at a stage at which it is proven to work.

Acquiring start-ups involves some convenient accounting. The buying corporation can pay for a start-up from its balance sheet rather than its income statement. That means they treat it as an asset instead of an ongoing expense.

It also means the corporation's earnings do not have to suffer from recurring expenses. Executives are often compensated based on their ability to maintain consistent growth in company earnings, so paying for start-ups instead of building technology internally is a strategy that's attractive to them.

Large corporations may also buy start-ups just to prevent a competitor from getting a certain technology. This kind of rationale is not something many big buyers would ever admit to, but it likely drives some portion of acquisition decisions.

For example, Google is notorious for buying promising start-ups and letting their technology sit unused on the shelf. Whether this is the product of a poor ability to integrate new technologies or a strategic move to prevent a competitor from getting promising technology is anybody's guess.

In addition to developmental or strategic reasons, large corporations often buy start-ups for irrational reasons.

It's common knowledge in academic circles that acquisitions seldom provide the benefits that acquirers initially expect. Most researchers blame this on a "principal-agent problem," where executive incentives diverge from shareholder interests.

Executives face two major incentives to make acquisitions even if they are not in a company's long-term interest. The first is the likelihood of getting a major bonus for making a deal go through. The second is the possibility of getting a higher salary and greater power over a larger fiefdom of cubicle serfs.

There's another school of thought that blames executive hubris for synergy disappointments. The theory is that executives systematically overestimate their ability to unlock the potential of corporate assets. They believe that they are superior managers than the schmoes running the acquisition target. Call it a crime of excessive self-esteem.

Yet deals keep getting done.

Price Determination

Determining what price to pay for a start-up isn't easy. There are three major problems with analyzing the value of an acquisition.

The first is the fact that small, irregular revenue doesn't fit into traditional, big-company valuation models. What's the right price to pay for a company that has recorded $5 million in sales during the previous year but is doubling its revenue each month? How do you account for a month with no revenue? Financial wizards can justify almost any valuation based on those numbers and a big swath of assumptions, but there's no science to their estimates.

Whenever an executive looks at a possible transaction, he or she will first consider the *comps,* or comparable deals that have been recently done. It's like asking a friend if your outfit looks okay. The answer provides a measure of reassurance that you're not going to look like a fool.

But what happens when there are no comps? A truly innovative technology may have no precedent in acquisitions or any public company to compare it to.[4] This is the second problem in evaluating a potential acquisition. When there is no baseline for a valuation negotiation, almost any price can be justified.

The third problem is the difficulty of understanding the potential synergy between the start-up and its strategic acquirer. Can they make one plus one equal three? Executives sometimes use the word "synergy" as a code word for layoffs when it comes to corporate combinations. But start-ups seldom see their staffs slashed. In fact, the acquiring company generally keeps most or all of the start-up's staff. Often that's exactly what it wanted to buy in the transaction!

A start-up, when combined with a big corporation, can take advantage of the corporation's existing business infrastructure to rapidly expand.

Imagine a small private company that has developed a big innovation that customers really want. Its founding team is taking sales calls left and right, and the money is starting to roll in. The CEO knows he needs to hire more salesmen, but can't seem to hire them fast enough to keep up with demand. Meanwhile the product is falling behind on its next iteration of development because the entire team is caught up in the sales process.

Suppose that a large, multinational corporation looks at the start-up and sees how well it is selling among early adopters. But what is it worth? The multinational may have a thousand salesmen around the world, as compared to the six guys currently selling the start-up's product. Imagine how much it could make if the start-up just had more salesmen.

It's not a logic that applies to every market, but it is a pervasive way of looking at acquisitions that can inflate the perceived value of any deal.

Trouble valuing small or irregular revenue, a lack of comps, and difficulties in assessing the synergy between a start-up and its acquirer make it hard to determine if an acquisition offer is good.

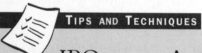

TIPS AND TECHNIQUES

IPO versus Acquisition from a Venture Capitalist's Perspective

The entrepreneur's dream used to be to ring the bell on the NASDAQ after taking his or her company public. These days, both company founders and their venture capital investors weigh different paths to success against each other. There are a few things to think about if you're in that position. For a list of considerations, see Exhibit 6.3.

EXHIBIT 6.3

IPO versus Acquisition

IPO	ACQUISITION
Requires disclosure.	Seldom requires any public filing.
Offers unlimited upside.	Comes in four flavors: All cash (no additional upside), all equity (upside is contingent on performance of acquirer), cash and equity (a little bit of both) and deal value with earnouts (upside is contingent on performance of start-up as a subsidiary).
May require the investors to maintain their board seats on the newly public company and expose themselves to potential shareholder lawsuits and additional government regulation.	Unlikely that the venture capitalists will take a board seat.
Company value based on public perception.	Company value based on acquirer's perception.
Takes at least 90 days from the start-up's first filing to its public listing.	Can literally happen overnight.
Lockup period of at least 180 days on insider sales.	Immediate liquidity.
Subject to approval by the listing market.	May be subject to approval by the Federal Trade Commission in certain circumstances.
Good for big companies, where legal and listing costs may be justified.	Good for small companies, where legal and listing costs may not be justified.

The IPO Crisis

"IPOs are the river Nile of the venture business: No Nile, no life," says Venky Ganesan, managing director at Globespan Capital Partners.[5]

Ganesan's assessment may sound a little dramatic, but venture capitalists have long relied on public market stock offerings to convert their illiquid preferred shares into publicly traded stock. Taking one of the companies they invested in public means a colossal payday. And just the threat of going public can always be held against a potential strategic acquirer to boost the price of any start-up's sale.

Equally important to the success of the venture capital industry is the role that a vibrant community of small, publicly traded companies provides. These companies are the most likely to adopt early stage technologies to get an advantage over their competitors and frequently rely on start-ups to sell them the tools to hone that edge. They also help spread the risk of technology investing to a wider base of public investors instead of just a handful of venture capitalists. And they can be relied on to grow, sometimes dramatically, after going public.

The IPO market, like the Nile, has always ebbed and flowed in cycles. During good years, the venture capital industry saw hundreds of its start-ups go public. These booms provided lush returns for investors and fertilized the next generation of innovation and start-up financing. During bad years, venture capitalists saw only one or two dozen companies go public and waited for their luck to turn.

Many investors, bankers, and entrepreneurs believe that the industry has fundamentally changed and that IPOs have dried up. It is cause for great concern to all involved who have seen great rewards from taking start-ups public in the past.

Proof of the change continues to mount. Consider the data presented in the November 2008 issue of the *Venture Capital Journal*:

> Analysis of historical IPO data from Thomson Reuters shows that the current decade has been atypically slow for VC-backed IPOs. The median number of annual VC-backed IPOs from 1970 to 2008 is 68, with an all-time high of 368 venture-backed offerings in 1986 and an all-time low of two offerings in 1975.

Besides the Internet bubble year of 2000, when 265 venture-backed companies went public, only two other years in this decade have recorded more than 68 IPOs: 2004 (with 94) and 2007 (with 86). Six of the past nine years have fallen well short of the median, with this year being the worst. Just six VC-backed companies have gone public in 2008, with only one in the past two quarters combined.[6]

The credit crunch and banking crisis conspired to make 2009 a tough year as well, with just 13 venture-backed start-ups listing.

Venture capitalists point to the IPO crisis as the number one culprit for a decade's worth of poor returns.

The causes for the crisis are not particularly well understood. We covered several of the most important reasons in the first chapter, such as investment banking consolidation, Sarbanes-Oxley legislation, and institutional investor growth. Others believe the IPO crisis is the product of major changes to the technology and rules associated with trading stocks that began prior to the dot-com boom.[7]

There are several proposed "fixes" that would solve the IPO crisis by reversing recent securities regulation, favoring small investment banks over their bigger brethren, or by creating a special trading market that would look similar to a stock exchange from 20 years ago.

Meanwhile, there are several ways in which venture capitalists and entrepreneurs have adapted to the problem and managed to make money despite the IPO drought.

Solving the IPO Problem

Different camps have come to different conclusions on how to overcome the IPO problem. There are three major suggestions, each with its own set of adherents.

NVCA "Four Pillar" Plan

The National Venture Capital Association (NVCA), a lobbying group funded by dues collected from venture firms, concocted a plan to revive the IPO market.[8] Industry veteran Dixon Doll headed the committee responsible for the plan, which arrived at four action points:

1. Promote "alternative ecosystem partners," banks, lawyers, and accountants that would tailor their offerings to young, high-growth start-ups.

2. Boost a new type of service that gives start-ups an introduction to financial institutions that may later support an IPO.

3. Ask Congress to give tax breaks to stimulate the IPO market and not to increase the capital gains taxes venture capitalists owe.

4. Call on the SEC to review government regulations, especially those that are costly to small companies.

The plan reflected two major venture capitalist complaints:

1. That big investment banks ignored them, and

2. The government was making it harder for them to make money.

It's a little like a heavy man who blames his weight problem on the fact that Nike doesn't make shoes that are comfortable to run in and that the gym doesn't smell nice.

To be sure, large investment banks have not found it lucrative to support venture capitalists or IPOs, thanks to consolidation and other changes in their industry. Venture capitalists bringing their business to small banks interested in serving start-ups may help recreate at least some of the conditions under which IPOs flourished in the past.

But by completely focusing on exogenous factors, the NVCA ignored venture capitalists' own culpability in the IPO crisis.

Grant Thornton's Opt-In Marketplace

Accounting firm Grant Thornton called for an "Alternative Public Market Segment" that would alleviate a lot of the headaches associated with going public.[9]

The plan stems from the accounting firm's research showing that market mechanics have caused the IPO crisis. The report received a lot of attention, primarily because it shifted the focus of the IPO crisis discussion away from Sarbanes-Oxley legislation and toward issues of how stocks are quoted and traded.

Grant Thornton's proposed alternative market would look like the stock markets of several decades before. The market would require specialist market-makers to trade $0.10 spreads via telephone and investors to execute trades through a stock broker. Investment banks that bring IPOs to the market would be required to provide ongoing analyst research.

Although many venture capitalists would no doubt like to see such a market brought to life, it is unlikely that it will ever come to fruition. As industry pundit Paul Kedrosky described the plan: "It's like hungry great white sharks proposing that newly speedier seals be fattened up, given weight handicaps and kept in open water, away from dry land & rocks."[10]

NASDAQ's Portal

Stock exchanges are businesses in their own right. They make money by charging fees to companies that choose to list shares with them. The major U.S. exchanges did very well during the dot-com boom and have been anxious to recoup the losses they've experienced from the decline in IPOs.

The NASDAQ's plan to make up its losses was to begin a special marketplace for certain types of investors to buy and trade otherwise illiquid securities. The idea was to connect qualified institutional buyers—those with over $100 million in assets—to securities they wouldn't be able to get on a public market.

They created a way for start-ups to get their shares into the hands of big buyers, similar to an IPO market. The major difference is that those big buyers can't turn around and sell the shares to the general public. This takes away the opportunity for a quick profit for institutional investors. But it also removes the cost of complying with federal regulation from the shoulders of start-ups.

The marketplace, called "Portal," takes advantage of Rule 144A, an amendment to the U.S. Securities Act of 1933, and securities traded through the Portal are sometimes referred to as "144A offerings."

As of this writing, the Portal is most frequently used by large foreign companies and has yet to host a significant number of venture-backed start-ups.[11]

Are Fewer IPOs a Bad Thing?

The accepted orthodoxy is that the lack of a strong IPO market for venture-backed start-ups is a bad thing. It depresses returns for venture capitalists, destroys the robust ecosystem of small public companies that were once customers for new start-ups, and hampers innovation and American competitiveness.

But the sky has yet to fall on the various Chicken Littles who have predicted the apocalyptic end of Silicon Valley and its business of fostering start-ups. The fact is that there has been little independent research into what fewer IPOs mean for the overall economy, job creation, the progress of innovation, or even venture capital returns. Most of the statistics generated and cited come from research groups either directly paid by industry lobbyists or from others hoping to benefit in direct proportion to the direness of the message they present.

Some venture capitalists have failed to produce attractive returns for investors, but many still receive investment from limited partners. There has yet to be a wholesale destruction of the asset class. Even during 2009, one of the worst years on record for financial institutions and the overall economy, 120 venture capital funds managed to raise $15.2 billion, according to data from Thomson Reuters.

Innovation hasn't died. If anything, it may be advancing faster than it would have with a strong IPO market. In a difficult IPO market, only the best start-ups are likely to get financing. That means start-ups don't fight with each other for customers or talented engineers.

In fact, there's reason to believe that private companies are actually much more efficient than their public counterparts. A private company does not have to provide audited financial statements each quarter, host earnings calls, or worry about managing its financials to appease stock analysts. For these reasons, it is often easier to pursue long-term projects and invest in growth as a private company.

Perhaps most important, fewer IPOs might help restore investor confidence in new issues. The start-ups that actually make it to a point where they are sufficiently viable to file for an IPO may be strong enough to reverse the decades-long trend of post-IPO underperformance.

Do Venture Capitalists Compete with Public Markets?

At root, going public and raising money from venture capitalists is not that different; it's just a matter of who buys the stock being sold. Either path provides the start-up with capital to grow.

But an odd thing has happened. Venture capitalists increasingly provide big financing rounds to start-ups that might have previously turned to the public markets.

In fact, it's possible to chart the decline of small, $25 million IPOs and the corresponding rise of large venture capital financing rounds (see Exhibit 6.4).

The success of venture capital firms in the early years of the dotcom boom allowed them to raise bigger funds from limited partners. More money floating around in venture funds meant that investors could write bigger checks for start-ups.

To a start-up, there may be big advantages to raising $25 million from a small group of private investors instead of going through the IPO process to raise the same amount of money. There's less disclosure, less time wasted pitching to institutional investors, and less financial scrutiny.

So if start-ups are able to raise massive amounts of expansion capital from private investors, why go public at all?

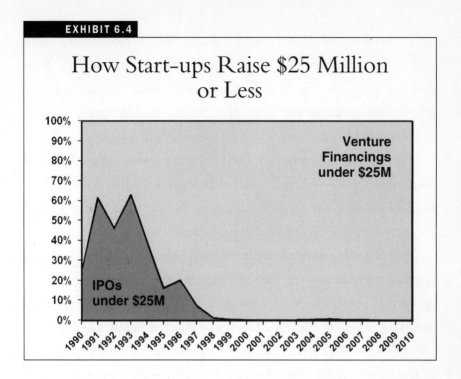

How Start-ups Raise $25 Million or Less

In late 2009, two major deals clearly illustrated the trend away from public financing to private financing. A video-game maker called Zynga raised $180 million from venture capitalists and other private investors, and a start-up looking to make recharging stations for electric cars called Project Better Place raised $386 million from venture capitalists and bankers.

Neither financing would have been imaginable 15 years prior. The start-ups would have either sold stock to the public or been out of luck. Even then, there's no certainty that the public market would have been able to accept such large financing for companies with such short track records. But now private investors can provide a viable alternative to public financing.

Firms focused on late stage, prepublic investing have been successful. This has helped them raise more money from limited partners and further decreased the need for small IPOs. They have captured the value that public market investors once got from IPOs.

Did venture capitalists kill the IPO market themselves? It would take some serious statistical analysis from an unbiased researcher to say definitively, but there is reason to believe that venture firms competed with IPOs to finance start-ups as early as 1997.

A funny thing happens when venture capitalists compete with the public market to provide growth financing for start-ups: Companies that do go public experience less post-IPO growth. IPOs used to be the place where public investors could buy into risky, high-growth opportunities, but that risk and its reward are increasingly going to late stage venture firms. Venture firms finance the start-up's rapid initial growth and wait until it has left its expansion stage before taking it public.

The absence of IPOs is a bit of a curve ball to many venture capitalists, particularly early stage investors. Yet some have evolved and adapted by applying new strategies.

New Strategies and Adaptations for Liquidity

There are many roads to Rome and venture capitalists are increasingly considering alternatives to the IPO and acquisition markets to achieve an exit. Not all of these transactions yield immediate liquidity for investors. In fact, some don't ensure any payout at all, but can improve a start-up's chances of success in the long term.

Mergers

Most people think of mergers right along with acquisitions. You will often hear the two lumped together as just "M&A."

Yet mergers hardly ever happen. A merger is a combination of two companies legally defined to be of equal value. This arrangement is very, very rare for any number of reasons: Finding equally valued companies is difficult, sharing power between executives is hard, and setting up a merger takes more lawyer time and is subsequently more expensive. It is just a mess.

People generally accept the term *merger* to apply more broadly to any combination of two companies of roughly equivalent size or stage. Legally, one company may acquire the other, but practically, they work together to reach a size that improves their competitive advantage.

With start-ups, one typically sees these combinations only when it is obvious that neither start-up is doing well on its own. If the market is robust, and both start-ups' products are selling, each may hope for its own lucrative acquisition offer from a large public company.

But putting two struggling companies together can help cut costs and prevent one start-up from price competing against the other. It is a strategy for desperate times—one that is often compared to tying two stones together and hoping they'll float.

Roll-ups

Combining two businesses in a merger may not necessarily improve their chances of survival in a difficult market, but what about rolling three, four, or even a dozen small companies into one big private company?

This strategy is called a *roll-up* and is becoming increasingly popular among venture capitalists sitting on large funds. A big venture capital firm may find a management team it likes and authorize it to acquire a number of other start-ups to consolidate their offerings into something the market needs. Think of it as giving a credit card to your teenage daughter and telling her to spend some money not just on a single piece of clothing, but on a whole outfit that matches and looks great together.

Roll-ups can take three major forms, each designed to bring the company using the strategy closer to becoming a monopoly.

The first is a horizontal integration of the market, where the acquiring start-up buys a handful of smaller, competitive start-ups. A horizontally rolled company can then exert market power and renegotiate more favorable contracts with both customers and suppliers. It can also reach a critical mass that no single start-up would be able to reach on its own.

A good example of this is Austin, Texas–based HomeAway. The start-up has raised more than $400 million from investors to consolidate online portals for vacation rental listings.

Before the company started making acquisitions, the market for online vacation rentals was extremely fragmented, with more than a dozen web sites catering to customers but nobody effectively controlling it. The lack of a centralized repository for vacation rentals made it difficult for potential renters to connect with homeowners and prevented renting from becoming a vibrant alternative to just getting a hotel room.

HomeAway started its horizontal roll-up in 2005 and over the next several years acquired A1 Vacations, TripHomes, CyberRentals, Holiday-Rentals.co.uk, VacationRentals.com, OwnersDirect.co.uk,

EscapeHomes, Homelidays, and BedandBreakfast.com. Now it has a comprehensive collection of properties for rent that was never before available in one place.

The second major type of roll-up is a vertical integration of start-ups that previously supplied each other. For example, a wireless network router–maker might benefit by bringing its semiconductor supplier and antennae supplier under the same tent. A vertically rolled company could face substantially lower production costs, which could translate into lower prices for consumers or higher profit margins for the company.

The third major type of roll-up is a "missing pieces" integration. In this scenario, an acquiring start-up is trying to create a product or service that has never before existed and needs to bring together a variety of technologies from smaller companies.

Each of these roll-up strategies puts the combined company in a better place than the individual start-ups would have been alone. Whether it eliminates competition, improves the supply chain or yields an opportunity for innovative new products, a roll-up usually works wonders.

Of course, giving your teenage daughter your credit card can have disastrous effects.

Disaster is the only way to describe the experience of a company called Pay-by-Touch, which was trying to create a biometric payment platform that would eventually replace credit cards. The company made thumb scanners, installed them at grocery store checkouts, and connected customer fingerprints to credit card accounts. It was marketed as an innovation of safety and convenience for the consumer.

Pay-by-Touch raised more than $300 million from venture capitalists and hedge fund investors and went on an acquisition spree, buying biometrics technology, credit card processing services, and whatever other pieces it needed to fill out its offering.

It installed payment terminals inside big grocery stores and signed up plenty of users. For a while, it looked like the investors were poised to make a good deal of money back on their investment. But Pay-by-Touch had serious problems. It burnt through cash relentlessly and its management proved itself not up to the task of executing such a major integration.[12] The company ultimately fell apart and the investors lost their money.

SPACs

Mergers and roll-ups don't always spell liquidity for investors—at least not immediately. Working with SPACs is one of the fastest ways to get money back.

A SPAC, or Special Purpose Acquisition Corporation, offers start-ups a hybrid of going public and getting acquired. At the end of the transaction, the start-up has been bought and becomes a public company.

Confused? It's actually pretty simple. A group of executives gets together and forms a shell company. The company has no operations and a vague sounding name such as "Technology Initiatives Corp." The executives meet with their lawyers and draw up the necessary legal documents to make an initial public offering for the shell company. The executives clearly communicate that they will use the proceeds of the offering to buy one or more private companies.

Public market investors buy into the offering for any number of reasons. They may trust the shell company's executives and their ability to pick good start-ups to acquire. Or they may believe that they will get access to a good company at a discount. Some investors will buy in solely because they automatically buy any new stock that comes to market.

Once the shell company has raised money from the public market, its executives begin to look for a promising start-up to acquire. This may take some time, during which the executives will be compensated from the proceeds of the IPO.

Meanwhile, there are always start-ups and their venture capital investors looking for a capital infusion or a quick path to the public markets. Combining with a SPAC can be a perfect way to get both.

Once the SPAC has found an appropriate start-up, it makes a bid to acquire it using its pile of cash. If the start-up agrees to the bid, it will become a public company and will have to start reporting earnings and disclosing other details about its operations. It will trade under the SPAC's ticker symbol, but will likely change the company's name to its own. Depending on what the situation calls for, the SPAC executives may or may not continue on with the consolidated company.

The SPAC's shareholders get stock in a company they might not otherwise have had exposure to, like a handpicked technology IPO they've bought into on the first day of trading. The SPAC's executives get a nice payday when they close the deal to compensate them for their efforts. The start-up gets a pile of money to help finance growth and doesn't have to go through a long SEC approval process. The venture capitalists see their illiquid preferred shares converted to common shares in a public company, which they can then distribute to their limited partners without a lockup period.

Foreign IPOs

Every several years, venture capitalists, bankers, and executives will "rediscover" SPACs as an alternative way of accessing the public market. So too with foreign stock exchanges.

An investor recently asked me what I had heard about the Toronto Stock Exchange. He was looking for any insight into whether it would be a good place to take one of his companies public. I confessed to him that I was generally skeptical of all foreign exchanges.

A stock exchange is a business and its clients are the companies that list shares on it. The more companies that list, the better the stock exchange does. It's this dynamic that drives exchanges to send representatives to Silicon Valley each year to drum up interest. NAS-DAQ actually has a permanent office on Sand Hill Road, right next to Silicon Valley's major venture firms.

I told the investor that I remembered a time five years prior when everybody was asking the same question about the London Stock Exchange's Alternative Investment Market (AIM). Venture capitalist interest in AIM was due, in large measure, to the recent Sarbanes-Oxley legislation. VCs were scared of the new U.S. government regulations that focused on board liability, financial certification, and disclosure.

Lawyers and consultants did a remarkable job of convincing investors that they could go to prison if one of their newly public portfolio companies was not adequately equipped to handle Sarbanes-Oxley provisions. So start-ups forked over more money to these service providers to help make them "compliant" with the new laws. NASDAQ and NYSE IPOs became more expensive and were perceived to be riskier than ever.

AIM offered an alternative to what was thought to be the excessive reporting requirements enforced on U.S. public companies. A company that listed on AIM reported its financials every six months, instead of the usual three-month period required in the United States. The United Kingdom did not have onerous Sarbanes-Oxley legislation and AIM's requirements for financial certification did not require as many expensive audits.

Venture capitalists imagined that they could help their start-ups raise money from the public market, obtain a measure of liquidity for themselves, and avoid any chance of going to jail. Some guessed that AIM's flexibility and friendliness to small companies would make it the new NASDAQ.

The hope and the hype never quite lived up to the reality. No more than a dozen U.S.-based, venture-backed start-ups ever tried for an AIM listing. Several that did later went out of business.

AIM did not work for venture capitalists for four major reasons:

1. Institutional investors perceived that AIM was a place where venture capitalists sent their dogs. If the start-up were truly a good one, it would have listed on NASDAQ, like a normal company.

2. AIM lacked sufficient post-market liquidity, making it impossible for the venture capitalists to sell their shares without the stock price taking a major hit.

3. Companies listed on AIM lacked adequate investment banking analyst coverage—a problem small companies listed in the U.S. face as well. Many large institutions won't invest in a public company unless analysts write opinions on how they think the company will perform.

4. AIM's listing requirements should have made it less expensive to put up an IPO, but the U.S. start-ups that listed there ended up financing their lawyers' learning curve on the foreign rules and regulations.

Running away from one set of problems meant running right into another set.

Investors want to believe that a foreign stock exchange will work out well for them and will invent any number of plausible sounding reasons. (The Toronto Stock Exchange "understands" the emerging cleantech space because one or two solar panel makers have already listed there and their stocks have gone up.) But offering shares on a foreign market will have its own set of issues, some of which will be impossible to anticipate.

There are no easy exits and darn few panaceas.

Buyouts

It isn't an everyday occurrence, but some start-ups financed by venture capitalists are actually acquired by another type of private equity investor—the buyout pro.

Buyout investors borrow money to buy a company and then use that company's profits to pay down the debt. They try to streamline operations to get the most cash out of the companies they buy. If they are acquiring a venture capital–backed start-up, it will likely be a mature one that produces plenty of cash.

Few start-ups have adequate recurring revenue to excite a buyout investor. Even an interested investor might not be able to raise the necessary debt to buy the company, since most start-ups have little in the way of hard assets to secure against a loan.

Still, it does happen.

Secondary Sales

Nobody wants to pet a wet dog and no venture capitalist wants to keep financing an old start-up. If a start-up isn't quickly advancing toward success within five years of its initial venture capital financing, it is unlikely to ever be a monster hit. Venture capitalists are seldom interested in convalescing an old and ailing patient when they can put their money into a healthy-looking new start-up.

Perhaps more important, venture capital funds have a 10-year lifespan. A firm has to get money back to its limited partner investors before that time runs out and may not be able to wait on an older start-up to pay off.

Secondary investors can provide a solution. These are specialized firms that raise funds from limited partners to buy companies and portfolios from venture capital firms. The secondary investor then has another 10-year fund cycle to get the start-ups it acquires either bought by a large corporation or to a point where they can go public. It's kind of like going into overtime.

Good secondary investors are able to pick start-ups with the fewest fleas, buy them at a discount of 10 percent to 40 percent, and then give them the help they need to be successful.

Secondary firms have garnered a lot of interest from limited partners in recent years as venture capitalists have had an increasingly difficult time finding quick liquidity for their investments (see Exhibit 6.5).

Secondary investments may sound a little boring, like picking up the scraps of companies that earlier investors couldn't make work out. But there's real money to be made here just by applying a little tender love and care. Consider Millennium Technology Managing Partner Samuel Schwerin's story about a recent investment that his secondary firm did in a venture-backed start-up:

EXHIBIT 6.5

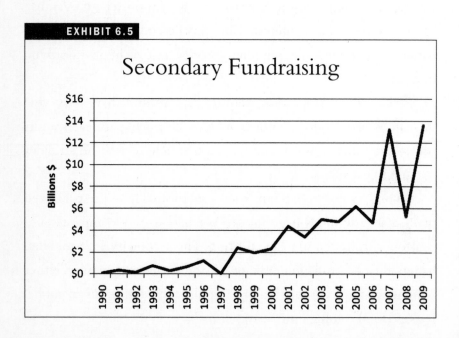

We bought 28% of a company from a hedge fund and investment bank. The company was shrinking, it went from $50 million to $16 million in revenue. We came in with the company's fifth CEO since it was founded 12 years before. It had tremendous value and we became the outsourced labor. We turned around the business and got in there and sold it. We made 27X our money. They [the company's venture capitalist backers] didn't make money on it, but they didn't lose as much money as they could have.[13]

Secondary firms have also grown in popularity as a way for a start-up's employees to cash out some or all of their vested stock options. The start-up itself may not need cash, but as it goes longer and longer without a liquidity event, employees can become frustrated. It's pretty inconvenient when the equity they've built up from working for the company cannot be converted to cash. Some secondary firms have been able to buy into big-name start-ups, such as Facebook, just by making it easy for the company's employees to trade their stock or stock options for cash.

Licensing Agreements

As I write this, venture capitalists, lawyers, and bankers are starting to talk about licensing as a potential path for investor liquidity in the cleantech industry.

The thinking behind this discussion is that a start-up that develops an innovative way of making high-efficiency solar panels may not want to go into the business of actually making them. A solar panel production facility can cost hundreds of millions of dollars and financing such projects with debt has been extremely difficult since the financial crisis of 2008. A start-up might prefer to have one or more established manufacturers incorporate its technology into existing products.

Such a licensing agreement might generate a stream of payments for a number of years, and the start-up could then distribute those payments to its shareholders.

It's unclear at this point how the details of such a transaction might work, or even that licensing agreements will catch on in any substantial way. The cleantech industry is still in its formative stages of development and may require new ways of thinking when it comes to investor liquidity.

Summary

Venture capitalists expect to either sell the start-ups they invest in or take them public within a number of years after their initial investment. Such a transaction is called a "liquidity event" because it turns the highly illiquid asset of private company preferred shares into either cash or public stock, which may be easily liquidated. Exactly how much money a venture firm makes from one of these deals is difficult for outsiders to accurately assess.

Going public is the process of selling shares not to the public, but to the large institutional clients of investment banks. Those institutions may then sell shares to the public on a major public exchange such as the NYSE or NASDAQ.

Start-ups file public disclosures on their financials and operations to the SEC and work with investment bankers to drum up interest for their offering. The bankers build a *book* of big institutions that might buy a number of IPO shares at a certain price. They use this process to determine at what price the start-up should sell its shares.

Investment banks may face a conflict of interest in taking companies public, offering shares for sale at a price below what they're worth. This led some investment banks to popularize the idea of a "Dutch auction" IPO.

Venture capitalists typically convert their preferred shares to common stock and are forced to wait 90 to 180 days after an IPO before selling these shares on the open market. This mandatory waiting period can be particularly frustrating if the stock "pops" after going public.

Large corporations may gain an advantage over their competitors by acquiring start-ups and will pay a premium to do so. Making an acquisition can help a big company cut product development costs and reduce the risk associated with doing research internally.

A big question that buyers and bankers tackle is how much to pay for a start-up. They often do not have sufficient financial data to make an accurate valuation estimate, lack comparable transactions, and may not be able to estimate the synergy possible between the two companies.

Venture capitalists have long relied on initial public offerings to convert their stakes in private companies to liquid public company stock. The market has always experienced cyclical variation, but some venture investors worry that IPOs are becoming rare.

Several factions have come up with potential fixes to the market structure that would reemphasize IPOs in the exit equation. There are three major proposals, each with its own group of supporters.

Despite the hubbub about the lack of IPOs, it may not be a particularly bad thing for innovation, the economy, or even for venture capitalists. It does not appear to have impacted the pace of innovation or the willingness of entrepreneurs to tackle big problems. If anything, fewer public offerings mean fewer unprepared or under-performing start-ups will get their shares into the hands of regular investors. Still, little if any unbiased academic research has been applied to determine the true effects of fewer IPOs.[14]

Venture capitalists are quick to point fingers when discussing why small-capitalization technology IPOs have disappeared. Yet there is good reason to believe that the venture capitalists themselves may have led to the IPO extinction.

In the run up to the dot-com boom, venture firms were able to rapidly increase their coffers and used their funds to create ever-larger financing rounds for start-ups. A company might have needed to go public to raise $25 million or more during the first half of the 1990s. In the second half of the decade, it could easily obtain the same amount faster and without the regulatory headaches simply by taking venture capital.

This trend has intensified and grown to the point where private financiers are putting together multihundred-million dollar financing syndicates.

Venture capitalists are adapting to the lack of traditional IPOs by pursuing alternative paths to liquidity. Beyond IPOs and acquisitions, there are several other avenues for investors to get their money back:

- Mergers are a rare type of business combination where two equally sized companies agree to work together.

- A roll-up is a series of acquisitions that can be used to consolidate start-ups.

- Special purpose acquisition corporations (SPACs) are a type of public company with no operations, but the intention to buy a private company.

- Foreign stock exchanges are perennially attractive to start-ups and their investors for any number of perceived advantages, including lower barriers for listing. These exchanges seldom live up to expectations.

- Buyouts are everyday events in industries known for having rich and regular cash flows, but seldom seen in technology start-ups.

- A secondary firm can swoop in to pick up a start-up that has been on a venture capital firm's books for too long, but it expects to acquire the company at a discount.

- Licensing has yet to take off as a way for investors to get their money back, but may be attractive to cleantech companies.

Notes

1. This gross example of underpricing, or perhaps of market euphoria, comes from the IPO of VA Linux, which offered at $30 per share in December 1999 and closed its first day of trading at $239.25, for a gain of 698 percent. Another example of a humongous first-day pop also comes from the dot-com boom, when theglobe.com went public in November 1998, offering at $9 per share. The stock price rocketed up to $97 per share before closing the day at $63.50, booking a first day gain of 605.5 percent.

2. John Batelle, "Doerr Interview Up," *John Battelle's SearchBlog*, November 20, 2007, http://bit.ly/bByhYO.

3. See, for example, Burt Malkiel, *Random Walk Down Wall Street, Ninth Edition* (New York: W.W. Norton, 2007), p. 242. This surveys the academic research and finds IPOs underperform the market by about 4 percent per year and that the poor performance begins at the point the lockup period expires.

4. This problem has led to some of the biggest misses in the history of the technology business. For example, Hewlett Packard (HP) missed out on the first iteration of the personal computer business because its executives did not have anything with which to compare the pitch they received from a young engineer who was obligated to offer any invention he made to his employer first. When HP decided against investing in the personal computer, Steve Wozniak quit and cofounded Apple Computer.

5. "Now What?" *Venture Capital Journal*, November 1, 2008, http://bit.ly/abP8iK.

6. Ibid.

7. See "Market Structure Is Causing the IPO Crisis," a publication from Grant Thornton's Capital Market Series, http://bit.ly/cCuXMB.

8. "National Venture Capital Association Releases Recommendations to Restore Liquidity in the U.S. Venture Capital Industry," press release, April 29, 2009, http://bit.ly/bJJ0fj. Also see the group's slide show presentation at http://bit.ly/c7Zbli.

9. See "Market Structure Is Causing the IPO Crisis," a publication from Grant Thornton's Capital Market Series, http://bit.ly/cCuXMB.

10. Paul Kedrosky is a Senior Fellow at the Kauffman Foundation and maintains a blog called "Infectious Greed." His comment comes from a November 10, 2009 post, "A Few Good IPOs?" http://bit.ly/azjsYW.

11. "Private Share Market May Supplant IPOs," *Investor's Business Daily*, November 10, 2009, http://bit.ly/aJwqJN.

12. Lawsuits at the time of Pay-by-Touch's bankruptcy filing indicate the CEO was a former felon and may have been using cocaine and harassing his employees. See "Turmoil Grips Pay-by-Touch Startup," *Los Angeles Times,* December 6, 2007, http://bit.ly/cdZW5y; and "Pay-By-Touch Investors Forgot Part About Due Diligence" *Alarm:Clock,* November 14, 2007, http://bit.ly/9npnQj.

13. "5 Questions with Samuel Schwerin," *PE Week*, May 4, 2009, http://bit.ly/9vbbLv.

14. Most of the economic research on start-ups, venture capital, and their impact on the national economy come from studies such as Global Insight's Venture Capital Impact Report, a study funded by the National Venture Capital Association, a lobbying group which maintains a pro-venture capital perspective.

CHAPTER 7

Booms, Bubbles, and Busts

After reading this chapter, you will be able to:

- Understand the cycle of venture capital investing.
- Develop strategies for investing in and around major trends.
- Spot a boom before it takes off.
- Identify the warning signs of overinvestment.
- Anticipate a speculative bubble's burst.

San Francisco sits near major tectonic fault lines that periodically shake the foundations of every building in the city. The tech industry is similarly situated on ever-moving ground. Innovations constantly rumble the basis for businesses in Silicon Valley and beyond.

Entrepreneurs and venture capitalists try to keep the ground shaking. They each face incentives that perpetuate a constant state of boom, bubble, and bust. Understanding how these tectonic movements happen will help you anticipate the direction of change and profit from it.

A boom starts with just half a dozen venture capitalists making small investments into a sprouting industry, such as digital media or cleantech. These investments can be designed to take advantage of some major macroeconomic trend or to fill some new need from corporations or consumers.

Within several months, the number of venture capitalists looking for start-ups in this new industry will swell to 20 or 30. Perception of the new investment thesis starts to shift. Investors begin to develop a "Monte Carlo mentality" and become desperate to put their bets down while they still can get in.

After 12 to 18 months, several hundred start-ups may receive several billion dollars of venture capital financing. The boom is either in full swing at this point or starting to turn into a bubble. Knowing the difference isn't easy.

An investment bubble happens when venture capitalists put too many dollars into too few real innovations. The amount of money invested starts to exceed the actual value of the new opportunity. Start-ups compete with each other for engineering talent and customers. The pace of innovation in the industry slows.

Bubbles burst when reality catches up to hype. That can be the product of a macroeconomic shock, an exogenous event, a lack of resources to continue expanding, or just a turn in the tide of public sentiment.

Timing a bubble burst isn't easy. But there are several warning signs that indicate when an industry boom has become a bubble and is trending toward bust. Busts are like forest fires that clear out the tangled mess of overinvestment and unsuccessful variants of the same idea or business opportunity. A bust is a healthy thing that fertilizes the next iteration of innovation.

The cycle of boom, bubble, and bust is the invisible heartbeat of the market. A venture capitalist once told me that a big boom happens every 12 to 15 years. His proof was more anecdotal than statistical, but seems to track pretty well for the past three decades and includes both the Internet boom and the personal computer boom of the early 1980s.

If the cycle is regular and predictable, it's useful to know how to tell which direction an industry is trending and how to make money from the next boom.

Riding the Waves

There are many ways to make money investing during a major business cycle and one sure way to lose it.

The worst thing you can do is to invest after a boom has already turned into a bubble and get stuck buying high and selling low. Venture capitalists who invest during the middle of a bubble typically get stuck overpaying for mediocre companies that will eventually go out of business. In the winner-take-all market of technology start-ups, these investors go home with nothing.

Nobody wants to be caught there, so investors try to develop a sense for where a technology is in its process and then invest accordingly. There are five major strategies on how to invest around trends:

1. Get in early.

2. Pick winners once they become obvious.

3. Back start-ups selling tools and services to boom chasers.

4. Get as far away from the booming industry as possible.

5. Pick up the pieces after the bust.

Get in Early

Investing early, before others realize that a new technology is gaining momentum, allows a venture capitalist to pick the best of whatever is available. He or she can select the best innovation, assemble a stellar team while talent is still cheap, and invest at a reasonable valuation.

Still, there are bound to be missteps along this path. Nobody has a full picture of any emerging technology. What features will resonate with customers? Who are the customers going to be? How much will it cost to produce?

It's a high-risk, high-reward strategy. Some investors believe they have the talent to discover the next big thing before everyone else sees it. Others "spray and pray," or try to put down as many bets as they can, gambling that one technology will make it big and make up for losses on other investments. A third group of investors actually tries to create booms after they have made their investments.

Growing Green Fools

In any bubble you need someone who believes that an asset is worth even more than what he or she pays for it. They pay an unreasonably high price for something, justified by the idea that somewhere out there is an even "greater fool" who will pay more for it than they did. Greater fools have an expectation that the price of a hot new stock, a condo in Miami, a tulip bulb, or whatever will continue going up after they've bought into it.

Foolish people buy high and sell low once the speculative bubble collapses.

Some venture firms move markets and can create an investment bubble just by hyping a new technology. Few do this better than Kleiner Perkins Caufield & Byers (KPCB). The firm most recently led the charge to stimulate cleantech investment and interest early in the industry's development.

KPCB determined that alternative energy and resource efficiency were attractive sectors primed for innovation and investment. The firm began quietly putting money into start-ups working on these technologies. After it had snapped up some of the most promising potential investments, it publicized its actions and heralded cleantech as the biggest thing since the Internet.

The firm held a cleantech innovation summit at San Francisco's Four Seasons Hotel in May of 2006, inviting 50 scientists and offering a $100,000 prize to anyone who could develop a major environmental policy or technology innovation. The firm announced that it had already invested $150 million into some 15 start-ups in the cleantech space.

The KPCB partners, usually taciturn, started talking about their newfound fervor for the field of cleantech to any journalist who would listen. Perhaps the most iconic image to come out of the media maelstrom was Partner Bill Joy's ecoboat, a 58-meter, $50 million testing platform for any number of green innovations that was photographed for *Newsweek*[a] and *Fortune*[b] within a matter of months. (As of this writing, you can charter the yacht for €225,000 a week from Camper & Nicholsons International.[c])

Then, in November of 2007, KPCB hired Al Gore as a partner. Gore went on to share the 2007 Nobel Peace Prize for informing the world about the dangers of climate change. His role inside KPCB is not clear, as the firm's web site does not list Gore as a board member on any of its portfolio companies.

These moves excited public sentiment about cleantech and its business viability. Other venture capitalists followed KPCB's lead and poured billions of dollars into cleantech start-ups. More importantly, public market investors have started salivating for cleantech IPOs, believing the KPCB hype.

[a] "The Color of Money," *Newsweek*, November 6, 2006, http://bit.ly/98nech.
[b] "The Green Sailor," *Fortune*, August 25, 2006, http://bit.ly/9UszUf.
[c] Camper & Nicholsons listing, December, 2009, http://bit.ly/bCOLQE.

Wait for Winners

Putting down bets before a bubble gets underway isn't for everyone. It takes either an iron stomach for risk or an almost irrational belief in one's ability to project which companies will be successful in the future.

Of course, some races have clear winners and losers after just one lap around the track. Investors can wait until a boom is in full swing and then try to pick the start-ups or industry segments that are most likely to come out winners.

Waiting for winners to emerge is less risky, but it also means buying start-up shares at a higher price. That can seriously cut into the returns that an investor expects to see. That makes this strategy particularly appropriate for late stage venture capitalists. They already spend their time deciding which start-ups deserve capital to continue growing and which should fall by the wayside.

Sell Tools

One of the most immediately lucrative ways to invest in a trend is to find and finance start-ups that sell shovels, picks, and denim blue jeans to the miners as they rush off digging for gold.

A venture capitalist who follows this strategy looks for what everyone else is going to need and then tries to invest in that. This concept can cut both ways. Selling shovels is a great business when there's a gold rush on, but what happens when the bubble bursts?

Avoid Booms

Some investors prefer to avoid fast-moving industries altogether. If you invest too early in a bubble, you may find that you've bet on the wrong horse. If you invest too late, you may be buying in when the bubble is at its peak and will only ever see your investments lose value.

Just as some people are content to go to Las Vegas and skip the casino, these investors are happy to stay away from the high-risk proposition of timing the business cycle. Of course, that can mean missing out on big rewards.

Or it can mean just picking a different type of risk to invest in. Venture capitalists who work in rapidly trending industries may not have time to train an untested CEO or coax a technical founder away from a cushy university research position. Yet avoiding a boom allows a venture capitalist the opportunity to deal with these and other problems. The payout from opting for this kind of risk may be just as lucrative.

Pick Up the Pieces

When the party's over, somebody has to clean up. In the venture capital business there's good money to be made investing in companies that have survived the aftermath of a bubble.

Busts are a lot like hangovers in that they cause people to stay away from whatever industry was booming. They may even irrationally avoid the place where money was lost, which is like walking around the block to avoid a bar where they once got sick from drinking too much.

That leaves opportunities for investors willing to stomach the memory of recent hardship. They're likely to see irrationally low valuations on companies that have real revenue and an opportunity for rapid growth even without a bubble pushing them forward.

Consider Amazon.com. The online retailer was soundly smacked down during the dot-com bubble's burst. By 2001, the company had seen its stock drop from over $105 per share to less than $6 per share. That would have been the right time to buy in. Ten years after the dot-com bubble burst, Amazon is trading at $130 per share.

Boom Beginnings

Since so much investment strategy depends on what stage an industry is in, it's important to know how the business cycle starts.

Booms begin when a new opportunity opens for companies to create real value and satisfy customer needs. There are five things which kick-start booms:

1. Macroeconomic shifts

2. Major news

3. Changing needs of big businesses

4. Evolution of consumer tastes

5. Some major proof that a new industry will be profitable, a flash-point that gets everybody's attention

These factors can act in tandem or alone, but the more they manifest themselves, the bigger the boom will be. Any one of them can cause venture capitalists to slough off skepticism in favor of optimism and to begin investing.

Macroeconomic Shifts

Any time the economy shifts, it opens opportunities for new products and services. The best recent example of this is the clean-tech boom.

It would have been impossible for novel forms of energy generation, fuel creation, or resource efficiency to take off during the 1990s. Oil was cheap. California had yet to experience rolling brownouts. China's industrial boom had yet to create massive demand for energy resources.

Fast-forward a decade and the need for energy innovation is obvious. Gasoline prices in California surged over $4 per gallon. The average price per kilowatt of electricity increased nearly 45 percent from 1998 to 2008.[1] As the price of energy increased, the demand for novel energy sources did as well. This became an unmistakable opportunity for entrepreneurs.

The rise of venture capital investment in cleantech was preceded by the immense success of industry incumbents who were able charge more than ever for their products and services. Success attracts competition and it is easy to see why entrepreneurs would have wanted to compete with large energy corporations such as Exxon. Exhibit 7.1 shows how a dramatic rise in Exxon's net income immediately preceded a rapid increase in venture capital investment in cleantech.

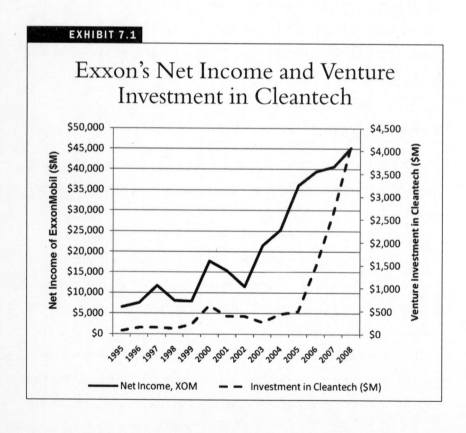

EXHIBIT 7.1

Major News

The world changed when terrorists flew airplanes into New York's World Trade Center towers in 2001. For the next four or five years, start-ups pitched venture capitalists on "security" technologies to solve all kinds of problems, both real and imagined.

Venture capitalists invested heavily in antispam, antispyware, and antivirus software. These digital security start-ups were hardly going to protect anyone from another terrorist attack. Instead, they played into an emerging national paranoia and attracted venture investment.

Another example of the power of news to insight an investment boom may be found in the market for vaccination technology. There's quite a bit of innovation in this business, especially in how to rapidly develop vaccines for new strains of flu.

Each time a flu scare hits the front pages of the newspaper, venture capital investment into the sector spikes up. See Exhibit 7.2 for a chart of the venture investment in immune response effectors and vaccines. The first spike comes after the anthrax scare of 2001. The next follows the avian flu scare of September 2005, when a United Nations official said it could kill 5 million to 150 million people. Venture capital investment in this industry more than doubled from 2005 to 2007.

The news changes people's perceptions and expectations. For venture capitalists, it signals a new opportunity that can be the beginning of a booming new market.

Changing Needs of Big Business

Large corporations are often a start-up's first customers. They can also be important strategic acquirers later in a start-up's life.

EXHIBIT 7.2

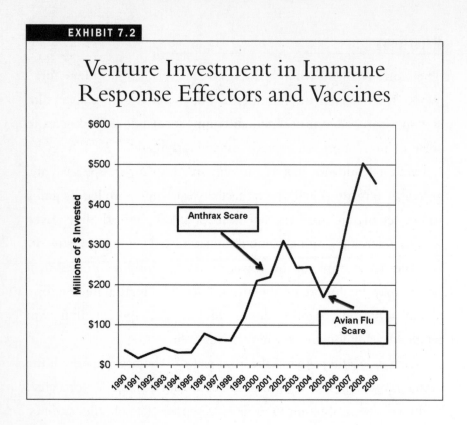

Venture Investment in Immune Response Effectors and Vaccines

Entrepreneurs quickly develop a keen sensitivity to what technologies these big businesses need.

When a group of large corporations all need the same type of technology, a venture capital investing boom may take root. This is what happened in the second half of the 1990s, when the large telecommunications companies needed better equipment. They were handling a massive increase in the use of their data networks coming from customers surfing the Internet and operating their first mobile phones. Start-ups came through with all kinds of innovations in fiber optics communications processing, and venture capitalists invested billions of dollars in their development.

The big telecommunications corporations paid for the new products and sometimes bought the start-ups. Eventually, the demand for additional bandwidth slowed. Telecommunications companies consolidated, the pace of entrepreneurship in this sector slowed, and venture capital investment ground to a halt.

Evolution of Consumer Tastes

Big businesses aren't the only customers start-ups sell to. Some focus exclusively on marketing to regular people. Booms can begin when folks start liking different things than they used to.

Tastes and preferences change subtly over time and can be difficult for entrepreneurs and venture capitalists to pick up on. Often, consumers don't know what they want until they see it.

An example of a changing consumer preference that launched a venture capital boom is the desire people had to "time-shift" television shows. A start-up called TiVo made it exponentially easier for people to record their favorite television programs and watch them later. The new technology changed people's perception of how television should be experienced: They wanted to watch whatever had been recently broadcast whenever they wanted to watch it.

The changing preference to "anytime" television led entrepreneurs to pitch related technologies. Video podcasting start-ups, video blogging start-ups, and Internet video sharing start-ups proliferated. Start-ups such as SlingBox offered consumers the opportunity not only to time-shift their television shows, but also to swap them between different media players.

It's difficult to say exactly how much venture capitalists invested in such technologies, but it is easy to see how a change in consumer preferences led to a boom in television-related start-ups.

Flashpoint

The Internet boom began with Netscape's initial public offering (IPO) in August 1995. The stock jumped 108 percent during the first day of trading and made everybody associated with the company rich—seemingly overnight. Netscape made it glaringly obvious that there was easy money to be made for investors willing to back Internet start-ups.

The stock market responded to the real demand consumers had to use the Internet. Netscape offered them what they wanted, albeit for free.

There were other factors at work beyond the success of a single company that led to the Internet boom. Still, Netscape stands out as the point from which every other dot-com dream was launched and its name was often evoked when entrepreneurs pitched venture capitalists on new start-ups to invest in.

Not all industries need a Netscape. But one proof point can help sway many investors who may be on the fence about the profit potential of an unknown and unproven business idea.

A different kind of flashpoint is the launch of a major new platform or successful product. The release of Apple's iPhone in 2007 is a perfect example. The company launched the device to much fanfare and it rapidly became successful with consumers.

Soon afterwards, Apple opened a programming platform for the device and invited software engineers to sell their creations through

Apple's iTunes store. It was like the sound of a gun going off at the beginning of a race. Entrepreneurs started dozens of companies to take advantage of this new opportunity and major venture financing soon followed.

Bubbles

Bubbles are characterized by a disregard for business metrics, rapidly escalating company valuations, and decreasing rates of technological or economic progress. They create winners and losers and are the inevitable product of the incentives entrepreneurs and venture capitalists face.

Bubbles also make people ridiculously rich. For example, Mark Cuban benefited big during the dot-com bubble. He started Broadcast.com, a company that hoped to stream audio over the Internet. He took it public in January 1998 and the stock rose 249 percent on the first day of trading. In April 1999, he sold the company, much of which he still owned, to Yahoo for $5.7 billion worth of stock. Yahoo never got the product integrated into its online offerings, but Cuban has gone on to own the Dallas Mavericks basketball team and several other businesses.

For a quick comparison, fast-forward to 2006. The dot-com bubble was a thing of the past when Google spent $1.6 billion to purchase YouTube. It paid less for something that actually worked a lot better. The Internet video sector was attracting a lot of attention but was not yet frothy with bubble speculators.

It's this difference that makes spotting a bubble a critical skill for venture investors.

Bubbly Start-ups

"When something generates a ton of excitement, at a certain point people are entering it because of the excitement not because there's anything solid there," iPhone application developer Dave Castelnuovo told the BBC.[2] He should know. Castelnuovo was one of the first programmers to develop a successful game for Apple's iPhone platform and has seen tons of people pile behind him, developing all kinds of games, tools, and miscellaneous junk.

Castelnuovo's insight is straightforward. Entrepreneurs with little innovation to offer push a booming industry to become a bubble. This process accelerates when entrepreneurs stop focusing on customer needs and try solely to make themselves attractive financing targets for venture capitalists.

Founders are hypersensitive to where growth capital is going and may choose to work on a problem they know venture capitalists are interested in solving. Early stage companies seldom have customers, so it can be easy for entrepreneurs to quickly pivot and tackle whatever market they believe venture capitalists will finance.

IN THE REAL WORLD

Boom Chasers

Some entrepreneurs are so desperate to get in on a boom that they will try to pitch venture capitalists on whatever appears to be hot at the moment. This is one of the things that turn a boom into a bubble.

I saw this firsthand in a start-up that had developed software for keeping track of and analyzing rapidly recurring data on computer networks. Such technology may sound wonky, but it was useful and could be applied to all kinds of problems.

When digital security was hot, the start-up said its technology was a great way of tracking cyberattacks in progress. The founders pitched it to more than 80 venture firms before finding financing.

But they were late to the digital security boom. The industry was already crowded with other start-ups and theirs didn't survive.

So one of the founders split off and recast the company's technology as a way of tracking a user's interaction with increasingly data-intensive web sites. His strategy was to get in on the Web2.0 boom that venture firms had just recently been frantic to finance.

But the entrepreneur was late to that party, too. The Web2.0 companies were making plenty of progress without the type of product he was offering so he never connected with customers and was unable to raise venture capital.

The experience of this unfortunate start-up highlights a major accelerant in the creation of overinvestment bubbles: entrepreneurs who chase venture capital trends instead of connecting with customers.

Bubbly Investors

But entrepreneurs aren't the only ones guilty of pushing booms into bubbles. Venture capitalists do it too. They invest in too many similar start-ups with too few real innovations. But why would a venture investor bet on a company knowing full well that it already has competitors and may be playing into an over-investment scenario?

There are two possible explanations. The first is that an investor may simply not know what his or her competitors are financing. Journalists generally do a good job of keeping track of what gets financed, and there are many free publications that can help people follow where venture dollars are flowing.[3] But a few stealthy start-ups can fly "under the radar" with only a handful of people aware of their existence for years after venture capitalists invest.

The second explanation seems more plausible. Venture capitalists invest in certain companies because it will look good to limited partners. It's a form of "resume padding" for the venture firm to be invested in areas that are perceived to be hot. A venture capitalist that can point to one or two portfolio companies in a promising sector may be perceived to be savvy.

Venture firm investment returns suffer when their partners come into sector-specific technology trends mid-bubble. They buy high and sell low. But the reputational value afforded to a firm for being involved in a rocketing trend may help it impress limited partners and raise bigger funds.

 TIPS AND TECHNIQUES

Spot the Splurge

COMFORTABLE EMPLOYEES

One of the warning signs that venture capitalists may have over-invested in an industry is the sight of comfortable employees working for start-ups. The employees of a start-up should always be a little afraid of losing their jobs if the company's innovation doesn't commercialize well or sales are too slow. Fear is a good thing in this context because it motivates the team to produce at its utmost ability.

It's like the old maxim about the rabbit and the fox. Which runs faster? Well if the fox slows down, he loses dinner. If the rabbit slows, he loses his life. Start-up employees should always feel more like the rabbit than the fox.

Employees stop feeling like the rabbit when they realize they have options. If one start-up fails, they can always go to work at one of its competitors. The people who work at start-ups are typically hyperaware of exactly what their company's competition is and how well it is doing. They watch closely for opportunities to hop from one company to another to get a pay raise or a promotion.

Watching start-up employees closely can give you an idea of just how many start-ups are competing in a given industry. Do they come to work late or go home early? Do they spend more time playing ping-pong than programming computers? Do they look worried?

It's important to distinguish "comfortable" from "confident." It's a good thing to have confident employees. They understand the risks and work hard, knowing they will win as long as they don't slow down.

CONFERENCES

Another symptom of overinvestment is the emergence of industry-specific conferences. It is a good indicator of how bubbly a technology sector has become. I have put on several industry conferences during my career and one of the first questions we always ask is "Will people come to this event?" There has to be a critical mass of entrepreneurs, investors, and executives interested in a sector or technology before you can sell enough tickets to make the event profitable.

If you lived in Silicon Valley in 2004, you would have been able to go to a handful of conferences related to various aspects of clean energy production each year. By 2007, you might have gone to a major, well-attended conference each week.

Busts

Once overzealous entrepreneurs and venture capitalists have pushed a boom to become a bubble, a rapid devaluation or bust is inevitable. Bubbles burst when one of three things happens: companies stop adapting, the economy takes a nosedive, or the people involved regain their sense of reason.

The first cause of a bust might be called "dinosaur disease." It's an inability of companies to rapidly adapt when the world around them changes. Sometimes it can be as simple as a key element of the environment disappearing or an assumption that executives held going up in smoke. Inflexible companies should expect extinction.

A macroeconomic shock, such as a major recession, can feel like an extinction-inducing meteor, and is the second big cause of a bust. It scares off would-be customers and can drastically impact start-ups' ability to either connect with strategic acquirers or go public.

The third cause of a bust is the "greater fools" getting wise to the idea they may be investing into nothing more than pixie dust and promises. Public sentiment is an ephemeral and elusive thing. Why people decide that they want a piece of the action one day and change their minds the next is anybody's guess.

Things Change and Companies Don't

A good business plan helps entrepreneurs to think through the assumptions that their start-up is based on. It also forces them to imagine alternative strategies if the environment changes rapidly. That's the whole idea of making the plan in the first place.

But it's not a perfect system. Some assumptions are so firmly established in our minds that we are unable to imagine a world without them. Entrepreneurs pitch an idea that is based on such a bedrock assumption and venture capitalists who share that view of the world finance the start-up without question.

A recent example of this is the rapid bust in ethanol investing. Ethanol, which is made from corn, can be used to power certain types of cars and trucks as a replacement for gasoline. Venture capitalists and entrepreneurs agreed on two major assumptions: the price of oil would continue to rise and the price of corn would remain relatively flat. Between 2005 and 2007, venture investors plowed over $1.3 billion into start-ups looking at distilling ethanol, according to data from Thomson Reuters.

The problem came in 2008, when the price of oil rose, but not nearly as fast as the price of corn. Suddenly the ethanol producers felt a tremendous squeeze on their margins. They had locked themselves into supply contracts that were no longer profitable and some start-ups went bankrupt. Venture capitalists lost boatloads of money.

The ethanol investment bubble burst when the environment changed and the assumptions that had driven it proved to be wrong. The companies that lost money were the ones that were unable to pivot when the margins from fuel production started to shrink.

A handful of start-ups were able to abandon the ethanol production market for a lower-volume, higher-margin alternative. They took their know-how and applied it to making chemicals for use in other products. Big consumer-focused companies, such as Procter & Gamble, had a great desire to make their products from "renewable" sources instead of petroleum and were willing to pay a premium for it. The former ethanol producers had just the solution for them.

Bringing down an investment bubble takes more than just faulty assumptions. It also requires inflexible companies unwilling to change or adapt in the face of a major market movement.

TIPS AND TECHNIQUES

Stay Paranoid

Our minds are hardwired to underestimate both the potential for adverse events and the magnitude of negative outcomes.[a] If a normal person is an optimist, then entrepreneurs and venture capitalists might be deemed "superoptimists." That can be a problem when it comes to evaluating the world and imagining where technology will take it.

Andy Grove, the former CEO of semiconductor maker Intel, is a master of anticipating negative outcomes and preparing for them accordingly. His maxim, later formulated as a book, was "Only the paranoid survive."[b] It's a good way of thinking about markets because it forces you to work through what would happen in any number of negative scenarios.

When investors stopped asking ethanol entrepreneurs what would happen if the price of oil went down and the price of corn rose, they walked into a bear trap. Both venture investors and start-up executives should be prepared to answer any number of what-if scenarios.

As I write this, it's currently popular for venture capitalists to put money into start-ups offering "social games" that you can play with your friends on networking sites such as Facebook. When the trend first emerged, some people were skeptical that Facebook would play nice with the ecosystem of start-ups trying to ride on its coattails. But two years later, nobody seems concerned that Facebook could change its rules overnight, could be eclipsed by some new social network, or could suddenly and unexpectedly go out of business.

And that all takes for granted that people want to continue playing social games. But what if they lose interest?

Healthy paranoia can be a good way for entrepreneurs and venture capitalists to stay prepared for rapid change.

[a] For more on the phenomenon of loss aversion and its effects on our ability to estimate value, see Dan Airely, *Predictably Irrational* (New York: HarperCollins, 2008).
[b] A brief synopsis is available from Intel's web site, (http://bit.ly/coMy40). The book is *Only the Paranoid Survive, first edition* (Doubleday, 1996).

Macroeconomic Shock

When I first moved to Silicon Valley, the people there seemed to believe that their businesses were more or less immune to federal monetary and fiscal policy.

The truth is that what goes on in Washington, Wall Street, and the rest of the world has a profound impact on Silicon Valley and the business of start-ups. Nowhere does this figure more strongly into the equation than in the burst of an investment bubble.

When the economy gets squishy, start-ups have a tougher time connecting with customers. Consumers drop nonessential spending and corporations lock down budgets. That slows start-up sales substantially.

Falling stock prices make it more expensive for strategic acquirers to buy start-ups and less attractive for start-ups to go public. The lack of a clear path to liquidity slows the pace of venture capital investment.

The financial crisis of 2008 seemed to be a world away from Silicon Valley when it first started.

The *Venture Capital Journal* surveyed over 60 venture capitalists and other service providers for their estimates of what impact the financial crisis would have in the industry.[4] This was a week after Lehman Brothers declared bankruptcy and about three weeks before Sequoia Capital gave its famous "R.I.P. Good Times" presentation to CEOs.

At the time, more than 80 percent of the investors surveyed said they didn't think the Wall Street crisis would cause them to slow their current investment pace. Some 16 percent planned to actually increase their rate of investment.

Yet the amount of money committed to start-ups fell 37 percent during 2009, according to data from the National Venture Capital Association.[5]

Investors had predicted that just 24 percent of their companies would see a lower valuation in their next round of financing. The reality was much worse. The majority of the investments made during 2009 came in either at flat valuations or as down rounds, according to data from Fenwick & West.[6]

The investors surveyed by the *Venture Capital Journal* were optimistic that cleantech would ride out the economic turmoil even if other sectors took a hit. "Our cleantech sector is looking a bit counter-cyclical, which may make our story a bit different than what you might hear from other sectors," one investor said at the time. It was a sentiment echoed by another survey participant as well: " . . . this really only affects a few of our portfolio companies. We invest across industries and think our industrial and health care companies will feel less of an impact than our IT portfolio companies."

Yet their optimism was misplaced. Big cleantech investments were the first casualty of the financial crisis. The "project finance" professionals that arrange loans for energy production facilities shut their wallets tight. Financing dollars for the sector fell by nearly half from 2008 to 2009. Cleantech ended up being one of the worst affected areas due to its reliance on large financing syndicates and big loans.

You can see the trend clearly defined in one of the most capital-intensive sectors in cleantech: thin-film solar investments. Thin-film solar companies promised to manufacture inexpensive photovoltaic panels based on breakthroughs in polymer science. You can see that the investment bubble crashed in this sector shortly after a handful of the major investment banks went belly-up in Exhibit 7.3.

EXHIBIT 7.3

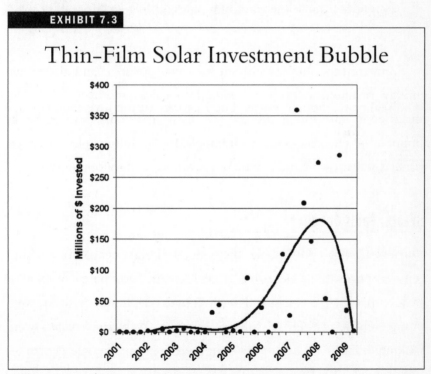

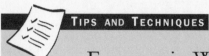

Tips and Techniques

Economic Warning Signs

You can track the general economy using any number of indicators, or by hanging on every word each of the Federal Reserve governors say. But those measures may not be as useful as more obvious warning signs.

One of the best indicators of an impending bust is a fluctuating stock market. A Dow Jones Industrial Average yo-yoing up and down makes people worry. It is like a patient that starts screaming in the emergency room: Nobody quite knows what's the matter, but things are going to get worse before they get better. Bizarre stock performance is the sort of thing that indicates something big is going on with the overall economy that will likely have a major impact on start-ups and venture firms.

Venture capitalist enthusiasm for thin-film solar and alternative energy production projects seemed to evaporate overnight. The macroeconomic shock and the fall of the major investment banks popped the emerging cleantech bubble and ambitious plans for solar panel installations, wind farms, and geothermal developments.

Greater Fools Get Wise

During the dot-com bubble, the general public engaged in a willful self-deception about the nature of the Internet. Most people wanted to believe that computers, linked together over telephone networks, were completely rewriting the rules of business. Web *wunderkinder* were making billions of dollars by simply connecting people. Fortunes were there for the taking, all that was required was an e*Trade account.

For whatever reason, it was an attractive fantasy. Until it wasn't.

Nobody knows for sure what causes a rapid change in public sentiment. There's always somebody pointing out the fact that the emperor isn't wearing any clothes. The problem is that during a bubble nobody listens. At least not until greed gives way to fear.

The cleantech boom nearly turned into a bubble when people started believing that Silicon Valley and American innovation had come to save them from the boogeymen of foreign oil and global warming. For a few months in 2007, prices at the gas pump spiked and Al Gore's "Inconvenient Truth" won an Academy Award. It seemed, briefly, that anything cleantech-related was a good investment idea.

But the euphoria was short-lived. Too many people were too focused on the underlying economics of the cleantech businesses. Could solar start-ups survive without government subsidies? Did growing corn to make gasoline really make financial sense? Could technology ever provide energy that would be cheaper than coal? At the time when the boom might have bubbled over, people were still skeptical about the new green technologies. Those who would have been the greater fools were not feeling foolish.

Summary

The process of boom, bubble, and bust is as central to the venture capital industry as a heartbeat. It measures off the rhythm of investment and dictates its nature. The process writes itself both large and small across industries and technology subsectors. It's impossible to say just how many little bubbles happen in venture capital investing during a given year, but the cycle manifests itself as a tradeoff between investor greed and fear.

There are several major strategies for investing in and around markets going through the business cycle. A venture capitalist can get in early and put down bets before prices become unreasonable; pick winners once they become obvious; or invest in start-ups selling tools and services to those chasing a boom. Some venture capitalists get as far away from a booming industry as possible, while others prefer to wait for the inevitable bust and invest in the remaining companies at a discount.

Booms create value for customers by rapidly creating new products and services that they need. They begin when conditions create a major opportunity for change. That can be the product of a macroeconomic trend, major news, the changing needs of big businesses, or a shift in consumer preferences. Yet few things stimulate a boom as much as a single big success, such as the Netscape IPO that kicked off the dot-com boom, or a major new platform such as Apple's iPhone.

Booms create wealth and bubbles redistribute it. The entrepreneurs and investors who get in before a booming industry starts to bubble stand to make massive profits from the irrational behavior of others.

Booms become bubbles when entrepreneurs try to pitch ideas they think will be attractive to venture capitalists instead of products people will actually pay for. These "me too" investments may be attractive to second-tier venture capitalists who are anxious to demonstrate to their limited partners that they are hip to the new thing, whatever it is. Such an investment may be a money loser in the long run, but can help a venture firm raise its next fund in the short run.

All bubbles eventually deflate or burst. This is a natural process that can clean out the excesses of over-investment and restore reason to the market.

Some busts happen when companies are unable to rapidly adapt to changes in the marketplace. Others are the product of macro-economic shocks that nobody could have predicted.

These reasons are relatively straightforward compared to busts that come from changes in public sentiment. Nobody knows quite how or why this happens, but at some point the "greater fools" get wise and stop buying into the idea of ever-increasing company valuations.

Notes

1. "Electric Power Industry 2008: Year in Review," *U.S. Energy Information Administration*, January 2010, http://bit.ly/bQbLbr.
2. "The Rise of the App Entrepreneur," BBC.co.uk, March 21, 2010, http://bit.ly/cZq586.
3. Thomson Reuters runs a free newsletter called *PEHub Wire* that tracks deals in the venture capital and private equity industries. You can sign up for it at www.pehub.com.
4. "From Wall Street to Sand Hill Road," *Venture Capital Journal*, October 1, 2008, http://bit.ly/aaLgGV.
5. "PricewaterhouseCoopers/National Venture Capital Association MoneyTree™ Report, Data: Thomson Reuters Total U.S.

Investments by Year Q1 1995—Q4 2009," January 22, 2010, http://bit.ly/acxeJl.

6. "Trends in Terms of Venture Financings in Silicon Valley (Fourth Quarter 2009)," *Fenwick & West*, February 16, 2010, http://bit .ly/9Kdk2y.

CHAPTER 8

Going Global

After reading this chapter, you will be able to:

- Work in countries other than the United States and appreciate how their venture capital industries evolved.
- Avoid pitfalls common to investors doing business abroad for the first time.
- Implement strategies for establishing a venture capital investing office outside the United States.
- Deal with cross-border taxation and currency issues.
- Establish realistic expectations for travel requirements.

One of the most profound changes in the venture capital business during the past two decades has been its globalization. Conventional thinking dictated that U.S. venture capital was a local business and that investors would either want or need to be in constant contact with their start-ups to help them grow.

Wrapped into that practical concern was a political philosophy—namely that venture capital was essential to the creation and support of technology start-ups that in turn assured American economic competitiveness. Exporting venture capital to other countries was tantamount to FedExing the gold bars right out of Fort Knox.

However, capital knows no ideology. It tends to flow to where it can multiply. And in the aftermath of the dot-com boom, Silicon Valley's soil seemed less fertile. Opportunity abounded abroad and venture capitalists soon sought it. The first part of this chapter covers their foreign investment strategies.

Each country has followed its own path in establishing an entrepreneurial industry and technology investing community. Some, such as Israel, managed to build a start-up culture during the 1990s. Other countries, such as Russia, have yet to make it work. We'll consider the development of several major venture capital economies in the second part of this chapter.

Despite the recent rise of venture capital in other countries, the United States remains the most active investor in start-ups. Over the past decade, start-ups in the United States have raised $488 billion from venture capitalists, according to data from Thomson Reuters. That's about 65 percent of all the money raised in the entire world from venture capitalists. Start-ups in Canada raised the next-highest amount of money, collecting $39 billion, less than a tenth as much, and still more than both China and India combined.

Strategies for Foreign Investing

The venture capitalist toolkit for going global is surprisingly limited given the diversity of locations, cultures, and industries of the world. Most firms have opted for one or more of several strategies:

1. Fly in, write a check, and fly out.

2. Open a foreign office.

3. Support an independent firm.

4. Affiliate with knowledgeable locals.

5. Subsume a foreign firm.

6. Let the government support you.

It is tempting to view one strategy as an evolution of another, especially when you see investor approaches to a country changing over time. But it may be better to think of these strategies as suiting different risk tolerances and different levels of involvement. The "fly in, write a check, and fly out" strategy is like dipping your toe into the pool to check the temperature. Subsuming a foreign firm is like diving in headfirst.

Fly In, Write a Check, and Fly Out

Investing takes a lot of trust. There's only so much any financier can do to make a company successful, and this is especially true for venture capitalists who make investments from half a world away.

For a venture capitalist to fly to a foreign country and make an investment takes almost complete faith in the local management team. This kind of trust is usually only allotted to executives who have already been successful in Silicon Valley.

This is one of the major reasons China and India gained such attention from U.S. venture capitalists during the past 10 years. Each country had a large community of entrepreneurs with Silicon Valley experience.

U.S. venture capitalists investing abroad must also have a good understanding of the technology or market a foreign start-up is pursuing. Usually that restricts "fly and buy" venture capitalists to industries that are well established in the United States.

For example, it's easier to invest in a start-up making semiconductors in China than one that hopes to open up a chain of Chinese fast food restaurants. It's easy to evaluate a semiconductor technology against what exists in the United States than to know what type of fast food will appeal to Chinese consumers.

Syndication is a classic way for venture firms to share risk and gain exposure to investments that they might not otherwise see. Yet syndicating in foreign countries is not always easy.

U.S. venture firms need strong partners whom they can trust in countries they hope to syndicate investments in. Yet there are few good firms established abroad and even fewer that have cultivated strong relationships with investors in the United States.

Investing in other countries from a home base in the United States also requires a lot of time on airplanes.

IN THE REAL WORLD

Travel

Arvind Sodhani runs Intel Capital, which is regularly one of the most-active investors in the world. The investment arm of the Santa Clara, California–based semiconductor giant has made investments in 35 countries. It has dedicated investment funds for China, India, the Middle East, and Brazil.

Sodhani spends a lot of his time on airplanes managing these investments. He says he books 250,000 miles on international and domestic flights each year.[a]

Don Wood runs Draper Fisher Jurvetson's global network of affiliate funds. Sitting in his office on Sand Hill Road, Wood keeps a map of the world on one wall, with pushpins indicating the locations of the 17 DFJ affiliates. The other wall has two framed Roger Broders original art deco travel posters.[b]

He has no idea how many miles he travels each year, but he does know that United Airlines has given him the distinction of being a "United Global Services" member. Details on the program are guarded, but this frequent-flyer status is reserved for the top 1 percent of the airline's flyers. It's one step above the customers who book more than 100,000 miles of travel each year.

Ajit Nazre discovered and supported India's Info Edge (operator of Naukri.com) as a partner at Menlo Park, California–based Kleiner Perkins Caufield & Byers. He was just past 40 when he worked with the Indian Internet start-up and helped to take it public. He visited India six times in 2006 to get the deal done.[c]

"Quite a few of the venture folks in the Valley have lifestyle problems when it comes to travel," he says. "I'm not one of those people. What are you going to do? Say no? That's the reality. All of our businesses have business everywhere. You can't avoid it. There's no substitute for face time."

[a] "Remaking Intel Capital," *Venture Capital Journal*, December 1, 2006, http://bit .ly/dpojQ6.
[b] "Balancing Act," *Venture Capital Journal*, July 1, 2007, http://bit.ly/db9P2q.
[c] "Ajit Nazre: The Man behind Kleiner Perkins' First Big Hit in India," *Venture Capital Journal*, March 2007, http://bit.ly/9nqntu.

Open a Foreign Office

Flying into foreign countries all the time is not easy. That's one of the major reasons that U.S. venture firms open foreign offices staffed with full-time investors.

It takes a serious commitment to send a venture capitalist to a foreign country. Beyond the cost associated with opening a permanent office, just getting someone to leave a cushy life in Silicon Valley isn't easy.

It may, however, be an amenable arrangement for a venture capitalist with substantial family or cultural ties to the foreign country. He or she may already speak the language. The fact that many successful venture capitalists have connections to China and India may be one of the major reasons investment into those countries has taken off.

One seldom sees a firm hire for a foreign position, at least not until it is certain it wants to stay in a given country. This may be because venture capitalists are reticent to share compensation with another partner or just because the firm wants to train a new investor in the United States first, in order to keep its operations consistent across countries.

Support an Independent Firm

This strategy first appeared around 2005 as well-known U.S. venture firms sought access to investments in China but were unwilling or unable to open offices abroad. Other firms were concerned that they had little or no experience with this emerging economy and would have a tough time gaining it by themselves.

Venture capitalists wanted trusted partners in foreign countries to syndicate deals with, so they helped create them.

U.S.-based New Enterprise Associates (NEA) had tested the waters in China with a pair of late stage semiconductor investments. But making late stage investments in prepublic companies is different from time-intensive early stage investments. Without people on the ground in Shanghai and Beijing, it seemed impossible to penetrate the early stage market.

So NEA joined forces with U.S.-based Greylock Partners, another well-known and respected firm, to help launch a $125 million fund targeted at China called Northern Light Ventures. The two U.S.-based firms acted as limited partner investors in the newly formed fund and handpicked the venture capitalists they wanted to run it, putting the pieces together in late 2005. The Silicon Valley venture firms turned to Chinese nationals whom they had worked with in the past, especially successful entrepreneurs with significant experience working in California, to staff the new firms.

Each U.S. firm introduced the Chinese investors to their limited partners to assist them in fundraising. They also offered the expertise of their general partners as a resource. In return, the expectation was that the newly formed Chinese venture capital firm would find good investments and syndicate them with the U.S. venture capitalists. That way, the U.S. firms avoided the risk of beginning their own office, but were able to take part in investments as though they were sitting in China themselves.

Other U.S. firms began their own affiliate partnerships in China around the same time. Silicon Valley–based Mayfield Fund announced in October 2005 that it was both a limited partner in and a coinvestor with Chinese venture firm GSR Ventures, which had a $72 million fund.

Both Northern Light and GSR have gone on to raise subsequent funds.

NEA did the same thing in India, putting former Intel Chief Engineer Vinod Dham in charge of its NEA IndoUS fund. Dham is considered to be the father of Intel's Pentium processor line and had been investing in India prior to partnering with NEA in 2006.

Affiliate with Knowledgeable Locals

This strategy is often compared to launching a chain of fast food restaurants. It's the McDonald's business model: A central organization dictates structure and brand and provides supplies in return for a big cut of whatever profits the local restaurant makes.

In the venture capital affiliation model, the central "parent" firm dictates branding and strategy to its affiliate partners. It helps them raise funds in exchange for a cut of their fees and carried interest. The affiliates also share attractive deals with the parent firm.

Affiliates are expected to maintain consistent branding with the parent venture firm and to share income into perpetuity. A particularly successful affiliate may later spin off into an independent venture firm, but doing so may be frowned upon by the parent firm.

Employing an affiliate strategy is halfway between creating an independent firm and opening a foreign office. An independent firm might do a portion of its investments with a U.S. firm as a syndicate partner, but an affiliate will do the majority of its investments in tandem with its parent firm.

U.S. venture firm Draper Fisher Jurvetson helped to pioneer this investing model during the 1990s. It began with affiliate funds in other parts of the United States and has since expanded into half a dozen foreign countries.

Its success with this strategy has been mixed. During the dot-com boom, it helped launch DFJ ePlanet Ventures, a $650 million affiliated fund with a global investing mandate. Over the subsequent half-decade the fund invested in Chinese companies Baidu, Focus Media, KongZhong, and Luxemburg-based Skype. Each led to a massively successful liquidity event that lined not just the pockets of the affiliate fund but also yielded ample returns to the parent firm.

The firm has had less success chartering affiliates focused on specific countries. Some have never made it off the drawing board, such as the Ukraine-focused DFJ Nexus or the Greece-focused DFJ Faros, while others, such as Brazil-based DFJ FIR Capital Partners, are still too early in their development to judge.

Subsume a Foreign Firm

Sometimes it is easier to buy a venture firm than to build one. That's the thinking some U.S. venture capital firms have employed as they expanded into unfamiliar territories.

Merging operations with a foreign venture capital firm already in operation can take away a lot of headaches. The investors at the foreign firm get along with each other and may have a track record of success. Perhaps most important, the partners of a foreign firm already have substantial connections to entrepreneurs and don't need time to come up to speed.

These reasons weighed heavily in the minds of the partners of Menlo Park, California–based Sequoia Capital and Kleiner Perkins Caufield & Byers (KPCB) when they decided to buy out venture firms. Sequoia subsumed India-based WestBridge Capital in 2006 and KPCB took on TDF Capital in China during 2007. Both WestBridge and TDF had successful investing track records in their respective countries and years of experience doing U.S.-style venture capital.

How such transactions work is not easy to learn—both firms have declined numerous inquiries to discuss specifics. However, it is clear that the strategy immediately exposed Sequoia and KPCB to top-notch investment opportunities in countries that have been difficult for other investors to crack.

Let the Government Support You

Foreign governments periodically attempt to recreate Silicon Valley's innovation ecosystem within the borders of their own country. Their efforts usually include some kind of incentive designed to import knowledge and investing talent from elsewhere in the world.

Both Israel and Russia have attempted to entice experienced venture investors during the past two decades. Each created a fund-of-funds structure with hundreds of millions of dollars designed to support the formation of venture funds in cooperation with foreign partners (more on this later).

Obtaining support from such a program has its plusses and minuses, but can be a good way for a venture capital firm to enter a foreign country for the first time.

Venture Capital Outside the United States

Knowing how to invest in a foreign country is one thing, but knowing which foreign country to go to is another matter completely.

Despite the recent rise of venture capital in other countries, the United States remains the most active investor in start-ups. Over the past decade, start-ups in the United States have raised $488 billion from venture capitalists, according to data from Thomson Reuters. That's about 65 percent of all the money raised from venture capitalists in the entire world.

The United States has developed a very attractive environment for small companies that no other country has yet replicated. People seem to be constantly asking: What makes Silicon Valley so successful at commercializing innovation? Some attribute the area's dominance to its proximity to Stanford University's major research and engineering centers. Others say it has to do with geographically centralized venture capital industry, or even the concentration of large tech corporations nearby.

But where else might such an innovation ecosystem emerge?

The number of start-ups financed in a given country might be indicative of its ability to sustain further investment. Exhibit 8.1 shows which countries have had the most active venture capital industries during the past decade.

Of course each country or region has its quirks, some of which have opened opportunities while others have made development more difficult. We'll consider several of the areas of greatest interest.

EXHIBIT 8.1

Venture Capital Investment around the World 2000–2010

Country	Number of Start-ups	Investment ($ Billion)	Country	Number of Start-ups	Investment ($ Billion)
United States	19,398	$488.1	Australia	809	$6.2
Canada	5,920	$39.0	Spain	716	$6.2
United Kingdom	3,234	$36.8	Sweden	892	$5.9
France	2,605	$23.5	Israel	522	$5.5
China	1,174	$18.5	Italy	433	$5.3
India	1,052	$15.9	Brazil	303	$4.7
Germany	1,692	$13.3	Hong Kong	179	$4.3
Netherlands	727	$10.0	Denmark	394	$4.2
South Korea	2,433	$9.5	Singapore	213	$3.4
Japan	451	$7.1	Rest of the world	4,599	$36.1

Source: Thomson Reuters

Israel

It's impossible to ignore the potential of Israeli entrepreneurs and technologists. The country has invested heavily on defense and technical training for its soldiers. And many of those who go through the compulsory military service end up applying their leadership lessons and technical know-how in the service of start-ups.

The military unit that mints the most entrepreneurs is also one of the most secretive. Unit 8200 of the Israeli Defense Forces is akin to the U.S. National Security Administration, only with more guns. It recruits its members starting in high school and attracts many bright people for work in intelligence.

Once Unit 8200 members finish their term with the military, they seem to find their way into management positions at start-ups. Their experience working with high-performance teams and cutting-edge technologies can uniquely equip them to take on the challenge of running a start-up. "I salivate over these guys," venture capitalist Jon Medved recently told *Foreign Policy*.[1]

A large number of successful technology start-ups can trace their roots back to the Unit, but the most well known may be digital security company Check Point Software. Company founder Gil Shwed spent four years in the Unit, according to reports.

Unit 8200 members have become acutely aware of the success of their peers in the technology business and have tasked the section's alumni association with the role of facilitating networking and job placement.[2] It may be one of the best-networked groups in the entire country.

To be sure, not all of the country's entrepreneurs are Unit 8200 members. Israel has done a remarkable job of stimulating technology start-up development and its entrepreneurs come from every walk of life.

Yozma Program

Israel may have been ripe for an innovation economy to flourish, but it took a government program to attract venture capital investment.

In 1993 the government began the Yozma program, which used $100 million in public funds to match venture capital investment in start-ups. *Yozma* means "initiative" in Hebrew, and the program was designed to jumpstart the nascent venture capital business. Its aim was to replicate the success of Silicon Valley by funding entrepreneurs with serious initiative.

The government started by inviting foreign investors to establish venture funds based in Israel that would invest solely in Israeli start-ups. It selected 10 firms it would support with public money, offering to contribute up to 40 percent of each firm's first Israel-focused fund.

When one of the supported venture capital firms picked a start-up to invest in, the government matched the venture firm's investment at its promised 40 percent contribution. The government bought an equity stake in the start-up, just like the venture firm did.

As a Yozma-supported firm's portfolio of start-ups grew and became more stable, the government's share became more valuable. But instead of reaping the upside of a successful investment, the government offered each venture firm the opportunity to buy back the government's initial investment in the fund.

When the government offered its investment back to the firm for sale, it was at a bargain basement price. It did not ask for a price that reflected the growth of the portfolio of start-ups, say double or triple what the venture investors initially invested; the government offered its stake in the venture fund at cost plus a modest annual interest.

That was a pretty good deal, effectively allowing a venture firm to almost double down if it was successful. If a venture fund turned out to be unsuccessful, the government shared in the downside. The government also made direct investments into start-ups, backing 15 companies, of which 9 enjoyed positive returns.

The Yozma program offered money to just 10 venture firms. Those firms demonstrated it was possible to make good investments with attractive rewards and their success attracted many other firms to the country. Moreover, many of the firms that got their start through the program have persisted and continue to invest today.

"Israeli Model"

Israel's entrepreneurs and technologists are top notch, and its government has supported the development of a vibrant venture capital community. The one thing Israel always seems to be missing is customers. As one entrepreneur explained to me, "You have to cross 1,000 miles of sand and desert just to sell something."

Customers are a key part of an innovation ecosystem. Beyond the obvious importance of exchanging money for goods and services, customers also play a critical role in the development and improvement of a start-up's product. Customers are the best testing ground for any innovation and regularly provide feedback to start-ups on how to improve their offerings.

Although many multinationals have offices in Israel, the country still lacks the large customers that its start-ups need to survive. But entrepreneurs have adapted to this challenge by developing what is often called the "Israeli Model."

Under this model, a start-up maintains its research, development, and production in Israel, but stations its CEO and sales team in a country with lots of potential customers.

Visiting an Israeli Model start-up is a strange experience. You meet with the CEO in a big office building in Redwood City,

California, and find out that he and the vice president of sales are the only two people working for the company in the entire building. You start to wonder where those millions of venture capital dollars are going. The developers, testers, support staff, and other employees all work from Israel, several thousand miles away.

IN THE REAL WORLD

An Area in Conflict

During the summer of 2006, the Israel-Hezbollah conflict revved up, sparking fears of a major military mobilization.

There was little immediate danger for many in the tech business though. The fighting focused on Israel's northern border, while most of Israel's technology companies are based in the southern city of Haifa.

But some start-ups still felt the effects. UCLT, a semiconductor start-up based in Karmiel, Israel, had to relocate most of its operations to be closer to bomb shelters, says investor Yoni Cheifetz of Lightspeed Venture Partners. Lightspeed invested $8.7 million in the company's first institutional round in January 2006. The start-up has had to postpone visits from foreigners concerned for their safety, Cheifetz says.

Meanwhile, the biggest strain on Israeli venture investors has been personal. Cheifetz says he has taken in friends from the embattled northern region just so they can get a decent night's sleep.[a]

Still, investors seemed undaunted in their pursuit of profits. U.S. venture firm Greylock Partners, for example, launched its first Israel-focused fund north of Tel Aviv during July 2006.

[a] "Greylock launches fund in midst of conflict," *Venture Capital Journal*, September 1, 2006, http://bit.ly/cdG6VE.

Pullback

Interest in Israel peaked during the late 1990s as the country helped lead the development of telecommunications networks. U.S. venture capital firms opened offices in Israel, added an Israeli partner, or established funds specifically dedicated to investing in the country.

But the results of the dramatic push into the country have been mixed. Only a few major companies have emerged from Israel in recent years. U.S. venture capitalists feel increasingly pressed to find returns even within their own country and are reconsidering foreign operations.

The result has been a slow pullback from Israel. It is not always easy to distinguish which firms have withdrawn their support and which are simply slowing their investment.

Most notable in the retreat has been Benchmark Capital, the U.S. firm known best for its investment in eBay. The firm had established an Israeli affiliate fund in 2001, but announced it would no longer be working with the affiliate to do deals in Israel. It isn't ignoring the country completely though; it still considers investments there through its primary fund.

A Future in Cleantech?

Israel's technology business has historically focused on information technology. Yet there is a great deal of interest from both entrepreneurs and financiers to work on alternative energy and resource efficiency start-ups.

Water has always been an issue for Israel, and many start-ups are looking to exploit the country's long history of working on desalinization.

Others are more interested in developing energy sources to replace oil. For example, Project Better Place is run by Israeli Shai Agassi and has received $550 million from investors, including large Israel-based firms. Its goal is to build a national infrastructure of battery swapping stations for electric cars.

China

When investors and entrepreneurs talk about China, they invariably mention the fact that the country has more than a billion inhabitants, many of whom are coming into a consumption economy for the first time. From this fundamental principle extends any number of suppositions and investment theses:

- China will be a tech giant thanks to the massive number of engineers that it trains each year.
- China will have more people connected to the Internet than any other country in the world—it will make the U.S. Internet boom look little by comparison.
- China's middle class is going to be bigger than the entire U.S. population and all you have to do is sell to just 1 percent of those consumers to make billions of dollars.

"The Rise of China" was recently rated the most written-about news story of the decade and the rapid expansion of the country's economy, which seemed only to accelerate in advance of the 2008 Olympics, has managed to sustain itself through the ongoing financial crisis.

A few adventurous U.S. investors began flying to China in 2000 to invest in deals that looked extremely similar to what one might have seen in Silicon Valley. Yet most venture capital investors did little or nothing to either leverage the country's base of engineers or tap its markets until after 2005. It was the point when skepticism finally gave way to greed, and soon many U.S. firms established either offices in Shanghai or started China-dedicated funds.

But just as soon as making money seemed easy, it proved to be hard. Competition for good investments heated up and talented entrepreneurs became harder to find. U.S. firms were faced with a choice. They could go all the way, hire local professionals, set up offices outside of Beijing and Shanghai, and invest in nontech start-ups. Or they could quietly pack up and pull out.

First Movers

The first iteration of venture capital investment in China filled a long-underserved need for capital there. Entrepreneurs versed in telecommunications migrated into dot-com start-ups, or worked on networking devices.

There was little to no domestic growth financing to support these start-ups and many U.S. venture capitalists were not ready to invest.

Most firms that were already successful U.S. investors were shy about visiting China. Many echoed the sentiment of Don Valentine, the founding partner of Sequoia Capital. In September 2004, he addressed an audience in Palo Alto, California about the opportunities he saw in China during a recent trip he'd made there with 19 other venture capitalists that had been sponsored by Silicon Valley Bank.

He made it clear that he thought it was a bad idea to invest there. "China has no laws, no accounting system, bankruptcy banks, and according to *Fortune*, a stock market that is made up of a den of thieves," he said. "You're about to see a bubble burst in the next five years, or sooner, that will make our bubble look meaningless."[3]

Many in the audience that evening nodded their agreement. But a handful of small, newly formed firms emerged to grasp the opportunity. Foremost among them was Granite Global Ventures (now called GGV Capital).

The firm raised its first fund in 2000 based on a new strategy. It pitched the idea of investing both in the United States and in China and focusing on mature start-ups.

GGV Capital planned to nose its way into deals on both sides of the Pacific based on the idea that it could help U.S. companies navigate the offshoring of certain manufacturing or software development to China and that it could help Chinese companies access U.S. consumer and capital markets. The firm was one of the first to open a permanent office in Shanghai.

The firm's aggressive move to capitalize on the opportunity in China paid off. Entrepreneurs there were yearning for capital to get their businesses off the ground. Larger U.S.-based companies wanted better access to Chinese manufacturing facilities and invited GGV Capital to invest, join their corporate boards, and help them meet partners in China.

The firm's first fund returned 2.3 times what it raised from limited partners, which is a good return. One or two investments might yield 10X or more in any given venture fund, but to get back more than twice the value of the entire fund is impressive. In fact, records show it was one of the top-performing funds investing anywhere in the world at the time, according to data from CalPERS.

But GGV Capital was an exception. Most U.S. venture capital firms didn't touch China at all during the dot-com boom or immediately after its bust. The few that did involve themselves did so only by sending junior investors on airplanes to report on what was going on there.

Baidu, Alibaba, Focus Media, and the Olympics

Investors are motivated by fear and greed. And fear was still very much in the air when it came to investing in China at the beginning of 2005. But the dam was weakening. Soon, a torrent of suppressed greed would be let loose on the country.

Thomas Friedman came out with the globalization manifesto "The World is Flat" in April 2005. It lauded the internationalization of business empowered by the Internet and the free flow of people and capital. You could not attend a Silicon Valley investor conference without someone reminding the audience that "the world is flat now," as though some fundamental physical principle had recently been reset.

Then the summer came and brought with it IPOs. Early China investor DFJ ePlanet Ventures took digital billboard advertising company Focus Media public in July. It jumped 20 percent over its offering price on its first day of trading on NASDAQ. After the IPO, the company was worth $1 billion and was still less than three years old.

China exploded into the psyche of U.S. venture capitalists on August 5, 2005. That was the day that Chinese search engine start-up Baidu offered its shares on NASDAQ via an IPO. The shares offered at $27 and closed that Friday at $123.90, up more than 350 percent during the day.

The next week Yahoo spent $1 billion to buy 40 percent of Chinese Internet auction company Alibaba. U.S.-based Granite Global Ventures had invested early in the company's development and received a substantial payout.

The boom was in full swing and everyone in Silicon Valley was talking about how to get in on the easy money. Entrepreneurs pitched China-focused start-ups that would take advantage of the country's rapid growth. The chief executives of every major tech company in Silicon Valley had to field questions about how they would approach China as either a resource for inexpensive labor or as a market to sell into. Venture capitalists who had said a year or two before that they'd never invest in China saw their firms launch dedicated Chinese funds, or establish satellite offices in the country's biggest cities.

But the sudden rush on Chinese start-ups exhausted the supply of competent managers. Venture capitalists started complaining about a shortage of executive talent. Even skilled Chinese leaders knew little about international financial accounting standards or how to effectively use stock option grants as an incentive for employees. Some people believed that Chinese start-ups would need to offer dormitory housing to attract employees. The learning curve on both sides of the Pacific was steep.

And everybody was concerned about the role the government would play.

To date, the Chinese government has provided little impediment to the free flow of capital both in and out of the country. Local governments maintain varying degrees of interest in the technology businesses within their borders, but there are few reports of problems.

The big problem for venture capitalists investing in China has been keeping up with the rapid pace of change.

Going Native

The first big change took place after the money started to seriously flow in to China. Venture capital firms soon found themselves competing as aggressively in Shanghai as they were in Menlo Park, California.

The first wave of investment in China, from 2000 to 2005, had helped release the pent-up demand for capital and had borne a wide array of successful start-ups. The venture capital firms that came first picked the ripest fruit.

The second wave, which lasted from 2005 to 2006, ensured that any reasonably attractive start-up got the funding it needed for growth. The venture capitalists picked any fruit that looked like it was edible. Native Chinese entrepreneurs living in the United States traveled home to take advantage of the opportunity.[4] The "invisible hand" of the marketplace had moved to stuff money into the pockets of any entrepreneur who needed it.

The third wave of venture capital in China began when all the edible fruit had already been picked from the entrepreneurial tree. Venture capitalists found few tech start-ups that needed as much money as they were able to invest. Even the start-ups that had been financed during the second wave still had more cash than they knew what to do with.

Once the venture capital spigot had been turned on, it was hard to stem its flow. The money sloshing around Shanghai and Beijing had to be redirected. The best firms found two solutions. They either piped their money deeper into China or sent it into companies outside the technology industry.

China's second tier cities are hardly household names in the United States. Still, Tianjin, Wuhan, Guangzhou, and Shenzhen have populations greater than that of Manhattan. Despite their size, they seldom see the level of foreign visitation that Shanghai or Beijing does. Just getting around takes a firm grasp of at least one Chinese dialect. And it was to these cities that venture capitalists went next.

Notably, native Chinese had an advantage over Westerners when it came to finding and financing opportunities in these regions. Firms that committed to China early and recruited Chinese investors found themselves increasingly successful.

Just as venture capitalists began to look beyond Shanghai and Beijing, they also started looking beyond the traditional technology industries. Larger, more mature businesses in manufacturing, agriculture, and retail needed expansion capital, and venture firms were anxious to put their funds to work. Kleiner Perkins Caufield & Byers, a firm well known for its technology investments such as Amazon, Netscape, and Sun Microsystems in the United States, invested in a Chinese T-shirt manufacturer. Sequoia Capital, backers of U.S. tech companies such as Apple, Cisco, and Google, bought into a publicly traded Chinese dairy company.

China may be gearing up for the next wave of venture capital evolution. It's difficult to say what form this may take, but there is reason to believe that the country may be developing its own base of institutional limited partners. Many are government-affiliated entities that have been encouraged to include venture capital funds as a part of their investment portfolios.

An increase in the available funds for Chinese venture firms could put additional competitive pressure on the market for good start-ups and eventually drive down investment returns. It might facilitate the growth of economies outside the major cities. One thing is certain: Adding money will send China's venture business in a new direction.

India

U.S. venture capitalists often talk about India in the same breath as China. Both countries have a base of well-educated engineers and a burgeoning consumer class. But the similarities end there.

India benefitted from a telecommunications infrastructure constructed to make outsourcing services reliable. Major technology companies established offices in cities such as Bangalore, first to take customer service calls and later to develop large swaths of complicated software. It brought millions of people in contact with computers and the Internet, many for the first time. That cleared the way for e-commerce and other online start-ups that venture capitalists have experience financing.

More important, it has contributed to education and employment in India. There were some 2.3 million software and service sector employees by the end of 2009, nearly three times the number employed at the end of 2004, according to the National Association of Software and Services Companies.[5]

And that's not just people answering customer support calls. According to reports, between 2004 and 2007, the number of workers engaged in software research and development grew by more than 75 percent to an estimated 144,000. This would explain why the number of patents granted to companies in the Software and Services sector grew 22X between 2005 and 2008.[6] Other technology sectors, such as semiconductors, networking gear, and mobile devices are seeing similar spikes in employment. That kind of innovation gives venture capitalists a good reason to lick their lips.

Demand for technical talent has fueled a surge in engineering students in Indian universities. Those students numbered just over 1 million in the 2003–2004 school year, up from the 590,000 enrolled during 2000–2001, according to a study by the National Council of Applied Economic Research. Engineering is the country's fastest growing course of study, the report shows.

And Indians are becoming increasingly connected to each other and the rest of the world. The number of people subscribing to broadband in India was 20 million in 2007, while the number of Internet users was about 40 million, according to the India Department of Telecommunications. That's where the United States stood in 1995 and it represents less than 10 percent of India's growing middle class. Mobile phone penetration is much further along. India broke the 100-million-subscriber mark in April 2006 and has since been adding new subscribers at a rate of 4 million a month, according to the Internet & Mobile Association of India.

Each of these factors—computer experience, large markets, emerging innovation, engineering education, and communications infrastructure—mirrors some part of what has made Silicon Valley successful and attractive to venture capitalists. An optimist might look at India and see many of the necessary components for a lucrative venture capital investment market.

Infrastructure Issues

For all there is to be excited about in India, there are several major problems that impede growth and have made the country difficult for venture capitalists to invest in. Foremost among the problems is the infrastructure issue.

Uncertain electrical power and a lack of transportation infrastructure top the list. India's manufacturing sector suffered as many as 17 power outages each month during 2004, which resulted in an estimated loss of 9 percent of its output, according to a study by the World Bank. Running a start-up is hard enough without having to worry about basics like keeping the power on.

It isn't easy for venture capitalists to even get to potential investments. As recently as 2007, the entire country had only 2,000 miles of four-lane highways, or about 20 times less than United States. Even if you can take the highway it isn't likely to help you much. The average speed on those highways is 20 miles per hour, according to the World Bank.

As if these issues were not enough to deter foreign investors, the business infrastructure problems are elephant-sized, such as the deficit of suitable office space or the time it takes to set up a dedicated high-speed data connection. There's weak intellectual property protection, making it difficult for would-be innovators to secure any defensible advantage from research and development. And Indian courts process legal claims at a pace that would put a snail to shame.

It is by no means Silicon Valley, where office space abounds, patent lawyers are a dime a dozen, and the San Mateo County Court works with deliberate speed. Yet that doesn't dampen the desire for investment capital. After all, it took decades before business infrastructure came south from San Francisco.

Investment Trends

Investor enthusiasm for India peaked in 2007. The country's stock market reached its apex during the first week of January 2008. At that point, the Sensex, India's version of the Dow Jones Industrial Average (DJIA), closed at over 20,800, more than 5.2 times higher than it had been during the same week five years before. To put that in perspective, if the DJIA had grown at an equivalent pace during the same time period, it would have topped out at over 45,680.

For India, it was a period of unprecedented growth.

Still, the venture capital opportunities remained somewhat limited thanks to a lack of management talent and too many entrepreneurs pursuing the same opportunities. For example, eight Indian online travel start-ups had raised venture capital by 2007. That's a lot of start-ups chasing a new market. What's worse, the market was still small because few Indians were online.

It seems clear that India will eventually develop a multibillion-dollar online booking business similar to the market Kayak, Expedia,

HotWire, and others serve in the United States. In fact, the market could eventually be much larger, not only because of India's population, but also because the process of buying travel tickets is more difficult to begin with. But having eight companies compete against each other makes it a lot harder for any one venture capitalist to make money.

Still, many U.S. investors were emboldened by the success of Info Edge, the company that runs online job site Naukri. The start-up raised money from Kleiner Perkins Caufield & Byers and Sherpalo Ventures. The two U.S.-based firms had invested together before in the United States, but the investment in Info Edge was their first foray together into India. The two firms collectively paid $6 million for 5 percent of Info Edge in April 2006.

It proved to be a lucrative investment. Info Edge went public on the Bombay Stock Exchange in October 2006 and closed its first day of trading at nearly double its offering price. The venture capitalists' stake was valued at $75 million. Not bad for just six months of investment.

Like Netscape in the United States or Baidu in China, many venture investors looked at this as proof that venture firms could come into India, invest, and get their money back via an IPO.

Every U.S. venture capitalist that had either been to India or was thinking about going there talked about Info Edge's Naukri job portal. It seemed a marvel to those accustomed to the high barrier for public companies hoping to get attention via a U.S. IPO. "A $20 million [revenue] company wouldn't get noticed on the NASDAQ, but in India it's huge because there's not that many Internet stocks there," says Deepak Kamra, a Menlo Park, California–based general partner at Canaan Partners.

Indian Stock Markets Garner Attention

The run up of the Sensex combined with the burgeoning supply of companies looking to list public offerings made the stock markets themselves attractive businesses.

The New York Stock Exchange (NYSE) took note. In January 2007, the NYSE Group said it would buy a 5 percent stake in the India National Stock Exchange (NSE) for $115 million. Two years later, U.S.-based venture capital firm Norwest Venture Partners invested $55 million into the NSE. "We are extremely bullish on the value proposition NSE offers shareholders at a time when India is on the cusp of global influence," Norwest Managing Partner Promod Haque said at the time.[7]

The strength of the NSE and Bombay Stock Exchange (BSE), both of which are based in Mumbai, prompted more companies to consider going public. It's relatively easy for an Indian company to go public. The minimum requirements to list are a market capitalization over $1.1 million with revenue of more than $600,000 in the past year and more than 1,000 investors after an IPO. The exchanges also don't have the Sarbanes-Oxley restrictions that have caused so much heartburn in the United States.

IN THE REAL WORLD

Mauritius Tax Pass-Through

If you're thinking about investing in India, then you need to get up to speed on the island Republic of Mauritius, 500 miles east of Madagascar and about two-thirds the size of Rhode Island.[a]

There you'll find Kleiner Perkins Caufield & Byers, Sequoia Capital India, and Norwest Venture Partners, to name a few. Well, you're not likely to find any of those firms' actual partners, but that's where they have incorporated their Indian investment vehicles.

Mauritius, which rhymes with "delicious," has been an Indian tax haven since April 1, 1983, when it entered into an agreement with India to avoid double taxation of its residents. India agreed not to levy a capital gains tax on the sale of shares of Indian stock owned by a Mauritius entity, under the Indian–Mauritius treaty.

The treaty is important because India taxes its residents differently than the United States. The Indian government collects a tax whenever an Indian asset is sold, no matter who sells it. The United States government taxes citizens for the capital gains they realize as income. "If you bought some stock in the Indian stock exchange, even when you don't live in India, you're subject to tax on the Indian shares," explains Fred Greguras, an attorney at Fenwick & West. "A lot of people have located their funds in Mauritius to avoid this."

Mauritius doesn't tax capital gains, so international investors that locate subsidiaries there completely miss out on any taxation on shares of Indian companies they sell.

[a] "Meet Mauritius," *Venture Capital Journal*, March 1, 2007, http://bit.ly/d8Agj3.

Russia

Venture investors periodically get excited about the potential of Russia. They see the country's strong scientific history, its defense-industry technical prowess, and the tenacious ability of its people. It looks like an attractive investment opportunity. But Russia has yet to develop a robust small company innovation ecosystem.

The latest craze for the country came in 2006, when the government took steps to actively promote the establishment of a venture capital industry.

Government Stimulus

In 2006, the Russian economy was in the midst of resurgence, averaging 6.4 percent GDP growth each year since 1998. The Russian Trading System, that country's version of the NYSE, was up 330 percent from 2003.

And it wasn't just the oil oligarchs making money. Personal incomes increased more than 12 percent each year since 2000, according to the CIA World Factbook. The middle class seemed to finally be coming into its own as an economic power, and people with greater income have greater freedom to both consume and take entrepreneurial risks.

At the same time, Russia's communications ministry was predicting computer penetration would quadruple and the percentage of people using the Internet would triple by 2010. There was going to be lots of money made in information technology and communications, the government assured anyone who would listen.

It was during this time that Russia's Communications Minister Leon Reiman announced that the government had launched a $500 million fund-of-funds to stimulate growth among technology companies in the region. The fund could expand to $1 billion, depending on the interest of outside investors.

The move was met with great optimism from U.S. investors. "This is the clearest effort to date from the government saying that Russia's future isn't just petrochemicals," Palo Alto, California–based investor Colin Breeze said at the time. "It's defining Russia's future in technology, communications, and services."[8]

Earlier Attempts

U.S.-based venture capitalists looked to embrace Russian entrepreneurs for decades with little success.

Perhaps the first venture capitalist to see opportunity in the country was Pitch Johnson. Johnson is famous in Silicon Valley for being one of the first west coast venture capitalists to open shop during the 1960s. He is considered a pioneer of the industry.

Johnson attempted a $10 million Russian-focused venture fund in 1995, which did well until the Russian financial crisis of 1998. After the correction, it made a handful of investments that are now getting serious revenue. These more recent successes may be enough to make the fund worthwhile, Johnson says.

Johnson's first trip to the country was in 1990, when he gave a talk about entrepreneurship to the Leningrad City Council. Johnson, an avid pilot, says he had wanted to fly his private plane into Russia for years and was excited to finally get the chance. It was a fortuitous meeting. Sitting in the audience that day was then–City Councilman Vladimir Putin.

When Putin became Russia's president, he was instrumental in turning around his country's economy and wanted to rev it up even more by fostering venture capital and entrepreneurship. The Russian government's fund-of-funds program was part of that effort.

Built on Yozma's Back

The government established the Russian Venture Corporation to invest the money associated with its fund-of-funds program, and its officials met with venture capital luminaries, such as Pitch Johnson, for guidance on how the program should work. Together, they agreed to model it on Israel's Yozma program.

The Russian Venture Corporation (RVC) planned to invest in 10 funds, owning just half of each one. At the end of the investment period, the Russian government would collect its principal back along with 3 percent of any of the profits made from investing it. Investors familiar with the arrangement likened it to a form of venture debt, where a bank lends money and gets a variable payback if the loan does well.

As similar as the Russian program was to the successful Israeli one, there was one key difference. The Russian government stipulated that foreign investment firms that wished to raise money through the program would have to apply in conjunction with a Russia-based partner.

Venture capitalists formed three firms that received the first round of promised government funds. U.S.-based Draper Fisher Jurvetson launched an affiliate fund called DFJ-VTB Aurora in partnership with Russian Bank VTB. Pitch Johnson's U.S.-based Asset Management firm partnered with Russian bank Vneshekonombank (VEB) to form Bioprocess Capital. Israel-based Tamir Fishman worked with Russian partners to establish a firm called Finance Trust.

The Problem with Partners

Partnership is a sure impediment to progress. Any action requires two sets of approval. Any policy needs multiple meetings to hammer out. It takes time to build a rapport and years to build trust. Problems among the international partners in the Russian venture market arose almost immediately.

It all started when Oleg Shvartsman opened his mouth. Shvartsman was a midlevel investor working on the Russian side of the Finance Trust firm established with Israeli firm Tamir Fishman. Shvartsman told a reporter that he used ties to government security officers to force private business owners to sell their companies below their market value.

It reinforced the worst fears of foreign investors, namely that Russia was a lawless place unfit to do business in.

The Israelis yanked their support from the fund.

Then Pitch Johnson ran into trouble with the firm he was working with in Russia. "They didn't want to do anything I'd call venture capital," he said.

Johnson's partners in Bioprocess Capital were not crooks. In fact, Johnson goes out of his way to stipulate that they were "square guys and on the 'up and up.'" The problem was that they were uninterested in financing start-ups or working with entrepreneurs.

"As the fund finally shaped up, with VEB in control, venture capital for start-ups and young companies was not high on the agenda, and investments in existing companies would be the primary activity," Johnson says. "While we Westerners were listed as 'experts' in the application [to receive funds from the RVC], our venture skills are not being utilized and I don't expect any further involvement."[9]

But such blows have not been fatal to the program. Bioprocess was still a going concern when Johnson left, even if it isn't making venture capital–style investments. Tamir Fishman returned to Russia with a new partner in June 2008. It launched Tamir Fishman Russia as a $100 million fund with help from Central Invest Group, a Russian investment bank.

Questions Remain

It's not clear whether technology start-ups and venture capital will take hold in Russia, even with government support. Universities have yet to embrace the idea of start-ups and technology transfer as a way of improving their balance sheets or increasing their prestige. The mindset of Russian business people, at least these days, is that the most valuable natural resource is oil, gas, or some other thing that can be pulled from the ground. They have yet to embrace the idea that it is the ingenuity and efforts of entrepreneurs that are the greatest resource of a country. Wealth in Russia remains a thing you take, not create.

This can change. Change, if it comes, will be a product of the Russian people and their will to build a different future. This matters more than government intervention, better business education, or well-defined and fiercely protected property rights.

Europe

Homogeneous markets are great for business—you make one product and many people buy it. But years after the advent of the European Union, selling products and services in countries with vastly different needs and cultures remains a challenge for start-ups. However, they have managed to raise $133.3 billion from investors over the past decade, according to data from Thomson Reuters.

That money has funded start-ups that have gone on to sell for billions of dollars. Perhaps the most dramatic recent example of this is Internet telephone company Skype, which began in Luxembourg in 2003. It was financed by an early angel investor in Denmark, quickly raised venture capital, and sold to eBay in 2005 for $2.6 billion with another $1.5 billion in earnouts.

There have been several other successes for both entrepreneurs and venture capitalists. U.K.-based online music start-up Last.fm raised $5 million from venture capitalists before selling to CBS for $280 million a year later in 2007. Swedish start-up MySQL raised tens of millions of dollars from venture capitalists in both Europe and the United States before selling to Sun Microsystems for $1 billion in 2008.

Rewind even further and you'll find a handful of dot-com-bubble-era successes, such as communications chipmaker Giga. The Danish start-up raised $2 million from European venture capitalists before selling to Intel for $1.25 billion in 2000.

Despite this appearance of success, European venture capital is underrepresented relative to the size of the combined European economies and has underperformed its U.S. counterpart. Even those successful venture investments owed much of their good fortune to the United States. The European start-ups raised money from U.S. venture capitalists, turned to U.S. customers for revenue, and later sold to U.S. corporations. This is not always the case, but there are several factors that hold European venture capital back.

Lack of Centralized Resources

Europe has its outposts of innovation, places where technology start-ups thrive and grow. Yet there is no central repository of investment capital and experience, no preponderance of strategic acquirers, nor even a single public marketplace that rises above all others as a place for high-growth technology start-ups to go public.

That's a weighty anchor on the innovation industry of Europe. A central place where start-ups can go to find financing, such as Silicon Valley's Sand Hill Road, can drastically cut down the time it takes to raise money. An entrepreneur can meet with several venture firms in a single day, just by walking down the street.

That not only speeds the time it takes to raise money, but also forces a higher level of competition between venture firms. That's good news for entrepreneurs, who will get better financing terms as a product. Next-door neighbors are more likely to compete than venture firms based in different countries.

The same logic extends to the lack of large strategic acquirers. Europe has large technology companies in every industry. Yet there are few local competitors anxious to get the edge over each other. That means fewer bidding wars to acquire start-ups.

The lack of a central stock market presents a more serious problem. A single market for fast growing technology start-ups is good for three things.

First, it creates a critical mass of investment banking analysts who can specialize in evaluating technology companies. That helps large institutions better understand these companies and their growth potential.

Second, it creates a group of public market investors interested in technology companies. For example, it's easy to imagine an investor who has money in Cisco, Amazon, and Microsoft taking a chance on a newly public Google.

The third thing that a central market is good for is increased trading liquidity. More liquidity means if an investor decides to either buy or sell shares, the stock price will not fluctuate greatly. A stable stock price can help companies plan for the future by ensuring they'll have a ready currency for making acquisitions or raising more money later on.

Cultural Impediments

It's difficult to say how an idea takes hold, especially when it is a broad idea about a diverse group of people. Yet investors in Silicon Valley have it in their minds that Europeans are unwilling to become entrepreneurs. They believe that Europeans are risk averse and that the business culture of Europe punishes those who try something new and fail.

I have sought out and interviewed some of the most successful entrepreneurs and investors in the region and found them as willing to try and fail as anyone I have ever encountered. Yet they were, at some level, importing the ideas of what it means to be an entrepreneur.

One well-known European investor deeply admired U.S. venture capitalist Tim Draper. He borrowed many of Draper's tropes and mimicked Draper's rhetoric about the importance of entrepreneurship.

A respected venture firm in Geneva saw the majority of its managing partners educated at Harvard Business School. They were decidedly European, but equipped with a U.S. education and appreciation for entrepreneurs.

Many of the venture firms themselves are U.S. exports. Europe-based Balderton Capital, DFJ Esprit, and Accel Europe all started as affiliates of U.S.-based venture firms.

Even a staunchly European venture firm, such as France's Sofinnova Ventures, keeps an office in San Francisco to be close to Silicon Valley.

The thing that many in the United States too readily forget is that the father of venture capital in our country was, in fact, French. General Georges Doriot was born in Paris, taught entrepreneurship at Harvard Business School, and began American Research and Development, which is considered by many to be the first venture capital firm.[10]

TIPS AND TECHNIQUES

Dealing with Currency Issues

At the end of 2007, Partech International was nearing the final close on its fifth venture fund but running into problems with its European limited partners.[a]

The San Francisco–based firm had relied heavily on its European heritage when raising past funds and anticipated that as much as half of the money for its new fund would come from Europe. But the U.S. dollar was rapidly depreciating. In fact, over the previous five years, the dollar had lost half of its value against the euro.

This was a big problem for the limited partners. The firm's last fund, which was raised in 2000, evenly split the commitments from U.S. and European investors. The firm called down money from its limited partners to write checks for start-ups over a period of several years. But as the value of the dollar fell, the

European limited partners effectively bought a greater equity stake in each start-up that Partech backed.

This became a point of contention when the start-ups were acquired and Partech had money to pass out. The European limited partners might have reasonably argued that they deserved more of the payout. After all, the value of their euro-denominated contribution to the start-up's financing was 50 percent more valuable than the dollar-denominated contribution from U.S.-based limited partners.

To avoid these problems in its next venture fund, Partech developed a structure to shield its limited partners from the effects of dramatic currency fluctuations. "That's the tricky part where we had to get pretty creative," says Managing Partner Vincent Worms. "It's very simple once you do it, but very complicated to set up."

The trick, Worms says, is to have each group of investors treated almost as though it has its own sub-fund within the firm's overall fund. Each sub-fund is denominated in the currency that the limited partners prefer, and then converted at the time an investment is made.

"We had to make sure that the U.S. investors were not favored or disfavored in terms of gains," Worms says.

[a] "Falling Dollar Hampers Partech Fund-raising," *PE Week*, November 26, 2007, http://bit.ly/bsK3nw.

Regional Policies Promote Cleantech

A highly fragmented marketplace for investors, acquirers, and stock exchanges is a problem for start–ups looking to grow. But it can also provide rich grounds for policy experimentation and a variety of government support programs.

Perhaps the most important facet of government policy for start-ups has been the feed-in-tariffs and other state-supported initiatives for stimulating demand for solar panels in Germany and Spain.

A feed-in-tariff is a way governments can skew incentives to stimulate a market for a new product. It gives tax breaks to anyone who makes a qualifying purchase. It works especially well when consumers are *price-elastic,* meaning that a little drop in price can greatly increase the quantity purchased.

These tax breaks have given the two countries vibrant solar panel industries, replete with both major energy corporations and start-ups. It has taken the industries in Germany and Spain beyond simple manufacturing and installation to real innovation.

A good example of this is Bitterfeld-Wolfen, Germany–based Q-Cells, which makes high performance solar panels. The company raised $15 million from London-based Apax Partners Worldwide, Good Energies, the venture capital subsidiary of Switzerland-based COFRA Holding AG, and others in 2004. Q-Cells went public the following year, raising $325 million on the Frankfurt Stock Exchange, and was worth over $10 billion within two years.

The start-up managed to get out in front of competition in the United States, thanks to the early sales it made in its home country.

The Future of Venture Capital in Europe

In January 2010, Boston-based Atlas Venture announced plans to shutter its operations in Europe. The venture firm had been investing there since 1992 and had financed over 120 European start-ups.

Atlas investor Fred Destin, who worked out of the firm's London office, initially said that the move was not a product of a bearish outlook on Europe. He pointed to the firm's recent success selling French pharmaceutical company Novexel to AstraZeneca at the end of 2009 as an example of a good reason to remain optimistic about European innovation. The start-up raised more than $125 million from European and U.S. venture capitalists before selling for $500 million.

But then, two months later, Destin blogged about the problems of making venture capital investments in Europe. He cited the lack of ambitious youth and political leadership, the weight of pension funds, continual talent loss, and other issues. "We're f—ed if we don't wake up soon," he wrote. "The rest of the world works harder, smarter, produces more engineers, is hungry, is globally mobile, has inherent competitive advantages we often don't have."[11]

Destin's frustration is something other venture capitalists have echoed over the past decade. Yet for each Atlas that leaves, there's an Atomico Ventures that launches.

Atomico formed in London in 2006 and began investing the money that Skype founders Niklas Zennström and Janus Friis earned from selling their start-up to eBay. In 2010, the firm raised its first institutional venture capital fund, weighing in at $165 million. "With the rise of companies like Skype, there's been a re-generation of people who had been working as product managers or in other positions who now are going out to start something new," Zennström said.[12] He plans to be the one that finances those entrepreneurs.

Atomico is one of the few examples of a European venture firm founded by successful entrepreneurs. Although this has long been the model for establishing firms in the United States, seeing entrepreneurs turn into investors in Europe remains anomalous.

But it does happen. Successful advertising entrepreneur Morten Lund put $50,000 into Skype shortly after it formed. He got more than $20 million when it sold to eBay. Lund went on to invest in over 80 start-ups during the next several years, including Danish data sharing company Zyb, which sold to Vodafone for $50 million not long after Lund invested.

The future of venture investment in Europe depends more on reinvestment from people such as Zennström and Lund than on imported capital from firms such as Atlas.

The Rest of the World

Israel, China, India, Russia, and Europe have garnered the most attention and interest from U.S. venture capitalists during the past decade.

Which countries will be attractive to venture investors in the future is anybody's guess. But there are a few countries that may be particularly well poised to rapidly ramp up their innovation industries and accept additional foreign investment.

Japan

Venture capitalists have traditionally had a difficult time penetrating the Japanese market. "It's historically been quite closed to outside investors," says Draper Fisher Jurvetson's Don Wood. "There's a tradition there where the smartest university graduates are tempted to join larger, stable companies. It's harder to attract talent to smaller companies there."

Still, Japan is the world's second largest economy, and entrepreneurship is starting to take root there, says Wood. He attributes the change to a critical mass of successful entrepreneurs whom new founders can emulate and a greater understanding of how start-ups work in the United States, gleaned from the Internet.

"People are no longer just looking in their own backyard," Wood says of Japanese entrepreneurs. "They have proof that you can raise venture capital, take your company public, make yourself a lot of money, and create a lot of jobs. That's really just occurred in the last three to four years."

Venture capitalists invested $7 billion into 450 Japanese companies during the first decade of the twenty-first century, according to data from Thomson Reuters. Yet nearly half of those investments were made in 2000.

One of the most attractive aspects of Japan is its Mothers market, a subset of the Tokyo Stock Exchange that promotes high-growth, small companies, says Wood. "It's a training-wheels public market. You could be public there with a $25 million market capitalization."

In fact, the average trading value on the Mothers market at the end of 2008 was just less than $14 million, according to the exchange. Mothers hosted 12 IPOs during 2008 and 23 during 2007.

The country has yet to host a runaway success that will prove its viability as an investment hub. One of the biggest recent new issues on the exchange was Internet services company Gree, which listed a

$143 million IPO in 2008. The company was founded by a 26-year-old, according to reports, and is one of the companies that are likely to act as an example for other entrepreneurs.[13]

Brazil

With the Summer Olympics heading to Rio de Janeiro in 2012, one can expect Brazil will see plenty of media attention in the coming years.

One of the things that may be most interesting to foreigners is the country's expertise in alternative fuels. Brazil has been on the forefront of ethanol development by distilling sugar since oil shocks in the mid-1970s.

U.S. investors flocked to invest in ethanol production facilities during the past decade, and much of the money that came into the country was from hedge funds.

Venture capitalists have focused on Brazilian Internet start-ups and wireless companies. Internet penetration has gone from less than 3 percent in 2000 to more than 34 percent in 2008, according to data from the International Telecommunication Union, and that has opened an opportunity to build companies and services similar to those that have been successful in the United States.[14] An example of this is Draper Fisher Jurvetson's $10 million investment in Power Ventures, which makes an online social network similar to MySpace or Facebook.

Other start-ups are carving out different parts of the information technology market. São Paulo–based Scua Seguranca develops digital security technologies and has raised more than $750,000 from local venture capitalists. Internacional Syst S/A operates an information technology consulting company and has raised just under $1 million from Brazil-based FIR Capital Partners.

Yet Brazil's information technology sector has been somewhat slow to get going, investors say. Venture capitalists invested $4.7 billion into 300 Brazilian companies during the past 10 years, according to data from Thomson Reuters, though this data may be inflated by one or two large investments primarily run by hedge funds with some little participation by venture capitalists.

South Korea

Samsung, Daewoo, and LG are all household names in technology. The country has a history of semiconductor production and one of the highest percentages of broadband penetration of any country in the world.

Venture capitalists invested $9.4 billion into 2,400 Korean companies during the past decade, according to data from Thomson Reuters. A third of those investments were made in 2000, but Korea has maintained a steady stream of investment since.

Only about half of the money going to South Korean start-ups came from South Korean investors. Part of the reason for this is that the South Korean government has carefully regulated its domestic venture capital firms. For example, prior to 2005 the government prevented local venture capital firms from owning more than 50 percent of any start-up they invested in.[15]

U.S. investors have been happy to step into the breach. Yet the South Korean government has not always welcomed this development. Large buyout firms were prosecuted for tax evasion in 2005 after the government discovered they had made large profits on deals done in the country.[16] Although it was not directly related to the start-up business, it may have driven down investment in this period.

One of the most promising sectors in South Korea is online gaming. The country's high broadband penetration positioned it to have a natural market of early adopters for online games. Nurian Software, for example, has raised $25 million from U.S. venture capitalists such as Globespan Capital and New Enterprise Associates among others. Seoul-based Wemade Entertainment, maker of "The Legend of Mir" video game, raised $28.9 million from South Korean venture firm Skylake Incuvest in 2008. It went public at the end of 2009 on the Korea Exchange.

Summary

Venture capital has a long history in the United States, stretching back as far as the late 1950s. Yet the past two decades have seen venture capitalists taking their expertise and money to other countries.

There is no simple way for a U.S. venture firm to "go global." There are several strategies that a firm might consider, depending on its preferences for risk, the makeup of its partnership or the nature of the country it aims to invest in.

Some firms prefer to keep their relations with foreign start-ups at arm's length. They fly to another country, pick a start-up in an industry they know with a management team they trust, write a check, and fly home.

Other firms prefer to open their own offices in a foreign country. This strategy may be particularly well suited to firms that already employ native language speakers.

U.S. venture firms have had some success partnering with each other to form new firms focused on foreign countries. Others have worked to affiliate themselves with local investors. Both strategies work well if the U.S. firm is a competent fundraiser and can help the local firm connect with U.S.-based limited partners. Other venture capitalists would rather get into the foreign market faster and may buy a successful foreign investment firm.

Venture firms hoping to syndicate across borders must be prepared to explain what useful things they will do, from making introductions to major customers to helping recruit experienced executives.

Governments periodically try to stimulate innovation and create incentives to attract experts, though these programs typically come with various strings attached.

Knowing how to invest abroad is one thing; knowing where to invest is another.

The United States remains the number one spot for start-ups and venture capital investing in the world. Many places have tried to replicate Silicon Valley's unique confluence of innovation resources, but few have succeeded. It may just take time.

Technology start-ups in Israel have benefited from the country's investment into military technology and training. The country's government launched a successful stimulus for technology investors during the first half of the 1990s called the *Yozma* program. It acted as a fund-of-funds investor to support foreign firms interested in opening shop in Israel. The country suffers from a lack of major customers and its start-up executives will sometimes set up shop in Silicon Valley just to make sales. Israel has seen foreign interest in its technology start-ups fade somewhat since the dot-com boom, but it may have a promising future in cleantech.

China's massive markets have attracted venture capitalists during the past decade and the first firms to invest there were richly rewarded. Even the most skeptical venture capitalists eventually relented and pursued a China strategy after several major success stories started to emerge from the country during the summer of 2005. Competition to finance Chinese start-ups increased, and venture firms were forced to go deeper in the country to find deals, invest in start-ups outside of traditional technology sectors, or give up on the country altogether.

India also experienced rapid growth in venture capital investment during the past decade thanks to early outsourcing efforts, growth in the number of engineering students, and the country's increasing use of communications technologies. Still, it lacks critical physical and business infrastructure. This has hampered growth. Some U.S. venture firms have been successful investing there, but one or two technology sectors have been subjected to overinvestment. Understanding the listing requirements of its stock exchanges and the way it taxes capital gains may require the help of a lawyer.

Russia is well respected for its technological prowess and potential to become a lucrative market for new companies. The country's recent economic boom led the government to create a program to stimulate start-up creation. It formed a fund-of-funds similar to Israel's Yozma program, but required foreign investors to partner with a Russian investment firm to qualify for the stimulus. This minor twist in policy caused problems when the partners didn't see eye to eye. U.S. investors involved with Russia say the opportunity there still needs time to develop.

Europe is made up of many smaller markets, none of which has the critical mass to create a consolidated pool of talent and investment money. Still, each country in Europe is free to pursue its own development strategies, and governments are able to establish policies that promote specific high-growth industries. The region still imports many of its entrepreneurial concepts from the United States but is slowly developing its own batch of home-grown expertise.

Other countries may become interesting to venture capitalists in the coming decade. Japan, Brazil, and South Korea each have experience in technology and may be primed to rapidly grow.

Notes

1. "Billionaire Boot Camp," *Foreign Policy*, September/October 2007, http://bit.ly/9Dnn7S.
2. "The Unit," *Forbes.com*, February 8, 2007, http://bit.ly/c13xxw.
3. "Sequoia Shrugging Off China," *SiliconBeat* (A *San Jose Mercury News* Blog), September 28, 2004, http://bit.ly/bfBz4L.
4. Entrepreneurs working or studying in the United States who returned to their native China to start companies were so prevalent that they merited their own term. They were called "sea turtles."

5. "Indian IT—BPO Industry Exports Touches USD 50 Billion Landmark," National Association of Software and Services Companies, February 4, 2010, http://bit.ly/aTgsdh.

6. Ibid.

7. "Norwest Venture Partners to Invest RS 250 Crores in National Stock Exchange of India (NSE)," *press release*, June 3, 2009, http://bit.ly/b9csNk.

8. "Russia Lays Out the Welcome Mat," *Venture Capital Journal*, October 1, 2006, http://bit.ly/ddm3gg.

9. "Pitch Johnson Retreats from Russia," *PE Week*, September 29, 2008, http://bit.ly/ccVDSK.

10. Doriot lamented the fact that there was no institution equivalent to Harvard Business School in Europe. So he founded INSEAD, a business school based in France that opened in 1958 and is now considered to be one of the best international institutions. For more on Doriot, consult *Creative Capital* by Spencer Ante (Boston, MA: Harvard Business Press, 2008).

11. Fred Destin, "A Cry for Europe," *Fred Destin* blog, March 17, 2010, http://bit.ly/djza8B. (Edited to censor vulgarity.)

12. "Q&A with Niklas Zennström, on Atomico Fundraise and European Venture Capital," PEHub.com, March 22, 2010, http://bit.ly/cflxcl.

13. "DFJ Moving on Japan," *PE Week*, July 13, 2009, http://bit.ly/9lXzYS.

14. "Brazil Internet Stats and Telecom Market Report," *InternetWorldStats.com* (accessed March, 23 2010) http://bit.ly/9DEXVt.

15. "Korea Opens Up PE Investing to All," *PE Week*, November 22, 2004. http://bit.ly/cIyASG.

16. "Korea Fines Carlyle, U.S. Firms for Alleged Tax Evasion," *PE Week*, October 17, 2005, http://bit.ly/dC2tIJ.

About the Author

Alexander Haislip specializes in venture capital and technology investment analysis. He is a columnist for *Forbes.com* and has been a senior writer at Thomson Reuters's *Venture Capital Journal* and *Private Equity Hub* for the past four years. He holds an economics degree and a finance certificate from Princeton University and a master's degree from the Columbia University Graduate School of Journalism.

Mr. Haislip has won awards from the New York Financial Writers' Association, the National Press Foundation, and the Western Publishing Association. The London-based Management Consultancies Association recognized him as one of the "Best Young Management Writers."

In addition to researching and writing, Mr. Haislip also conducts conferences and moderates panels of experts on topics such as venture capital, cleantech, energy, buyouts, fundraising, and private equity.

You can find more information about Mr. Haislip at his web site, www.AlexanderHaislip.com.

Index

Index

Index